The Power of Discord

Also by Ed Tronick, PhD

The Neurobehavioral and Social-Emotional
Development of Infants and Children

Also by Claudia M. Gold, MD

The Developmental Science of Early Childhood
The Silenced Child
Keeping Your Child in Mind

The Power of Discord

Why the Ups and Downs of Relationships Are the Secret to Building Intimacy, Resilience, and Trust

Ed Tronick, PhD, and Claudia M. Gold, MD

Little, Brown Spark
New York Boston London

Little, Brown Spark
Hachette Book Group
1290 Avenue of the Americas, New York, NY 10104
littlebrownspark.com

First Edition: June 2020

Little, Brown Spark is an imprint of Little, Brown and Company, a division of
Hachette Book Group, Inc. The Little, Brown Spark name and logo are
trademarks of Hachette Book Group, Inc.

The publisher is not responsible for websites (or their content)
that are not owned by the publisher.

The Hachette Speakers Bureau provides a wide range of authors for speaking events.
To find out more, go to hachettespeakersbureau.com or call (866) 376-6591.

ISBN 978-0-316-48887-7
LCCN 2019953318

10 9 8 7 6 5 4 3 2 1

LSC-C

Printed in the United States of America

CONTENTS

Introduction: Origins   3

1. Repair as Food for the Soul   33
2. Aiming for Good Enough   63
3. Feeling Safe to Make a Mess   84
4. Stopping the Blame Game   107
5. Resilience Reconsidered   130
6. Games We Play: Learning to Belong   151
7. Technology and the Still-Face Paradigm   171
8. When Meaning Goes Awry   184
9. Healing in a Mosaic of Moments over Time   210
10. Finding Hope in Uncertainty   225
11. Through Discord to Connection and Belonging   237

Acknowledgments   251
Notes   253
Index   267

For the faculty and fellows of the University of Massachusetts Boston Infant-Parent Mental Health Program

The Power
of Discord

INTRODUCTION

ORIGINS

THE POWER OF DISCORD offers a new way to think about ourselves and our relationships. Over decades of research and clinical experience, we were motivated by some fundamental questions: How is it that some people enjoy a range of satisfying, intimate social connections while others suffer from painful feelings of disconnection and loneliness? Why are some human beings sad, withdrawn, and lacking in self-esteem, whereas others are angry, unfocused, and brittlely self-assertive, and still others are happy, curious, affectionate, and self-confident? How is our ability to feel a sense of belonging and attachment to other people linked with the way we develop our individual sense of self? Perhaps most important, how can answers to these questions, which we uncovered in the course of our work, guide us in finding connection and intimacy when we feel lost and alone, an experience everyone has at one time or another? Before we begin to show you what we've learned, let us introduce ourselves by telling our separate stories and how we came to write this book together.

CLAUDIA'S STORY: FROM MANAGING
TO LISTENING

The year was 2004. As the generally acknowledged behavioral specialist in my busy small-town pediatrics practice, I increasingly felt that neither my pediatrics training nor my almost twenty years in practice had given me the tools to address the wide range of challenges that arrived in my office. Asking questions and offering guidance, advice, and behavior management often resulted in a sense of frustration and failure both for me and for the families I worked with. Then two visits — one with a "defiant" teenage boy and another with a three-month-old girl with "colic" — changed everything.

After meeting alone with fifteen-year-old Alex for about twenty of the thirty minutes typically allotted for an "ADHD evaluation," I invited his parents, Carmen and Rick, to join us. Alex sat huddled on a corner of the exam table, wrapping himself tightly in his coat and silently staring at the floor. Carmen and Rick stood, arms across their chests, as far apart as possible. The small space could barely contain the anger and disconnection on display.

For that first visit with Alex and his parents, I followed the typical procedure of taking a history in line with standardized diagnostic assessments for attention deficit hyperactivity disorder. Their answers to my questions seemed to indicate, according to the ADHD rating scale, that Alex might meet the diagnostic criteria for the disorder. We scheduled a follow-up visit for further evaluation and to discuss treatment.

But in our second meeting several weeks later, my approach was different. I had begun studying with the newly formed Berkshire Psychoanalytic Institute that year. As part of a program designed to train psychoanalysts, the institute offered a scholars track for people who were not mental health clinicians but worked in related fields. I was encountering a range of new ideas that had not been covered in my pediatrics training. Pediatricians get surprisingly little education in the critical foundational role of relationships in growth and development.

One of the most important influences on my thinking from that time forward was the work of pediatrician turned psychoanalyst D. W. Winnicott. Winnicott developed his ideas in post–World War II England, where, as in most Western societies at that time, a mother was thought of mainly as a provider of basic care — feeding, bathing, and dressing. The mother-child relationship itself was accorded little value. Children were routinely removed from their families to keep them safe from the threat of bombings in London during World War II without anyone giving much thought to the consequences, and hospitalized children were separated from their parents for long periods. Winnicott was among the first to introduce a different way of thinking.

Around the time of my second visit with Alex and his parents, I was reading a paper about what Winnicott termed the *true self*. He described how parents' own issues may cloud their view of who their children really are and of what their children's behavior is communicating. Another mother in my practice offered a striking example of the concept. She was highly distraught by her older son's need to always be first. Getting out of the house with a five-year-old and two-year-old was becoming increasingly difficult. After several visits, she wept as she told me of the death of her older brother when she was a little girl. Her family had moved across the country to get away, and never addressed the loss. The experience of parenting two children of similar age brought all the grief flooding back. Her son, who had been quietly drawing on the floor while she shared this story, climbed on her lap and handed his mother a picture of a person in a field. Offering a great example of the adage "out of the mouths of babes," he said, "This is you, not me." His behavior had its origins in typical sibling rivalry, but his mother's unprocessed grief had clouded her perspective, and she was escalating the situation with her outsize reaction. Once she had told this story in the safety of my office, she was able to respond to her son's "true self," calmly setting limits on his behavior. The intensity of the sibling rivalry dissipated.

While I do not recall purposefully changing my approach — it was more by accident — my studies gave me a new framework for understanding transformative moments, such as what followed with Alex and his family, that were starting to occur. Later I could deliberately duplicate what I had discovered. These first steps began my journey from managing to listening as the primary objective in my work. I started to see that behavior problems occurred when, for a range of reasons, a parent and child did not connect — a situation I would later come to understand in Ed's language as *mismatch*.

When I took time to listen to parents together with their child, parents were able to access the feelings that were in the way of their viewing their child's true self, often some combination of shame, anger, and grief. I was learning to simply listen with curiosity instead of jumping directly from diagnosis to treatment. Rather than searching for "What is it?" and "What do we do?," I asked more open-ended questions, such as "How was your pregnancy?," "What was your child like as a baby?," and "Does she remind you of anyone in your family?" With this invitation to talk, parents opened up, and the stories flowed. Holding my lessons from Winnicott and others in mind, I listened for what would help us find meaning in the problematic behavior. How could we make sense of what the child was communicating? As families and I shared powerful moments of reconnection, dramatic transformations occurred in relationships and in behavior. This was what happened next in my work with Alex and his family.

Several minutes into that second visit, Alex's mother, upset by a comment from her husband, stormed out into the waiting room. After the door closed behind her, Rick hardly acknowledged the disruption but instead unleashed a litany of complaints about his son. "He's lazy. He never listens. He doesn't care about anyone but himself." Wanting to validate Rick's experience of distress while protecting Alex from the intensity of his rage, I navigated this difficult moment by redirecting the conversation and asking some simple things about Rick's day. What was his work, and when did he usually get home? How much time did he have with the family? With an opportunity to tell his story, Rick calmed down and opened up. The quiet space filled not with questions from a rating scale but with time to listen. I observed father and son visibly relax, their body postures shifting away from tension and anger. For the first time, they looked at each other. As I stayed quiet, they began to talk directly, face-to-face. Rather than attack Alex, Rick seemed to feel safe to share his sadness about the widening rifts in his family and his feelings of helplessness in his desire to connect with Alex now that he was well into his teenage years. Longing and relief emanated from Alex as he told his father it frightened him to hear his parents fight, often about him. Preoccupied by these disturbing experiences, he found it difficult to pay attention in school. I now recognized the situation as a downward spiral of missed cues and miscommunications. Carmen and Rick saw a lazy, resistant boy; Alex saw parents who were constantly angry and disappointed in him. His behavior became fodder for his parents' fighting, digging the family into a deeper hole of disconnection.

I transformed my critical feelings that bubbled up in response to Rick's hostility toward his son into curiosity, recognizing that no matter how bad things appear, parents love their children and wish to do right by them. This stance allowed me to join Rick. The connection with me seemed to give Rick a new way to think about his son's behavior and, in doing so, to reconnect with him.

When Carmen returned from the waiting room, she seemed surprised by the dramatic shift in mood. After laying out expectations of confidentiality regarding my visit with Alex, I offered to meet with Carmen and Rick alone in a few weeks. At that next meeting, they told me that the problem behavior, which they had termed *oppositional* but now recognized as a reaction to tensions in the home and stresses in school, had significantly declined. They saw his behavior as a form of communication. They acknowledged strain in their marriage but felt an ebb in its intensity. Carmen and Rick sat side by side, turning to face each other as they shared with me their newfound joy and relief at changes in their relationship with their son. The healing in the father-son relationship had opened up a connection between Alex's parents. Moving through the mess of disconnection to reconnection led to a moment of growth and change for the whole family. No great interpretation was required. I simply created a calm space for them to think, to be curious about what was going on.

In the next few years of my studies with the Berkshire Psychoanalytic Institute, I discovered the work of other great thinkers in the fields of psychoanalysis and child development. Now a close colleague, psychoanalyst Peter Fonagy of the Anna Freud Centre in London offered profound insights that shifted my understanding of my clinical experience. Fonagy described how the ability to recognize that other people have different motivations and intentions from one's own, or what he termed *mentalization,* is a developmental achievement with its roots in early childhood relationships. When I first learned of Ed Tronick's research, it occurred to me that he offered scientific evidence for the profound truths Winnicott distilled from his clinical work, ideas that had so influenced my own thinking.

I learned that trust develops by exactly the process I observed between Rick and Alex. Moving from misunderstanding to understanding — repairing the disconnection — allows us to form deeper attachments in our larger social world. A path of trust opened between me and Rick during our second visit because, rather than judging him for his anger or trying to change his behavior, I validated his experience. In turn, he opened up to understanding his son. We all moved together from anger and judgment to listening with curiosity.

This dynamic would become typical in my practice. I came to recognize that once parents and I together discovered the meaning in the behavior, parents usually knew what to do. Behavior problems resolved.

The work with Alex and his parents was a kind of aha! moment for me and left me hungry for more. As the field of pediatrics exploded with diagnoses of ADHD and the newly discovered pediatric bipolar disorder, I experimented with creating a space for families to move from disconnection to reconnection. In part, this change was concrete. I started reserving fifty minutes for an appointment rather than the standard thirty and saw families in a larger, more comfortable office. I recognized that the amount of time for the visit and the safety of the physical space played a critical role. As I shifted from asking questions and giving advice to simply listening, frequently sitting on the floor with younger children, I saw families move from anger and disconnection, sometimes through deep sadness, and then to moments of reconnection. A young child would spontaneously run into his mother's arms to receive a hug. Often I felt a tingling in my arms, and my eyes filled with tears in the presence of rediscovered joy and love. Motivated by the power of these moments to share my discoveries with both parents and my pediatrician colleagues, I began writing. These experiences gave birth to my first book, *Keeping Your Child in Mind*, written for an audience of parents and professionals.

The second encounter that fundamentally changed my thinking and approach to my work occurred when I saw a three-month-old, Aliyah, for management of colic. A pediatrician from my practice who knew that I was immersing myself in new ways to work with struggling families referred the family to me. She understood that this case would involve more than instructions on what to do about colic. A common concern for parents of young infants, *colic* is not an illness or a disorder but a description of a behavior, excessive crying. *Colic* is often defined by the rule of threes: crying more than three hours a day, more than three days a week, and for longer than three weeks. For Aliyah, standard techniques for treating colic, including being carried, white noise, various different colic drops, and changes to her mother's diet, had failed.

Jaclyn, Aliyah's mother, had recently been diagnosed with postpartum depression. The obstetrician had recommended an increase in Jaclyn's dose of antidepressant medication. But Jaclyn already felt not entirely herself on the medicine; she feared a higher dose would interfere with her ability to be fully present with her baby, and so she was reluctant to take that path.

She came to the visit with her wife, Kayla, who was back to work full-time and struggling to figure out how to deal with Jaclyn's persistent and deepening sadness. Kayla offered a vivid example that brought me into their world. The morning of our visit, an apple had fallen out of the bag of groceries Jaclyn was bringing in from the car, and she collapsed on the ground sobbing.

Rather than offering the standard advice about managing colic, I sat down on the floor with Jaclyn and Kayla and observed the baby's behavior. Aliyah had been what is called a "late preterm," born at thirty-six weeks. In the hospital, she had been in the regular nursery, not the special care nursery, and none of the doctors or nurses had told Aliyah's parents to expect anything unusual. Yet pediatricians know that babies born even a week or two early can have relatively immature nervous systems that make their behavioral signals more difficult to read. While the three of us sat on the floor observing the baby, Kayla sneezed. Aliyah's whole body became disorganized as her arms flew over her head. In an instant, she transitioned from quietly sleeping to all-out wailing. Jaclyn immediately scooped up the screaming baby and started walking back and forth across the room, rocking Aliyah vigorously. Kayla looked at me imploringly. "See?"

"Yes," I replied. I joined their experience of a baby who went from calm to crying in an instant and appreciated along with them how exhausting this could be. We sat and waited, and in a minute or so Aliyah was quiet again. I shared my observation that, likely in part related to her prematurity, Aliyah was more sensitive to sensory input than most babies and thus required more support from her parents, especially in managing disruptions and transitions. Both moms nodded in recognition. Now that Jaclyn had a new way to understand Aliyah's behavior, her guilt and feelings of inadequacy, her certainty that the crying meant she was a bad mother, began to subside, and she felt a release from the grip of worry and self-doubt.

Much to my delight and a bit to my surprise, the next time we met, Jaclyn said that she felt 100 percent better. While I had not added any treatment for colic, the time and space for listening and understanding seemed to have resulted in a transformation in Aliyah's behavior, in Jaclyn's mood, and in their relationship. Aliyah was still having bouts of crying, but Jaclyn felt that she could manage them. Jaclyn's depression was being treated only by medication, so I had given her the name of a psychotherapist. But she had not gone that route, preferring to spend the time taking a yoga class. She had increased her medication dose for a few days but then decided that she didn't need it and was back to the lower dose.

Jaclyn had walked into my office grinning at Aliyah, who gazed up at her with adoration from her car seat. I saw their joy in each other. "What do you think made the difference?" I asked. She explained that during our last visit, she had felt she was being heard by both me and Kayla. Jaclyn sensed that Kayla understood her experience and could support her in a way that felt real and not forced. Jaclyn also understood that Aliyah's intense crying was not all her fault and did not represent her failure. Her decreased feelings of self-doubt together with Kayla's validation of her struggles gave Jaclyn strength to be more responsive to Aliyah. In turn, she said, Aliyah seemed calmer and the intense crying had lessened.

"I feel as if Aliyah were just born," Jaclyn told me. She described a complete transformation in their relationship. Jaclyn had been contemplating going back to work but now was rethinking her plans because she felt that for the first time she and Aliyah were really connecting.

As I continued working with children from infancy through adolescence with a full range of emotional and behavioral problems, I heard story after story of relationships that derailed very early in development. And I began to see that, even if the roots of troubles were deep, as long as I protected time for listening and reconnection, relationships could heal no matter the child's age. I recognized that behavior problems in an individual child were rooted in relationships with important people in that child's life. When I focused my work on healing relationships rather than on changing behavior, development could take a different path.

Unfortunately, recognizing the significance of relationships in making sense of behavior frequently gets translated into blaming parents. People may wonder if a child's behavior is a result of poor parenting. A more constructive approach begins with accepting that when relationships falter, individuals will struggle. While a particular problem may be located in one person — for example, Aliyah's relative prematurity and difficulty settling herself — the caregiver's response to the problem becomes part of their relationship. In every relationship, each person has a role to play and, through that role, influences the other. Not only as children but throughout people's lives, seeing struggles in the context of relationships, without judgment or blame, helps all of us connect and our relationships succeed.

Shortly after my visit with Aliyah, a faculty member of the Berkshire Psychoanalytic Institute told me about a new program in infant mental health, a growing field that integrates research and knowledge at the interface of developmental psychology, neuroscience, and genetics to inform models of prevention, intervention, and treatment. When I looked at the program website, I knew immediately that it was something I had to do. It was modeled on a similar program on the West Coast led by Ed Tronick and nurse-practitioner Kristie Brandt, and Ed was also the chief faculty member for this new version on the East Coast. I had heard him speak a few years earlier and recently learned about his still-face paradigm in one of my classes at Berkshire Psychoanalytic Institute. I applied to be a fellow starting in the fall of 2010. For a year, I participated in monthly three-day weekends where I learned directly from leading researchers from all over the world. In intimate, intense discussion with thirty other international fellows from a wide range of fields, including nursing, psychiatry, early intervention, social work, occupational therapy, physical therapy, and early childhood education, I found new ways to understand my observations and clinical experiences. Immersed in Ed's body of research, which dated back to the early 1970s, I learned about a new model of development and began a collaboration that would lead to the creation of this book.

ED'S STORY: THE STILL-FACE PARADIGM

One Minute, Thirty Seconds

A young, dark-haired woman enters a room, her eleven-month-old daughter on her hip. She scans the room, sees a high chair, approaches it, eases the now squawking child into the seat, and carefully buckles her in with the sky-blue straps. Then the woman sits down facing the child, leans in to make eye contact, and strokes both sides of her head with her hands.

"Are you my good girl?" she croons.

The baby, now calm, raises her eyebrows and coos a sound of agreement. Then she points over her mother's shoulder with a decisive "Da." The mother turns her head to see where her daughter is pointing, then turns back to her smiling, acknowledging that she has seen it too.

She holds the baby's feet and tickles them. The girl smiles as the mother spider-walks her fingers up her legs. The mother takes the child's hands, clicking her tongue to keep her attention. Mother and daughter are engaged in a graceful dance of interaction.

The mother turns her head to the side far enough that her daughter can see only her dark wavy hair. When she turns back around, her face is an expressionless mask, like a robot's.

The baby immediately looks wary. She smiles at her mother, but her mother does not respond. The baby tries to engage her by pointing again. This time, her mother does not turn her head to see what is of interest. Her face is leaden. Her only facial movement is blinking occasionally.

Sixteen seconds have passed since the mother stopped responding.

The baby strains forward against the straps of the chair, reaching her hands out to her mother. Her mother does not reach back or alter her expression. The child, now in distress, tries smiling one more time, though this time her smile is wan. She tries clapping. Nothing.

A minute and eighteen seconds have passed.

When her mother continues to stare impassively, the baby screeches. She puts her hands in her mouth and looks away anxiously. She turns back to her mother and reaches for her again in a gesture of pleading. Her mother remains stone-faced.

Finally, the baby gives up and begins to cry. She arches her back and turns away, desolate.

At this point, the mother's face comes back to life. She looks at her baby with a smiling, doting expression again. She reaches for her baby's hands and croons, "I'm here, I'm here," in the same singsong tones she used earlier.

The baby, still wary, hesitates a moment. Then she smiles shakily and reaches out. Mother and baby are together again.

One minute and thirty seconds have passed.

This scene comes from a videotape of a psychological experiment that has become known simply as "the still-face." I didn't realize it at the time, but the experiment would turn out to be a landmark, a first in the study of infant development and, later, in the study of human relationships more broadly.

Without knowing it, you show a still-face many times each day to express displeasure or to disconnect from family members, friends, enemies, or strangers. And others show it to you. Usually it's less dramatic than what happens in the experiment. Typically, both the still-face you offer to others and the ones you receive from others are out of your awareness, shown and experienced unconsciously. Nevertheless, the still-face is part of everyone's repertoire. It is in all of us.

In 1972, when I first did the still-face experiment, the finding was revolutionary. Prior to that, setting up my lab at Harvard Medical School as a new faculty member, drawing on my experiences thus far, I had been brewing an idea. I had a hypothesis that the infant was a much more active participant in the parent-child relationship than was commonly thought at the time. Psychiatrists and psychologists had come around to the idea that infants were deeply bonded to their primary caregivers. They knew that a disruption in that relationship could have negative repercussions for a child. But all the emphasis was on the mother's behavior. Was she consistent in her responses or was she preoccupied and emotionally unavailable? Did she behave in ways that were confusing and unpredictable? No one was looking at the infant's role in the relationship. It was assumed that the connection flowed in one direction, from mother to child; the baby simply received whatever was dealt. Yet after observing the extraordinary social competence in newborn babies in my work with pediatrician T. Berry Brazelton, I had begun to wonder if this perspective was wrong.

As an experimental psychologist, I decided that the natural next step was to set up an experiment to test my hypothesis. I played around with a number of possibilities — have the mother look away from the baby, frown, not talk — but these all seemed too subtle. Then I came up with the idea to have the mother not react to the baby at all. It was a big perturbation. It turned out I was right, that the infant reacted in a dramatically strong way. I was amazed to find just how much infants had to tell about what was happening to them. (While our original research was done with mothers, the results, as you will see throughout this book, have relevance for fathers and the full range of different family constellations.)

Based on everything I had been taught up to that point in my career, my expectation was that if mothers tuned out, as I asked them to do in the still-face experiment, their infants would simply follow their mothers' lead. Babies wouldn't plead, whee-dle, or express outrage. They wouldn't do anything.

Together with my colleagues, I set up the first still-face exper-iment. We studied seven mothers and their infants, who ranged in age from one to four months. In all seven pairs — or *dyads*, as we call them in scientific studies — the result was the same. When the mothers "turned off," the babies brought out a bag of tricks — smiling, gurgling, pointing, screeching, crying — to actively try to reengage them.

And given the babies' age, it couldn't have been something they'd learned. They hadn't had time. The little girl in the open-ing scene of this section, the version most viewed on YouTube, was eleven months old. Research subsequent to the original experiment has captured a similar reaction in infants as young as one month, and some have seen it in newborns. These babies have not learned social skills. The drive to connect arrived with them at birth, ready for action in these first relationships. They were *wired to demand* that back-and-forth connection that we saw when the mother and her baby in the opening story were responding to each other.

At a minimum, the babies' reaction meant two things: First, the field of psychology's primary assumption that the mother con-trolled the interaction while the baby remained passive was wrong. Instead, the baby turned out to be hugely active, making great efforts to induce the mother to tune back in. This single experiment undermined one of the most widely accepted beliefs in contemporary psychology; theories based on this assumption would have to be completely rethought. Second, there was a huge piece of human development that psychologists had missed entirely — something that researchers in the field knew *nothing* about.

And the experiment raised so many questions. What was happening in this interaction? What were the consequences of too little — or too much — connection between mother and child? How much of a broken connection could a baby endure? When would a baby simply give up trying to reestablish the link? After five minutes? Ten? The length of time it took to answer a doorbell? What was normal? We didn't know.

My research on the still-face went on at Harvard for several more years. My colleagues and I broadened the experiment to include studies with older children and even adults. In an effort to gain insight into the process, we asked pairs of adults to play the baby and the mother and enact the still-face experiment. We learned a tremendous amount. The adults who played the part of the baby described feeling panicky, angry, and helpless. The adults who played the mother felt guilty and anxious. Several actually apologized to the "baby."

The adult experiment revealed the fundamental importance of social connection. Our drive to connect inhabits our emotional core. Even though the subjects knew what was going on — there was no deception, and both adults received the instructions together — they still had strong emotional reactions. Adults who took the role of the infant described feeling just as dismayed by the experience of being emotionally stonewalled as the actual infants appeared to be. Adults asked to play the mother role were also upset. "*He* made me do it," they'd tell the participants playing the infant's role, pointing at the experimenter, me. While the real-life mothers we recruited found it fascinating to observe their infants' reactions, often saying, "I didn't know he knew me," they never liked the experiment either. And unlike the role-playing adults, these mothers had no way to explain their behavior to their babies.

By 1975, I still didn't know entirely what this all meant but I was sure that I was onto something important, so I decided to take it public. With some trepidation, I prepared to present the results of the still-face experiment at the annual conference of the Society for Research in Child Development, a professional society for clinical child psychologists and researchers. How would they respond to what I had discovered?

It was a daring move, and one I wasn't entirely comfortable with. I was thirty-two, and I'd had a charmed career in child development so far.

Learning from Giants

I was lucky to begin my research career in 1965 by training in the lab of Harry Harlow, one of the leaders in developmental psychology. While Harlow was semiretired by that point and the lab had a new director, his influence was pervasive. As a professor of psychology at the University of Wisconsin in the 1950s, Harlow famously, and somewhat controversially, proclaimed that he planned to study love. He began with the topic that had preoccupied psychiatry and psychology since Sigmund Freud: the relationship between mother and baby. The field was opening up to the idea of attachment theory, in large part as a result of the work of British psychologist John Bowlby. Bowlby had concluded that a strong emotional attachment between baby and mother would produce a psychologically sound, well-adapted child. And he said that the reverse was also true — if mother and baby did not develop this profound attachment, the child would suffer.

Harlow wanted to explore this idea of attachment, but instead of using human mothers and babies as his subjects, he chose monkeys — rhesus macaques. Once he'd established that humans and rhesus macaques behaved similarly in many respects, he performed the experiment that made him famous. He took the mothers away from their babies and replaced the mothers with facsimiles made of either wire or cloth. He found that babies with fake mothers not only were considerably more anxious and less capable of forming relationships than those with real mothers but, when they grew up, they were less capable of parenting their own infant monkeys. His now classic studies poignantly and painfully proved his point: that love, in this case a mother's, is vital to an infant's emotional and psychological well-being. All of this was about what mothers brought to the relationship; no one was looking too carefully at what the babies brought.

What I learned from Harlow, and what I saw in the labs, where the smell of monkey was ever present, was that a mother's love, or lack thereof, early in life had a long-term, intergenerational effect. The monkeys raised on surrogate mothers grew up to have abnormal peer relationships and sexual behavior. If the females became pregnant and bore offspring, they showed disturbed parenting behavior. They dragged the babies around, ignored them, pushed them away, or threatened them.

In an effort to understand the impact of parent-infant relationships, I began to study infant perception. I was already becoming curious about how infants make sense of their experiences. Inspired by the work of renowned psychologist James Gibson suggesting that infants were born with the capacity to perceive danger, I designed a low-tech experiment: A ball mounted on a cart was pulled by a string toward a light source, and the shadow of the ball was cast onto a translucent screen in front of the infant. The results showed that infants had a defensive reaction — putting their hands in front of their faces — when the ball appeared to be looming at them. They organized a response to the experience, making meaning of it as dangerous, although of course it was not actually dangerous.

Another lucky event had occurred earlier, in 1965, during my first year of graduate school in Wisconsin. I attended a talk by a visiting psychology professor from Harvard, Jerome Bruner. He studied language and was interested in the process by which babies make sense of the world around them. Bruner called this *meaning-making*, a term I later adopted in my own work, as you will see. I talked to him for hours after his presentation, probably way too much, but the next day my adviser told me that Bruner wanted me to come to Boston to work in his lab when I graduated from Wisconsin. I had just started, but already I had secured a job at Harvard!

Before I could conceive of my own still-face experiment, I needed one more teacher. That turned out to be pediatrician T. Berry Brazelton. We met when we were both fellows at the Harvard Center for Cognitive Studies in the late 1960s. Bruner was its director, and as a mentor to Brazelton and me, he would support our creation of the child development unit at Boston Children's Hospital in 1972.

Brazelton was becoming one of the most respected and influential pediatricians in the country. Not unlike those of fellow pediatrician D. W. Winnicott, his ideas grew out of the experience of studying psychoanalysis while simultaneously immersing himself in the lives of the infants and parents in his pediatric practice. It was Berry who, on our Saturday visits to the maternity ward at Mount Auburn Hospital, in Cambridge, Massachusetts, opened my eyes to what newborns were capable of.

Today, newborns usually room in with their mothers, but at that time they were kept in a nursery while their mothers recovered in the hospital, typically for five days. On these Saturdays, I would meet Berry and we'd walk together to the nursery. Often Bruner joined us. The newborns, ranging in age from a few hours to five days old, were swaddled in the usual pink-and-blue-striped blankets and placed in plastic bassinets that were lined up facing the viewing window. The cloying sweet-and-sour smell of baby powder, bath soap, and full diapers filled the air.

Berry always carried a man's toiletry kit under one arm on these visits. It was stocked with his tools, which included a flashlight and a plastic box filled with just the right number of popcorn kernels to serve as a gentle rattle, among other things.

When we stepped into the nursery, I'd trail behind Berry and watch as he scanned the rows of sleeping infants and then picked one to focus on. He would talk softly to the babies, pick them up in his large hands, shift their body position, shake the rattle near their ears, and flick the flashlight above their faces to elicit their reactions. He'd tap at reflex points — the palm of the

THE POWER OF DISCORD

hand to trigger the grasp reflex, the cheek to trigger the rooting reflex, when the infant turns toward the source of touch to locate the breast or bottle.

Much of what he did was standard stuff for a pediatric exam. But Berry added his own twist; he assessed the babies' social capacities by noting such things as the way each engaged with a face and voice and the ability to self-comfort. What was also uniquely Berry's was the way he would tune in and observe. These babies had his complete attention. As I watched, I saw that the babies visually followed both inanimate objects and faces, tracking their movement. The babies' expressions changed, as did the movement of their extremities, depending on whether they were looking at objects or people. At just a few hours old, babies could differentiate between people and things! How did they know? What meaning did they make of their world? Clearly, there was a lot more to these tiny people than I had expected.

Watching Berry, I also saw that babies were not simply awake or asleep. Berry's careful observations revealed to us that babies had six distinct states, ranging from deep sleep through quiet wakefulness to active crying. We noticed that each baby had a particular way of transitioning between these different states of consciousness. Some gradually went from sleep to quiet wakefulness to active crying. Others cried and cried and then were suddenly and instantaneously asleep. Still others seemed not to follow any consistent pattern.

In his visits to the nursery Berry somehow could see the individual inside the baby — who the infant already was and who the infant might become. While current variations of these sets of observations, including the Neonatal Behavioral Assessment

Scale (NBAS), Newborn Behavioral Observations (NBO) system, and the NICU Network Neurobehavioral Scale (NNNS), typically include parents, at that time, parents were not present for the exam. However, even though it was not standard to examine babies with their parents present, Berry saw the value of sharing these observations with them. It wasn't uncommon for him to handle a baby for a while and then go and chat with the parents. He would tell them what their baby was like to give them a sense of the baby as a unique individual. He recognized how important it was for parents to have protected time right from the start to learn about a baby's way of communicating. He would give the parents a sense of what their babies were sensitive to, whether they were capable of self-soothing, and how they liked to be held. Sometimes he would tell them difficult things that he thought they should know, for instance that when their babies were upset, they had trouble calming down.

His goal was to get the parents to see their babies as the unique people they already were — not the wished-for baby or the fantasy baby, but the baby they had. Parents would listen in awe as Berry revealed what he had learned about their child in the brief time he'd spent with them.

Berry wanted to systematize the way he examined babies so that doctors and nurses in other hospitals could do it too. He hoped these practitioners could reveal infants to their parents as the complex, capable creatures they were.

My role was to observe and help Berry systematize the exam. I did this, but it was far from just an exercise in note-taking. Every Saturday, I was awed anew by what he was showing me. This was as much art, intuition, and empathy as it was science. I often thought of him as a baby whisperer, somebody who could somehow speak the babies' language through a look, a touch, and his personal warmth.

I had arrived in Boston from Harlow's lab having read every paper about infants in the literature. I thought I knew everything there was to know about babies, although the only infants I'd handled until then were Harlow's infant rhesus macaques. The truth, I soon realized under Berry's tutelage, was that I knew close to nothing. What he was showing me on these Saturday jaunts defied everything that psychologists at that time believed about infants.

Few of the behaviors Berry was eliciting from these babies had ever been described before. In fact, they were doing things that psychologists "knew" infants could not do. Babies would turn their heads a full ninety degrees to both the right and the left to find their mothers' voices. Babies who became overwhelmed by sensory input could close their eyes and turn away to calm themselves. Babies appeared to come into the world with a remarkable capacity to engage in relationships!

I wanted to test our observation that, rather than being a passive recipient, a new baby was an active participant in relationships. That's what prompted me to devise the still-face experiment. According to the experts at the time, the mother was in complete control of the infant; she called the shots in the interaction. What would happen, I wondered, if I removed the active player, the mother? What would the baby do? With the original experiment, I knew almost immediately that, as the still-face video demonstrates, the conventional view of infants was wrong. It was stunning — and marvelous.

I knew that this finding had to be shared beyond my laboratory; I would have to present this work to my colleagues. But that prospect was terrifying. Scientists are notorious for ruthless criticism of those who introduce different ways of thinking and looking at the world. The experiment, and my view of why its implications were so spectacular, would force psychologists to abandon some long-held beliefs. When I presented this work, I might be publicly applauded — or ridiculed. I put my odds of success at fifty-fifty.

On the day of my presentation at the child development conference, I was the last of four researchers to step up to the lectern. I watched nervously as three of my colleagues discussed their work, all completely in line with what we all presumed to be true. The sequence of speakers was planned that way, perhaps defensively. The organizers were collaborators from my laboratory who supported my hypothesis and knew what I was going to say. Finally it was my turn to stand up and face the audience of more than four hundred child development experts from all over the world. I was about to share with my colleagues something they had never seen.

I started by showing a video clip of the still-face experiment. In 1975, this was not easy. Projecting videotape wasn't possible then. I had developed an innovative but crude technique for videotaping my experiments and devised a way to transfer the tapes to film so they could be viewed on a large screen.

When I turned off the projector in the room, there was dead silence. I stood, clutching the lectern, trying to sense the mood of the crowd. I wasn't sure I could get from the stage to my seat without falling down in a heap. Obviously, it had been too big a risk. I saw what appeared to be four hundred still-faces. I should never have let these results out of the lab. My career was over.

Then thunderous applause rippled across the auditorium as the scientists in the audience realized what they had just seen. My career wasn't over. Really, it had just begun.

Decades later, as the life lessons of my body of research took shape, I realized I wanted to bring the ideas to a general audience. The fellows in my infant mental health program who brought their rich clinical experience to our learning process helped me recognize the broad applications of my research. One of these fellows was Claudia Gold, who also happened to be a writer and a pediatrician who dealt with people's real-world problems every day. I asked her to write a book with me, and here we are.

RELATIONSHIPS AS BUILDING BLOCKS

The still-face study evolved into a broad-based theory that explains something critically important about human behavior and relationships across the life span. It has revealed how people's first unremembered moments of learning to relate to others shape every relationship they will ever have. It shows how the ability to repair the tiny rifts of moment-to-moment relationships forms the texture and fabric of experience, building one's character and way of being in the world. Perhaps most important, the original still-face study and subsequent decades of research using that paradigm give us insight into how each of us can move from having unfulfilling or troubled relationships to having relationships that are intimate and connected.

You do not have to be a psychologist or a physician to grasp the insights of the still-face experiment. Nor do you need a sophisticated understanding of human relationships. And you do not need to be troubled to benefit from the practical applications of still-face research. You simply need to be a human being who has relationships with others. When people understand the still-face paradigm and its import, it changes the nature of all of their relationships — with spouses, parents, children, work colleagues, friends, and even casual encounters with strangers.

At first viewing, the still-face experiment can generate worry, pain, and fear as we are moved by the infant's experience of loss. We may reexperience our own losses and feel guilty as we reflect on the way we failed to connect with our children and other loved ones. Some people react dramatically to the experiment, even calling it cruel and questioning how it could get beyond the Institutional Review Board (IRB), the administrative body established to protect the rights of human research subjects. The original experiment — when of course we did not know what would happen — was approved by the IRB, and the experiment continues to be used in IRB-approved research around the world today. The fact is that the experience is not unfamiliar to the infant; it happens when a caregiver is driving, preoccupied by a worry, or not present in some other way. And babies get distressed all the time. It is not a stress that exceeds their typical day-to-day lives.

The primary message of the still-face is one of hope. The baby communicates in her quick recovery that this experience of mismatch, while magnified and dramatic in the experiment, is familiar to her. She knows what to do to engage her mother. She has done this many times before but in ways that went unnoticed. When we slow things down in the still-face experiment, we are able to see the infant's tremendous capacity to act on her world to make it better. She knows what's going on and how to repair it.

It turns out that babies react to the still-face experiment in different ways depending on the quality of their early interactions with their caregivers. Not all babies show a hopeful response. The still-face experiment and the decades of research that followed offer answers to the questions we raised in the opening paragraph of this introduction. Our sense of ourselves and the quality of our relationships throughout our lives are embedded in our experiences, in our moment-to-moment interactions starting at birth with our earliest love relationships. Our emotional well-being derives from a fluid process that changes as we immerse ourselves in a network of relationships.

As we will elaborate on in detail in subsequent chapters, the false dichotomies of biology versus experience, of nature versus nurture, collapse under the weight of research evidence showing that our genes, brains, and bodies develop in relationships. Expression of our genes and wiring of our brains occur in an interactive process. It used to be thought that brain wiring was predetermined, that the brain had a fixed wiring plan. But now we know this is not true. In a process called *neuroplasticity*, the brain can change throughout a person's lifetime. The formation of new neural connections, the "wires" that make up the brain, is flexible and messy. No two brains are wired the same way. Child development researchers use the term *neuroarchitects* to describe caregivers of young infants. A baby's earliest relationships determine the nature of the wiring — they literally build the brain. When infants move through the experience of disconnection to moments of reconnection, accepting and embracing the inherent messiness of human interaction, their brains grow and change.

OUR COMBINED STORIES: THE AIM
OF THIS BOOK

In *The Power of Discord*, we integrate Ed's research with Claudia's clinical work and add some personal experiences to the mix to reveal the full significance of what has come to be known as the still-face paradigm. While the two of us have worked on separate career trajectories over different periods, for the purpose of simplicity, in the rest of the book we speak with one voice as collaborators, using the pronoun *we* whether or not a given context actually involved both of us. For all the vignettes, which span from infancy to old age, names and identifying details have been changed to protect privacy. Using these stories to demonstrate the central lessons of our work with babies and parents, we present a new understanding of human development.

This book is not meant to replace care given by professionals. It is not meant as a form of medical, parenting, or psychological advice. In fact, as we will show, blanket advice that's given without addressing the complexity of individual experience can get in the way of growth and development. The central takeaway of this book is that discord in relationships is normal; in fact, your sense of self and your ability to be close to others emerge by welcoming it. We want to alter your view of your relationships and of how you make sense of yourself in the world. There is not a single way but lots of ways you will learn to think differently.

In chapter 1 we introduce the concept that discord is not only healthy but essential for growth and change. We offer research evidence of how the process of mismatch and repair is central to human development. In chapter 2 we expand on the importance of imperfection, contrasting this with our contemporary culture's expectation of perfection. In chapter 3 we show what leads to either a sense of safety to engage in the mess or a fear of disorder. In chapter 4 we further address the myth of biology versus environment — that is, nature versus nurture. We describe how both your sense of self and your capacity for intimacy emerge in moment-to-moment interactions in your earliest relationships and continue to develop in new relationships throughout your life span. In chapter 5 we offer a new spin on resilience, suggesting it is neither an inborn trait nor a response to adversity but rather a quality that develops as each of us works through countless moments of interactive mismatch and repair. In chapter 6 we show how repeated patterns of interaction — the games people play — contribute to a sense of belonging in families, workplaces, and culture as a whole. In chapter 7, we show how technology is changing those games in ways that can be scary, and we draw on the still-face paradigm to manage and embrace these changes. Chapter 8 offers a new and different way to think about emotional suffering in the context of derailed relationships. Chapter 9 shows how people heal by protecting space and time for countless new interactions with opportunities for new meanings. In chapter 10 we address the danger of certainty and of clinging to simple answers; we reveal the value of uncertainty in promoting growth and change. Finally, in chapter 11, we link our model to current social ills and show how the still-face paradigm can help communities and society in general find a path to hope and resilience.

1

REPAIR AS FOOD FOR THE SOUL

JENNIFER HAD BEEN PREPARING dinner for her boyfriend, Craig, for hours. The tasks of whisking, chopping, grating, and mixing steadied her despite the growing tension between them. Approaching their one-year anniversary, they had been careful with each other for months, afraid to disrupt what felt like a precarious alliance. After the initial bliss of falling in love, it seemed they were stalled, unable to move forward in their relationship.

The quiet of the day allowed a mess of troubled thoughts to swirl in Jennifer's mind. She relived the moments over the preceding months when Craig appeared distracted and not emotionally available in the way she felt she needed. In this honeymoon phase of their romance, Jennifer had learned to suppress the hurt she experienced. But as they settled into what seemed possibly to be a committed relationship, her distress grew. Her silent cooking masked a bubbling anger.

Craig puttered about the house, occasionally stopping in the kitchen to give his girlfriend a gentle hug from behind as she worked at the stove. To him, it was a scene of blissful domestic-ity. While he had noticed the increasing distance between them, his approach was to ignore it and simply carry on. He had grown up in a large family with four siblings where hurt feelings came and went like the ebb and flow of the tide. He was used to pay-ing attention to several people at once. Unaware of the painful memories Jennifer brought from her past troubled relationships, he remained oblivious to the brewing storm.

Jennifer, an only child, had little experience with discord. In her family, clashes were avoided at all costs. Her stoic father, a veteran of the Vietnam War, silently held his feelings in. Her mother took great care not to provoke him, as he could go from calm and quiet to explosive in an instant. In the face of any kind of disagreement, her parents would withdraw from each other and from Jennifer. Though physically present, they disappeared emotionally. She had vivid childhood memories of sitting alone in the back seat of the family car in the stony silence that fol-lowed one of her father's angry outbursts. She felt completely lost when her parents withdrew like this, almost as if she herself had ceased to exist. Jennifer brought a reflexive fear of discord to her adult relationship with Craig. She craved the connection she found with him but feared its loss. Silence and avoidance seemed safer than open discord.

At the table, just as Jennifer was quietly placing the finishing touches on their meal, Craig looked down at his cell phone to read a text from one of his siblings. This behavior was not atypi-cal for him, but in that moment, Jennifer felt a wave of rage rise within her, and this time she did not hide it. While she could not have put the idea into words, in the preceding months of their relationship, she had developed a sense that Craig, who was so different in many ways from her parents, would not disappear if confronted with anger. Impulsively and without thinking, she gave this impression its first test: she knocked her elegantly laid-out meal onto the floor.

Initially Craig reacted with shock, bewildered by this unfamiliar display of emotion. But his brief flash of anger quickly dissipated when Jennifer burst into tears. He ran to her and they held each other. As Jennifer's sobs subsided, she began to share her fear that discord meant loss. Sitting on the floor next to the mess of the ruined dinner, she told him that she feared that their relationship could not withstand conflict. More powerfully, the memory of her sense of self faltering in response to her parents' emotional withdrawal led her to fear that she herself would disappear. The trust that she had developed in Craig in this new and very different relationship gave her access to these previously unexpressed and complicated feelings.

This moment became a turning point for them. She saw that she had interpreted his behavior as rejection when that was not his motivation at all. Craig saw Jennifer's tendency to detach in a different light. His approach of waiting for disturbances to pass, which had for the most part worked in his large family, wouldn't fly in this new relationship. Jennifer increasingly trusted that Craig would not disappear in the face of discord. She learned to engage with him instead of withdrawing in moments of miscommunication. They brought their respective different intentions and motivations into their relationship, each giving space and time to the other to be seen. Their relationship grew in the moments of mismatch and repair that followed over days, months, and years.

The mess of baked scallops, mashed parsnips, and buttered

string beans could serve as a metaphor for the role of mismatch and repair in human development. Just as nutrients provide fuel for physical growth, the energy produced by moving through the mess of mismatch to repair fuels emotional growth. Mismatch and repair figuratively (and sometimes literally) feed us.

MISMATCH AS THE NORM

An idealized notion of parental love might be epitomized by da Vinci's *Madonna and Child*, in which Mary and her infant son gaze lovingly into each other's eyes. In one of Raphael's depictions of the same pair, more tellingly, Baby Jesus looks at a book in Mary's hand while she gazes distractedly toward the ground below. Similarly, an idealized notion of romantic love is conveyed in Fred Astaire and Ginger Rogers's dancing; we get the impression that in good relationships, people step together perfectly in sync. But the partnership of Jennifer Grey and Patrick Swayze in *Dirty Dancing*, where at one point she steps on his toes and he pokes her in the eye, is closer to the truth. The mess of missteps is necessary for the creation of the graceful, coordinated dance of the final scene. For Jennifer and Craig, the laughter they shared while cleaning up the mess and ordering pizza captured the joy and intimacy that comes with navigating through mismatch to repair.

Moving through messiness turns out to be the way we grow and develop in relationships from earliest infancy through adulthood! This might seem counterintuitive, as you might think that in healthy relationships, there is no place for discord. Shouldn't two people in a good relationship always get along?

The dramatic findings of the original still-face experiment

had uncovered a new way to understand babies and parents, but there was still so much to learn about this primary relationship. Previous infant research had reflected the assumption that the more synchronous and attuned the interaction, the more optimal, or clinically "normal," the relationship. To many people's surprise, the research revealed that messiness holds the key to strong relationships!

We began by videotaping typical parent-infant interactions. In subsequent frame-by-frame analysis of these videos, we slowed down the tape, gaining a window into the moment-to-moment interactions that we could not appreciate in real time. We expected to see healthy mother-infant pairs in perfect attunement, meeting each other's gaze, turning away from each other at the same time, reaching for each other in sync, and in general matching each other's every move. With this preconceived notion of how relationships work, we drew neat graphs of moments of connection, dismissing as irrelevant any data that showed disconnection and did not fit this tidy pattern. But after months of research, we were unable to deny the actual pattern. In typical healthy parent-infant pairs, on average 70 percent of the interactions were out of sync! Disconnection was an inevitable part of the interaction.

In one sequence we observed, for example, an infant was looking at a strap on her high chair and comforting herself by sucking her finger. When her mother tried to get her attention, the infant avoided her. The mother then took the baby's hand from her mouth and moved back slightly. Their eyes met, and both smiled. The mother then moved closer and the infant looked away. A new dance had begun.

Does it seem right to you that most relationships are

mismatched 70 percent of the time? We found this again and again. In the field of developmental psychology, this seventy-thirty split has become famous, with some practitioners referencing it without actually knowing its origin. It comes from our detailed observations of the primary love relationship. Our expectation of attunement initially led us to see mismatch as a problem when in fact it was the norm. In analyzing these videotapes, we discovered that the most important part was not the mismatch but the repair.

REPAIR IS WHERE THE ACTION IS

We came to recognize that repair is the crux of human interactions. Repair leads to a feeling of pleasure, trust, and security, the implicit knowledge that *I can overcome problems*. Furthermore, repair teaches a critical life lesson: The negative feeling that arises from a mismatch can be changed into a positive feeling when two people subsequently achieve a match. One does not have to get stuck in a negative feeling state. And the belief that one can or cannot change an emotional state develops in an infant's earliest interactions.

We drew on observations from typical interactions to get a clear picture of what was going on when we performed a set of experiments using the still-face paradigm. We first observed parent-infant pairs engaging naturally in some kind of play that was typical for them, such as a clapping game or a counting game. We found that later, in the experimental setting of the still-face, these infants used the strategies they had learned through the mismatch-repair process in play to signal their mothers. When confronted with a stressful situation, they could apply a style of interaction drawn from the everyday exchanges with their caregivers. While they did not yet have the capacity for language or conscious thought, they were able to draw on their countless moment-to-moment interactions to cope with the stress of caregivers' unfamiliar behavior.

We came to understand mismatch and repair as a normal and ongoing experience fundamental to our species' development as social beings. What a relief to learn that in primary love relationships, humans are in sync only 30 percent of the time! That the number is so low should relieve the pressure many people feel to seek perfect harmony in their relationships as adults. As long as there is an opportunity for repair, mismatch in 70 percent of interactions is not only typical but conducive to positive and healthy development and relationships. We need the normal messiness in order to learn to trust each other.

Most of the interactions we observed in our videotape analyses were repaired to a matching state in the interchanges immediately following the mismatch. In other words, typical infants and their caregivers are constantly moving into mismatched states and then repairing them. Repairs may be small — microscopic, in fact — but there are lots of them in the countless moments of interactions.

The central lesson of the decades of research that followed the original still-face experiment is that this process of moving through mismatch to repair is not only unavoidable but essential if relationships are to flourish rather than stagnate or fall apart. As Jennifer discovered with Craig, we need to let the mess happen. We need mismatch because without it we cannot experience repair.

MISMATCH, REPAIR, AND MEANING-MAKING

Throughout his childhood, through countless moments of mismatch and repair in his family of origin, Craig had developed a core sense of hopefulness — or, to use the term we borrowed from Jerome Bruner, he *made meaning* of the world as a hopeful place. In contrast, Jennifer had a paucity of experience with repair, and that led her to construct a less hopeful meaning of herself in the world. A guarded sense of caution characterized her approach to relationships.

We see differences like these emerging in the early months of life. Recall that in the original experiment, we watched the infant employ different strategies to engage her mother. This behavior reflected an ongoing context of mismatch and repair. The baby had learned that she could act on her world to make it better. Even at the tender age of eleven months, she, like Craig, had made meaning of her world as a hopeful place.

When we performed the experiment with parent-infant dyads for whom the mismatch-repair process had derailed, we did not see this robust response. Parents and infants made different meanings. Some mothers, preoccupied by their own distress, made less effort to repair the inevitable mismatches. Others, overwhelmed by anxiety, rarely allowed space for mismatch. Still others behaved intrusively — for example, repeatedly touching the infants even when they pushed the mothers' hands away or gave other signals of becoming overwhelmed. When confronted by mismatch, infants who'd had a paucity of opportunity for repair did not make the same efforts to reengage, to repair the gap.

While growing up, Jennifer, like those infants, had suffered from a lack of opportunity for repair. She had not developed

40

strategies for managing the inevitable rifts that occur in human relationships. Instead, she had learned to protect herself from the deeply distressing experience of her parents' sudden emotional absence. She spent time alone in her room, immersing herself in homework or books. She excelled academically, using her intellect to hold herself together, but became emotionally guarded and closed off.

Initially, Jennifer had repeated this pattern of behavior with Craig. But Craig was a very different interactive partner than either of her parents. She observed in his interactions with his family that discord did not throw him. He took her tendency to withdraw in stride, never lashing out. She developed enough trust that, when the anger built up beyond her ability to tolerate it, rather than close herself off completely, she could let the mess happen.

The smashed dinner represented a conscious welcoming of mismatch and repair in their relationship. As they survived this disruption and many others that characterize the normal messiness of love, Jennifer discovered a different way of being in a relationship. She made new meanings of the world as a safe and hopeful place. She could have an argument, knowing she would be closer to Craig on the other side. While Craig's meanings going into the relationship were not as troubled as Jennifer's, he too had room to grow. He became more mindful of his distracted behavior, taking steps to be more consistently present once he understood the origins of Jennifer's tendency to react. He learned from her that relationships beyond the safe enclosure of his family of origin were not always so simple. He learned to pay attention.

WHAT IS MEANING-MAKING?

What does it mean to *make meaning*? We may use a term like *understand* or *make sense of* to capture the idea, but these words imply conscious thought in the form of language. Jerome Bruner, who first described the concept, was a cognitive scientist and so viewed meaning-making primarily in terms of language symbols and cognition. The still-face research revealed that people make meaning well before they have the ability to put those meanings into words. They make meaning at multiple levels of psychological and biological experience, including the sensory system, genes, autonomic nervous system, and motor system. From the multilayered levels of feeling — perceiving, thinking, reaching, looking, and even smelling — they elaborate their sense of themselves in the world. The information they incorporate in their relationships with others is composed of multiple layers of sensations, movements, and emotional experiences as only humans can process.

Louis Sander, psychoanalyst and pioneer of infant research, described what he called an *open space*, a figurative space between infant and caretaker filled with possibilities from which the infant's sense of self emerges and grows. In that space, a baby's own unique self develops in interaction with primary caregivers. The moment-to-moment engagement with people, as babies misunderstand and then reevaluate others' motivations and intentions, is the process by which they make meaning of themselves in the world.

The still-face experiment dramatically demonstrates that infants are born with the ability to influence their world and possess innate skills to interact with their environment. Confronted with a mother's unfamiliar blank expression, a baby responds with a number of strategies to reengage her. The still-face paradigm represents an experimental situation in which infants are challenged in their ability to make meaning of their experience. If they had words, they might say of the mother's failure to interact, *This does not make sense.* While the duration of the still-face portion of the six-minute experiment varies in different research protocols, the average length is two minutes. Try staring expressionlessly for two minutes at a friend or family member who wants your attention — it will seem interminably long! For the purposes of our experiment, this prolongation magnifies the response, offering a window into the infant's meaning-making process.

A baby who has experienced successfully moving through mismatch to repair will, when confronted with the stress of the still-face experiment, use various strategies to manage that stress. She points, screeches, and engages in a range of behaviors to reconnect. She shows *agency,* defined as a sense that she has control over her life and the power to act effectively on her world. If she could put words to her experience, she might say, *I don't know why Mom is ignoring me, but I know I can get her attention if I keep trying.* Rather than a sense of helplessness, an infant who has moved through countless moments of error to reconnect develops a hopeful way of interacting with her world. She has made a specific meaning of her experience, one of optimistic expectation, which gives her a sense of resilience (a concept we explore further in chapter 5). In contrast, an infant who has experienced mismatch but has limited experience with repair creates negative meanings: *You don't love me* or *I can't trust you* or *I am helpless.* (We explore this in depth in chapter 8.)

It turns out that patterns of interactive coping, the patterns that create meaning, are quite stable over time. We performed the still-face experiment with fifty-two infants and their mothers twice ten days apart, and we saw the infants use the same strategies on both occasions to engage their mothers and comfort themselves. In mother-baby pairs who did not have the opportunity to move through disruption to repair, babies exhibited behavior consistent with sadness, withdrawal, or disengagement. They seemed to have trouble holding themselves together; either their movements were disorganized or they collapsed and became very still. Both responses suggested that they felt helpless and ineffective.

We gained a new level of insight into the significance of our original findings when we applied the still-face paradigm in research with parents struggling with depression. We gave potential participants a screening questionnaire for depressive symptoms, and those who scored high were interviewed to determine if they were clinically depressed. We then analyzed videotapes of pairs of nondepressed mothers and their infants and depressed mothers and their infants, looking for matches (infant and mother doing the same thing together, such as mutual smiling and gazing) and mismatches (infant and mother doing different things with each other, such as the infant looking and smiling at the mother and the mother having a sad facial expression). We figured out the average time it took a dyad for a mismatch to be repaired into a match and found that when mothers were depressed, not only were there more mismatches, but it took much longer for the mismatches to be repaired. We also found that the longer the time to repair, the higher the level of the stress hormone cortisol (measured in saliva) in the infant.

The babies of depressed mothers appeared to turn inward,

relying on themselves or looking to objects for comfort. Such patterns of relating are incorporated early into a baby's way of being in the world and are carried forward into new relationships as the baby grows and develops.

But as we explore in depth in chapters 9 and 10, for adults, the main significance of these findings is that early relationship patterns are not fixed or permanent. You can continue to change and grow throughout life by engaging in the messiness of interaction with children, spouses, friends, teachers, therapists, and the wide range of other people you have the opportunity to bring into your life. If your early relationships were characterized by insufficient opportunity for repair, you can heal by engaging in a new set of moment-to-moment mismatch and repair with both your original caregivers, if they are available and open to change, and new partners in a range of relationships.

When you find yourself repeatedly stuck in problematic relationships, when you carry meanings of anxiety or hopelessness, you may feel you do not have the power to change your circumstances. But agency, like hope, is instilled by the iterative, repeated process of moving through mismatch to repair in relationships with people close to you.

STARTING FROM BIRTH

Meaning-making begins in a person's first moments. Consider the early dance of breastfeeding. Let's look at it first from new mother Aditi's perspective, then from that of her newborn daughter, Tanisha. All of these interactions occur, not over hours or even minutes, but over seconds that, strung together, build one's sense of self in the world.

Aditi had anticipated Tanisha's arrival with excitement and fear. This was her first baby, and she wondered how she would know what to do. Hours after giving birth, she tried to put her screaming infant to her breast. But Tanisha's arms got in the way and her movements became increasingly disorganized. Aditi began to speak softly to Tanisha while wrapping her tightly, and soon she felt Tanisha's body go from tense to relaxed; the incessant crying slowed and finally stopped. Tanisha slept and then woke and vigorously latched on to nurse, and Aditi experienced a peaceful calm that until then had eluded her. The meaning she made of this experience, if she'd put it into words, might be *I can do this* and *I know my baby.*

Now consider the same scene from Tanisha's perspective. Her tiny body wriggled. She screamed again and again as her arms flew over her head. Something was in her mouth, but she didn't know what to do with it. Then Tanisha heard a soft, gentle whisper and was wrapped in a warm blanket. Her breathing slowed. Now she could rest her arms on her chest and stop their wild movements. Her body relaxed as her need for help settling her immature nervous system was answered, and soon she drifted off to sleep. After a brief nap, her body felt calm and restored. When her mother again put her to the breast, she latched on without struggle. The meaning Tanisha created might be expressed as *I am safe* and *I am whole.*

In this early moment of figuring things out together, Tanisha and Aditi began to fall in love. Aditi recognized that Tanisha was tired and her nervous system was stressed. She needed help from her mother to calm down and a brief nap to refresh her before she would be ready for a meal. Allowing time for the process to work itself out literally fed Tanisha while also nourishing

Aditi's growing new identity as a mother, building her sense of confidence and self-efficacy. Moving from mismatch to repair provided actual nutrition for Tanisha and for Aditi a kind of food for the soul.

This shared experience is well captured by the phrase *moment of meeting*, coined by Louis Sander. In 1977 he wrote, "Current research in early infancy is beginning to provide provocative evidence that human existence normally begins in the context of a highly organized relational system from the outset. This relational system interfaces two live, actively self-regulating, highly complex, living (and adapting) components — the infant and the caregiver, each already running, so to speak." He painted a picture of the newborn period as a time when two separate unique individuals — infant and caregiver — got to know each other. When together Tanisha and Aditi worked through their first moments of mismatch, the pleasure of that moment of meeting fed them both.

Moving through mismatch to repair is more important than anything in particular that we do or say in the face of any given challenge. It is the process that matters.

A UNIFYING THEORY

In our moment-by-moment analysis of parent-infant interaction, we observed again and again that first love relationships are characterized not by synchrony but by error, and we wondered, "What purpose could this error serve?" We found the answer in a scientific theory with broad application to a wide range of disciplines, from physics to psychology.

Open dynamic systems theory describes how all biological systems, including humans, function by incorporating information into increasingly coherent and complex states. Systems that fail to gain complexity lose energy and fail to grow — say, Uncle Harry at Thanksgiving dinner who holds rigid political views and shuts out the different perspectives of other family members. Systems that are successful in gaining information grow — for example, Cousin Sue and Cousin Pete, who take time to listen to each other's stories and hear each other's respective motivations and intentions, and in working through their differences develop new understanding and insight. The energy produced by acquiring new information fuels growth and change.

This idea applies not only to human relationships but also to the origin of life itself! In his book *A Brief History of Time*, renowned physicist Stephen Hawking explains how life on Earth evolved out of errors. Initially the Earth's atmosphere had no oxygen and was thus incompatible with life. Primitive life emerged in the oceans through chance combinations of atoms into complex structures called macromolecules. Hawking tells how errors in reproduction eventually led to new structures:

> However, a few of the errors would have produced new macromolecules that were even better at reproducing themselves. They would therefore have an advantage and would have tended to replace the original macromolecules. In this way a process of evolution was started that led to the development of more and more complicated, self-reproducing organisms. The first primitive forms of life consumed various materials, including hydrogen sulfide, and released oxygen. This gradually changed the atmosphere to the composition that allowed

the development of higher forms of life such as fish, rep-
tiles, mammals, and ultimately the human race.

The macromolecules in Hawking's model of the origins of
life represent an example of open dynamic systems. Those mol-
ecules, through a process of multiple errors over time, organized
in such a way as to produce oxygen. Humans bump into each
other in a way analogous to those early macromolecules, developing an ever more complex sense of themselves in the world
out of the errors inherent in their interactions.

New information is not simply absorbed. Again, macromolecules provide a helpful image. They don't simply shift — they
bang into each other, get disrupted, and reorganize into new
configurations. New information disrupts humans too, forcing
them to reorganize their old sense of self in the world. New and
different meaning is created out of the disorganization.

When people experience this process of reorganization
along with another person — whether a caregiver when they are
young or with friends, colleagues, and partners as they get
older — they co-create a new way of being together, of knowing
each other. If people don't allow for disorganization, or mismatches, they fail to grow and change and do not get to know
others deeply.

The process of mismatch and repair in human interaction
generates the energy — the calories, so to speak — for development. The information we gain about others and about ourselves
through this messy interactive process provides the nutrients
that allow our minds to grow.

When applied to physics, open dynamic systems theory is

"cold." But human experience is "hot," driven by emotion. When the theory is applied to humans, the experience of deep joy and sense of wholeness from reconnection follows the disappointment and sense of loss of mismatch. The profound pleasure of repair becomes the fuel that drives growth and development.

Dysfunctional patterns of interaction in relationships represent closed systems. Their rigidity allows people to hold on to a familiar level of complexity and coherence that gives them an illusion of safety. But if they do not feel safe to engage in the messiness of relationships, they may remain in fixed patterns of interaction that do not promote growth and change. In chapter 3, we explore how to achieve that sense of safety. As Jennifer and Craig found, rigid patterns keep us closed off from each other, but when we open ourselves to discord, we gain new sources of energy.

MAKING MEANING IN OUR GENES

Billions of years ago, the process of mismatch and repair created life on Earth. Darwin's theory of evolutionary change describes how mutations, or errors, occur in the base pairs of DNA of living organisms, leading to individual variations. Like Hawking's macromolecules, some variations reproduce and thrive, leading to the remarkable array of different species uniquely adapted to their particular environment. This mismatch-and-repair process happens over millions of years.

And it turns out that an individual's genes change their function even within that person's own lifetime! Putting a new spin on the nature-nurture debate, research in the exploding new field of study called *epigenetics* teaches that genes are not destiny. Genes are specific sequences of nucleotides in DNA. While the DNA itself does not change, genes are turned on and off in response to the environment. A molecule, usually a methyl group, attaches to a nucleotide and changes the way a gene is expressed, a process referred to as *methylation*. For example, a particular gene may lead to depression in a stressful environment but not in an adaptive environment.

You may remember being taught in biology class that genes make proteins, not meaning. But these proteins do determine how we respond to our environment. The changes in proteins affect such things as how we metabolize nutrients and how we respond to stress. For example, when genes start to make too much cortisol, our bodies and brains may experience this change as anxiety. The following story offers an example of making meaning in our genes.

In what has been termed the Dutch Hunger Winter of 1944, Dutch railway workers went on strike with the hope of halting the transport of Nazi troops, and as punishment, the Nazis cut off the food supply to the Netherlands. By the time the war ended, in 1945, more than twenty thousand people had died of starvation. But a study of the children who were conceived during the famine and whose mothers survived their pregnancy tells an interesting genetic story.

A large body of research has closely examined these children through the years. When they reached adulthood, they were a few pounds heavier than average. In middle age, they had higher levels of triglycerides and cholesterol, higher rates of obesity, and higher levels of metabolic illnesses such as diabetes. One long-term follow-up study of men between the ages of eighteen and sixty-three showed that those who were in utero during the famine had a 10 percent higher mortality rate than those who were not.

Because the period of starvation had a defined beginning and end, in effect, it constituted an unexpected genetic experiment. In this epigenetic — literally, "above the gene" — process, the expression of a certain gene was altered in utero to adapt to an environment of scarcity. Rather than a change in the gene sequence, such as occurs in genetic disorders like cystic fibrosis and muscular dystrophy, changes occurred in the expression, or programming, of the gene.

One particular gene, *PIM3*, is involved in burning the body's fuel; it produces proteins that play a role in metabolism. The *PIM3* gene was likely turned off in utero in an adaptive process, slowing the metabolism of the fetus in response to the severe shortage of nutrients. The fetus, in a sense, "predicted" a future environment of scarcity. But after the war, when food was more abundant, these babies' slowed metabolic process meant that they gained more weight than their siblings raised in the same household. Their bodies still expected famine even in the face of plenty, but the children who weren't in utero during the famine did not have this genetic alteration and did not develop metabolic problems or obesity.

In the Dutch famine, the mismatch occurred between the in utero environment and the world into which the infants were born. Epigenetic research also shows that environmental effects on gene expression can be passed through the genes to subsequent generations.

FINDING HOPE IN EPIGENETICS

Does the idea that your life experience is embedded in your genes and that you take on the experiences of your ancestors make you feel worried? We encounter people who find this idea discouraging, especially if past generations have experienced trauma. But on careful consideration, we see that the lesson from epigenetics is one of hope. For just as gene expression can change to adapt to one environment, it can change over time to adapt to a different one.

Many parents have expressed to us fear that a toddler who has frequent tantrums or in other ways causes trouble will continue to be difficult, that he'll "turn out like Uncle Billy," for example, who suffered from a range of mental health problems. You inherit half your genetic material from each parent, and genes do get passed from generation to generation. But epigenetics research teaches us that while a child may carry the same genes as Uncle Billy, the effect of those genes on his behavior and development will vary according to the environment in which he grows up. Rachel Yehuda of the Icahn School of Medicine at Mount Sinai has studied a population of children and grandchildren of Holocaust survivors to determine how intergenerational transmission of environmental influence on genes works. The following story of an adult child of Holocaust survivors offers an example.

Hilda and Karl were both imprisoned at Auschwitz as children (although they did not meet then); after the war, they each immigrated with surviving family members to New York, where they met and raised their own new family. During the war, one way Hilda's and Karl's bodies made meaning of the constant real threat to their existence was through epigenetic processes, altering their reactions to stress. The expression of cortisol-producing genes was magnified in response to the environment. In that setting, the hypervigilance and constant high state of arousal produced by bathing the body in cortisol was adaptive, even lifesaving. These epigenetic changes — the hyper-activation of the cortisol-producing genes — were passed on to their son Eric in his genes.

But Eric, living in the relative safety of New York City, didn't require this heightened stress response. The excessive cortisol was no longer needed. The epigenetic meaning made in response to war trauma, planted in genes passed down to him from his parents, did not match the safe environment into which he was born. It would take Eric time and multiple new moment-to-moment opportunities for new meaning — countless opportunities for mismatch and repair — to change the meaning embedded in his genes. These moments were necessary to repair the mismatch between his genes and his relatively safe postwar environment in America.

In his late thirties, Eric had by all appearances a perfect life: a stable marriage with his wife, Devorah, a satisfying career in finance, and two healthy sons. Yet he was plagued by feelings of anxiety and burdened by relentless self-doubt. He was highly self-critical, and despite external measures of success, he had no sense of himself as an effective person. He got no pleasure from his accomplishments.

He spent most of his free time working out at the gym, thinking that if he could feel more comfortable with his body, that nagging insecurity would loosen its grip. But as his fortieth birthday approached, the grip tightened. He became obsessive about his diet, consuming only protein shakes for breakfast and lunch and ruining everyone else's enjoyment of family meals with his dictates about healthy eating.

Eric's troubles had roots in both his genetic inheritance and his experiences growing up. At a young age, Eric had learned that for his parents, feelings of distress generated anxiety and were met with immediate efforts to shut them down. By the time he got to college, he knew that when his mother asked how things were going, the answer had to be "Fine." If it wasn't, she would bend the conversation in that direction so it concluded with "But you're okay, right?" He would relent and say, "Yes, Mom, it's all good." His father had always felt remote. As he learned more about the losses his father had experienced during the war, Eric recognized his father's driven work ethic as an effort to stave off feelings of sadness. Both parents went to great lengths to make their world orderly and safe. Whenever the subject of the Holocaust came up, his father would point to how well his life had turned out, steadfastly refusing to associate the word *trauma* with the experience.

Eric's rigid behavior around exercise and eating was disrupting his family life intolerably. Devorah recommended that Eric seek help from a therapist. She did not want to re-create for their two young boys the environment of tension and fear that she knew had characterized Eric's childhood. Eric saw that Devorah was right, that he needed to do something. But nothing he had heard about psychotherapy prepared him for his first encounter with Dr. Olds.

STARVED FOR MEANING

After Eric's first session with Dr. Olds, he felt a powerful connection that, he reflected many years later, was due to a sense of safety that had previously eluded him. About halfway through the visit, he sensed that Dr. Olds would accept and help contain the mess of painful feelings churning inside him. Fear of discord had kept Eric relatively closed off. While both he and Devorah were devoted to their children, their relationship with each other was distant and strained. Eric felt at ease with the boys, but the expectation of emotional intimacy with his wife made him anxious.

Following that first visit, Eric experienced a phenomenon common in psychoanalytic psychotherapy. A patient regresses to what Winnicott termed a *position of dependency*. In this therapeutic relationship, many dynamics play out that are similar to those of the parent-infant relationship. This new relationship allows patients to access and then change unhealthy patterns of relating.

It was as if for forty years, Eric had been working hard to hold himself together — to deny any big messy feelings — and now the full intensity of his emotional experience rose to the surface. In the days between his twice-weekly therapy sessions, he could function as his adult self. But then Dr. Olds went on his first vacation following the start of their work together, and the strain was too much for Eric. He mysteriously lost the ability to eat. He literally struggled to put food in his mouth. The symptom resolved the moment Dr. Olds returned from vacation, but it reappeared the next time he went away. As this problem faded over the years they worked together, Eric came to recognize that he had felt "starved" for meaning. When he found a person to engage in the messiness of an intimate relationship, he felt "fed" for the first time. The abrupt withdrawal of that nourishment before he had an opportunity to understand his feelings about it led to his inability to take in real food in Dr. Olds's absence.

Given Eric's parents' history, it isn't surprising that they offered him a paucity of opportunity for repair. His mother hovered, and his father just never got involved. Both avoided the everyday mess of interaction. His parents' worlds were fixed and brittle. But Dr. Olds was different. Though at that first visit Eric could not fully articulate it, he knew he could bring all his feelings of rage, love, and fear and Dr. Olds would stay with him. He would listen without insisting that everything was okay.

Perhaps most important, Eric could move through mismatch and repair with Dr. Olds, who was not afraid of and was willing to acknowledge his own errors. Once, early on in Eric's therapy, there was a misunderstanding about an appointment time. Eric was devastated when he arrived to discover a locked door. Flooded with an almost unbearable feeling of dread, he feared something terrible had happened to Dr. Olds. Like the infant confronted with the still-face, he struggled to make sense of his experience. Eric's dearth of exposure to surviving friction in relationships led him to fall apart in the face of this major mismatch. But later, as Eric and Dr. Olds worked through this disruption, their relationship deepened, and it proved to be a critical moment on his path to healing.

In Eric's relationships with others, not only Devorah and his parents, his pattern was to withdraw in moments of discord. But this pattern took its toll. Though it was out of Eric's conscious awareness, shutting out unpleasant and negative feelings was hard work. The symptoms of rigid eating represented an adaptation, a way of holding himself together. But if he wanted intimacy, he would have to let his guard down. Dr. Olds provided a safe space where together they could put his reactions, which up to that point lived only in his body, without conscious thoughts attached, into words.

Eric's story of healing is confirmed by psychotherapy research showing an association between what is termed *repair of alliance ruptures* and healing. Psychoanalyst Leston Havens notes the importance of "survival of collision" between patient and therapist, an idea that echoes the earliest open dynamic systems described by physicist Stephen Hawking. The concept of survival of disruption in human relationships echoes the dynamics of the formation of the universe as a big bang!

Over five years of therapy with Dr. Olds, Eric survived many moments of disruption, both large and small. In the process, his sense of himself as a whole person grew. His obsessive need to control what he ate dissipated. Now that things being messy and confusing no longer frightened him, those rules were no longer necessary. Similarly, he could tolerate moments of disruption with Devorah instead of resisting any discord or exploding with rage. As their intimacy grew, the entire family increasingly felt like a coherent whole rather than fragmented separate parts. By the time Eric ended his therapy with Dr. Olds, he had a community of friends and colleagues with whom he could comfortably move through mismatch to repair. The trust he developed in his interactions with Dr. Olds opened up a path that allowed him to trust others, giving him access to a wider social world.

He was also able to make peace with his parents' limitations and rediscover joy in his relationship with them. Their rigidity no longer frightened him and he could take pleasure in the intellectually satisfying, though still emotionally remote, relationship he had with his father. He could indulge his mother's need for everything to be "okay" without losing himself in the process.

Many people live for decades in relationships that feel more or less fine but lack a certain level of intimacy. Similarly, as we explore in depth in chapter 8, people may have a sense of not being fully themselves. They become aware of this difference when, as Eric did in his often-tumultuous relationship with Dr. Olds, they encounter relationships in which they feel safe enough to engage in the mess without fear that they'll lose themselves in the process.

MULTIPLE WAYS TO MAKE MEANING

The paradigm of meaning-making offered by the still-face experiment shows that infants have the ability to make meaning well before the parts of the brain responsible for symbolic thought and language develop. As we saw in the Dutch famine story, even a fetus without a fully formed brain can make meaning.

Meaning-making occurs across a continuum of physiology, behavior, and conscious thought, as exemplified by the expression "Trust your gut." The sensory system, motor system, autonomic nervous system (the control system that regulates bodily functions), endocrine system, immune system, genetics, and even the microbiome, the trillions of microorganisms that live in the gut, all have a role to play in the process of making sense of experience. All of these meanings exist side by side along with explicit meanings conveyed in words.

Stated in words, Eric's inability to eat in Dr. Olds's absence did not make sense. Although as a young child he had been fed, his body held a memory of the lack of emotional nutrients. His rigid eating pattern preceding the start of therapy had the same origins as his extreme reaction to Dr. Olds's vacation. Creating a story in words was not sufficient to change Eric's way of being in the world. Discussion of his parents' war trauma occupied only a fraction of Eric's time with Dr. Olds. As much as, if not more than, the actual words exchanged, it was the experience of mismatch and repair in moment-to-moment interactions that fueled the change in Eric. He needed to learn, both in his body and in his mind, a new way of being in a relationship, one that was not characterized by rigidity and fear of mess.

When an airplane hits turbulence, your rational brain usually tells you not to worry. But your lurching stomach, clammy hands, and instinctive gripping of the armrest say otherwise. While you may tell yourself, *No one dies of turbulence*, your body reacts as if death may be imminent. Likewise, a chance meeting with a former boss who treated you badly years ago may produce a startling pounding in the heart, tremor of the hands, and difficulty thinking clearly, even though in your conscious mind, the upsetting experience has been pushed aside. Young children with natural creativity and high energy levels who are asked to conform to a rigid school structure probably do not think in words, *This is beyond my ability to cope*. Instead, they may develop flare-ups of eczema as their immune systems struggle to process the experience.

Fears and phobias that seem irrational, that don't make sense in words, may have origins in early, pre-language emotional experience. Eric could barely remember family outings to Rockaway Beach in his childhood, but he had an abiding fear of the ocean, of being thrown by a wave or stepping on a jellyfish. Those concrete fears were the expression of the tension and anxiety that simmered below the surface of his early childhood. After his work with Dr. Olds, he discovered a new love of the ocean. He could delight in the crashing of the waves, laughing gleefully with his boys as together they jumped into the surf. The meaning of fear and dread that he had made of the ocean had, over time and in the context of a range of new relationships, transformed into a meaning of joy.

MAKE MISTAKES

In the next chapter we explore how modern culture's emphasis on perfection flies in the face of the central lesson of the still-face paradigm. In fact, mistakes offer opportunities to heal and grow. In a recent interview for a magazine article, Claudia was asked, "What is the secret of success?" and she answered without hesitation, "Do not be afraid to make mistakes." Error is necessary for growth. Working through the inevitable small and large disruptions strengthens you and enriches your life. Something new and unforeseen emerges.

Sigmund Freud famously said, "Love and work are the cornerstones of our humanness." What enables some people to love freely and engage in satisfying and meaningful work while others become stuck in unhealthy relationships and struggle to find purpose in life? The research that followed the original still-face experiment offers a surprising answer. As parents, partners in a couple, siblings, teachers, therapists, or business associates at a brainstorming session, most people carry the idea that things must go smoothly to go well. But expecting life to go smoothly, whether in the realm of work or love, inevitably leads to trouble. Drawing on careful observation of the earliest love relationships, our research demonstrates that growth and creativity emerge out of the countless inevitable errors that occur in human interactions. Through repair of moment-to-moment mismatch, people build trust and intimacy. Together they make meaning of their experience. In contrast, lack of opportunity for mismatch and repair leads to anxiety and mistrust. People fail to grow and risk descent into hopelessness.

With this understanding, we can create a definition of *success* applicable to all cultures, one that includes the full range of ways in which people choose to live their lives. Success, broadly conceived of as the ability to form intimate relationships and find meaning in life, is founded in moving through and past the inevitable mismatches in our most passionate relationships, starting from birth.

2

AIMING FOR GOOD ENOUGH

WHETHER RAISING A CHILD, plunging into a romance, navigating relationships in a new job, or facing any of the infinite challenging moments on life's path, all of us inevitably miscalculate. We blunder, making choices and taking actions that in hindsight were mistaken. And from infancy to old age, we draw energy from human relationships, with all their inherent imperfections, for the strength to move through discomfort and distress to coherence, complexity, and creativity. It is the pleasure of reconnection that produces the energy necessary for growth. This idea may surprise you, as many people carry an expectation of perfection for both themselves and their relationships. The concept of being in sync with people who matter to them has a kind of mythic quality. They aim for perfect attunement and may experience profound disappointment when they do not achieve it.

One video from an experiment using the still-face paradigm demonstrates how perfectionism trips us up. The opening scene shows a mother and her two-year-old daughter in perfect attunement. They complete each other's sentences as they play a game with stuffed animals. It's as if each knows what is in the other's mind. They are in exact synchrony, with no miscommunications. It is a pleasure to watch. But as soon as the still-face segment of the interaction starts, the girl completely disintegrates. Her movements become increasingly frantic. The experimenters, who have observed a wide spectrum of reactions in this situation, find the scene so disturbing that they cut the still-face segment short. When the mother returns as an interactive partner, unlike the infant in the original study or other toddlers, the little girl cannot collect herself. She gasps for breath and is unable to process her mother's efforts to calm her. The child hits her in anger, saying, "Why did you do that?" Given the experiment, it's a tough question to which there is no easy answer. But rather than recognizing her daughter's distress, her mother responds, "Don't hit." She doesn't acknowledge her daughter's anger but says instead, "You were sad, weren't you?" The emotion conveyed by her daughter's behavior is obviously not sadness, so perhaps the mother is inserting her own expectation of what her daughter might or should be feeling. Rather than hearing the communication and addressing it, she injects her own thoughts. Neither mother nor daughter can repair the mismatch.

One has the sense that for all the initial perfection of their interaction, a lack of experience with mismatch and repair has left the toddler unable to manage the brief loss of her mother. It's as if we are watching the toddler's emerging sense of herself in the world dissolve in the temporary absence of her caregiver.

A baby who experiences typical mismatch and repair develops into a person with an internal voice that says, *I can change things.* When people move through mismatch to repair over and over again in relationships, whether as infants or adults, they develop agency, defined earlier as a sense that one has control over one's life and the power to act effectively in the world. They come to new situations with a hopeful feeling, armed with a positive affective core. But when they carry an expectation of perfection, they miss out on the success of moving through a bad moment to a good one, of bumping the boundaries of their own selves against the boundaries of another.

A caption under the photo of six-month-old Jeremiah as he is embraced by his three-year-old sister, Ayana, might read, *What's going on?* While Ayana has clearly already grasped the social convention of smiling for the camera, Jeremiah's wide-open gaze conveys a combination of wonder and puzzlement, not only about having his photo taken but about the whole world around him. Fast-forward twenty years, and a similar pose shows both siblings smiling as they hug, each one's facial expression communicating an emerging young adult identity to the world. How does this developmental process occur? How does a baby learn about the world and, in doing so, become uniquely "Jeremiah"?

The moment-to-moment mismatch and repair is the process by which baby Jeremiah grows into young adult Jeremiah and then continues to develop into old man Jeremiah. Working through mismatch to repair is fundamental to the process of developing boundaries that differentiate "me" from "you" and from everyone else. We can turn to Winnicott for further wisdom on the subject. He captures the way in which that sense of self emerges by bumping up against the boundaries set by a child's caregivers. Far from offering the perfection of attunement, a normal child produces disruption and disorder on his path to growing up. In an essay for parents, Winnicott writes:

> What is the normal child like? Does he just eat and grow and smile sweetly? No, that is not what he is like. A normal child, if he has confidence in father and mother, pulls out all the stops. In the course of time he tries out his power to disrupt, to destroy, to frighten, to wear down, to waste, to wangle, and to appropriate.... At the start he absolutely needs to live in a circle of love and strength (with consequent tolerance) if he is not to be too fearful of his own thoughts and of his imaginings to make progress in his emotional development.

In an environment that makes room for big, messy feelings, a child's development progresses in a healthy direction; he has a robust, positive sense of "I am." Setting limits on behavior but taking care not to squash a child's soul, the caregiver communicates a sense of safety, in essence saying, *I'm okay with your big feelings. I will stay with you. You will not be alone.* In the scenario that opened this chapter, the mother's apparent intolerance of mismatch, her need to be perfectly available, may impinge on her daughter's emerging sense of self. The sense of agency and the sense of self are closely linked.

NECESSARY IMPERFECTION

Twenty-seven-year-old Mai might have been the envy of her friends. She had followed plans laid out by her parents, gotten excellent grades, and participated in a range of extracurricular activities, all of which had landed her at a good college. Her mother and father, both successful academics, had encouraged her to pursue a career in teaching, which she dutifully did. She took the predictable path to graduate school. She began dating a high-school teacher whose agreeable demeanor fit well with her family culture. Her parents welcomed him with open arms, and soon she felt a subtle pressure to marry and start a family. She didn't challenge any of the assumptions that others had for her future — until her relationship ended. It turned out he was perfect for them but not for her.

For the first time in her life, with the encouragement of a close friend from elementary school, rather than continuing to present a glossy front, Mai gave herself time to live precariously in a painful state of uncertainty. Sad and lonely, yet still with a dose of hope sufficient to get her out of bed, she joined the local gym. On her newly free weekends, she resumed swimming, an activity that she had enjoyed as a child. One day by chance she met up with members of the masters' swim team, who invited her to join them. On Saturday mornings as she pushed herself physically alongside her teammates, slicing through the water stroke after stroke, she experienced a kind of coming fully into her body with a calming and organizing sense of her own movements. Even when she flubbed the turn, she kept on slicing. As psychiatrist Bruce Perry (see chapter 5) describes, rapid alternating movements such as walking, running, and swimming play a role in organizing brain, behavior, and emotions. Mai's emerging sense of herself was also enhanced by the adrenaline-fueled camaraderie in the locker room post-workout.

The energy she gained from both the activity itself and these new relationships gave her courage to switch gears professionally.

A longing for deeper, more complex connections emerged. She decided to pursue a career as a social worker. During her training she met Chasten. In contrast to the smooth and uneventful relationships of her past, with Chasten she moved through, rather than around, moments of discord. This resulted in a deepening sense of intimacy and connection.

Who am I? Where do I fit in? What does it all mean? are questions that drive us from childhood and that remain relevant throughout our lives as we grow and change. In a paper entitled "An Elegant Mess: Reflections on the Research of Edward Z. Tronick," psychoanalyst Steven Cooper wisely asks, "How can two people really be that in synch when, in fact, adults as individuals don't understand what they intend much of the time anyway?" In our efforts to connect, we find ourselves by bumping up against the boundaries of other people.

Mai reflected on her life, from her childhood characterized by a veneer of perfection to the disruption precipitated by the breakup with her boyfriend, and found she hardly recognized her past self. Over time, Mai's new experiences and relationships led her to begin to build a more complex, more genuine sense of self.

For Mai, the change in her life came about primarily through swimming, finding new friends, helping clients in her new profession, and being in a relationship with Chasten. Her cognitive understanding of the impact of her childhood on the troubles she had after her breakup played a minimal role.

Relational experiences themselves become part of your body and change the meaning you make of yourself in the world. For instance, as we'll explore in depth in the following chapter, many people find profound healing through singing with others. While a choir rehearses, there are countless cycles of mismatch and repair within individual sections, in the choir as a whole, and between the choir and the conductor. The inevitable mistakes as members work through the complexities of the music together are essential for the creation of a quality performance, and the hard work of moving through the mess to create a complex and coherent chorus leads to pleasure for the choral members, a joy that is then communicated to the audience along with the musical notes.

IMPERFECT FROM THE START

Drawing on his observations and insights about the cosmos, physicist Stephen Hawking recognized that "one of the basic rules of the universe is that nothing is perfect.... Without imperfection, neither you nor I would exist." Hawking understood that the reproduction errors produced when macromolecules collided were needed to create life on Earth. While Hawking observed the necessity of imperfections in the world of physics, Winnicott observed exactly this process in human development, starting from birth.

Unlike other mammals, humans are uniquely helpless in the first weeks of life. Their arms fly up over their heads at random moments in a primitive startle reflex. Sleep patterns have no rhyme or reason. Babies eat and poop around the clock. This behavior is the result of an immature brain that, in order to allow the head to move through the birth canal, does 70 percent of its growing outside the womb. A newborn baby relies completely on caregivers to organize his world.

For this reason, as any new parent can tell you, taking care of a newborn is a 24/7 job. Winnicott observed that when a mother is herself cared for and supported (an experience often lacking in our culture), she is more closely attuned with her baby. He referred to the "ordinary devoted mother" as one who is, in a normal, healthy way, preoccupied by her infant's every need. These early weeks when the infant is completely helpless, in circumstances in which a mother herself feels held and supported, offer parent and child a sense of oneness.

But this attunement, in situations of health, is temporary, lasting for about ten weeks, until the baby begins to acquire the capacity to manage himself. As his brain develops and his body grows, the primitive reflexes subside. His movements become more organized. Winnicott notes that at this point, the mother must, to use his word, "fail" to meet the infant's every need in order for his development to progress. She will fail, inevitably, but she has a new task, one summed up by the term he coined, the *good-enough mother.* Winnicott recognized that, just as most mothers are naturally preoccupied with their babies when they are completely helpless, most mothers are also naturally "good enough." These qualities are not something learned in books.

The concept of the good-enough mother often gets translated into simplistic, quick reassurance about caregivers being okay with their mistakes, but it reflects a more profound truth, which is that imperfections are necessary for healthy development. The truth Winnicott wisely identified is that failure — or, in Hawking's language, error — is not only inevitable but essential. A mother should not aim to be perfect but, rather, good enough. In accommodating their mothers' failures, infants begin to separate and learn to manage the inevitable frustrations of life. The boundaries between self and others start to form.

This is where the foundations of self-regulation, so critical to learning and social competence, develop. As we will explore in depth in chapter 4, self-regulation emerges out of the process of working through errors or failures with another person. In his book *Playing and Reality*, Winnicott wrote:

> Taken for granted here is the good-enough facilitating environment, which at the start of each individual's growth and development is the *sine qua non*. There are genes which determine patterns and an inherited tendency to grow and to achieve maturity, and yet nothing takes place in emotional growth except in relation to the environmental provision, which must be good enough. It will be noticed that the word "perfect" does not enter into this statement — perfection belongs to machines, and the imperfections that are characteristic of human adaptation to need are an essential quality in the environment that facilitates.

In addition to his academic writing, Winnicott communicated regularly with parents, acting as a kind of British Dr. Spock. In one such essay he wrote:

> I would rather be the child of a mother who has all the inner conflicts of the human being than be mothered by someone for whom all is easy and smooth, who knows all the answers, and is a stranger to doubt.

Winnicott combined his observations as a pediatrician, where he was immersed in real-time relationships of parents and children, with his work as a psychoanalyst. His adult patients, lying on the couch hour after hour, in his words "regressed to dependence," as Eric did at the beginning of his work with Dr. Olds. Many experienced deep anxiety around even brief separations. They reacted intensely to slight violations in attunement, such as a prolonged pause preceding a response from him. But rather than (or in addition to) crying in distress, they could explain what was happening. They brought emotions carried from early caregiving relationships into their relationship with Winnicott in a process originally described by Sigmund Freud as *transference*. These interactions offered insights into the impact of their emotional lives as preverbal children.

Out of these experiences, Winnicott developed the concept of the *true self* and the *false self*. He listened to adults who, like Mai, seemed to lack a solid sense of themselves. His experience with adults and children led him to recognize that if a mother fails to meet her baby's needs, not always getting what her baby is communicating but taking the time to figure things out, she paves the way for the child to adapt to the uncertainty inherent in all social interactions. The baby thus develops an emerging sense of self.

In contrast, he observed that a false self might develop in "compliance" with a caregiver who, for a wide range of reasons, is unable to tolerate imperfections in relationships. In the video of the toddler who is angry but whose mother insists she is sad, we can imagine that in repeated interactions where the child's feelings are not tolerated, she might comply, denying her true feeling of anger and instead becoming sad in an effort to join her mother. In Mai's story we sense this kind of compliance. Following the smooth path her family expected had distorted her developmental path to her true self.

THE TOO-GOOD MOTHER

The good-enough mother enables a baby's healthy development by failing to meet their needs in proportion to their growing ability to manage that failure. The too-good mother, however, in her anxious striving for perfection, may thwart growth through mismatch and repair.

When Sarah called a therapist and left a message to set up an appointment for help with her three-year-old son's difficult behavior, she said she could speak on the phone only between two and two thirty, when she could be sure that Ben would be napping. She explained that from eight to nine in the morning, Ben had breakfast and then played before his morning nap. Lunch had to be at noon and his walk was at twelve forty-five. He got ready for his nap at one forty-five and finally, at two o'clock, he would be asleep. "I could talk then," she said. She conveyed a profound anxiety as she described organizing her day around his every need.

Ben and Sarah's relationship had gotten off to a rough start when Sarah experienced complications from a cesarean section and had to stay in the intensive care unit for a couple of days. While she recalled this time as emotionally painful, after that, his infancy was, in her words, "perfect bliss." Once he entered toddlerhood, however, things began to unravel. Now their days and nights were filled with battles as she tried in vain to be perfectly available to him in the way she had been during his infancy. He struggled to go to sleep, fell apart easily in preschool, and descended into tantrums at the slightest violation of his expectations, such as having chicken for dinner when he wanted pasta. When Sarah spoke about her experiences in therapy, at first it seemed that the origins of this pattern might lie in the early disruption in their relationship and Sarah's guilt about having "abandoned" him during his first weeks when she was too ill to care for him. But on further reflection, Sarah recognized that her own mother had felt a similar pressure to be perfect with Sarah and her brother. She described her mother as having sacrificed her own needs, her own self, to give everything to her children. Sarah had felt stifled and recalled her anxious mother as being distant and emotionally unavailable.

The pattern of relating in which Sarah and Ben were stuck was likely in part due to her wish not to disappoint him the way she felt she had in those first days. But it ran deeper, as she repeated the kind of mothering she herself had received. As Sarah became aware of this intergenerational pattern of the too-perfect mother, she saw not only that the perfection she strove for was unattainable but also that it made her nervous and worried. She wondered if Ben's behavior might be a reflection of her anxiety. When she saw the effect of her perfectionist striving on her emotions and Ben's, Sarah experienced a profound relief, a kind of freedom to relax.

As Sarah allowed herself to tolerate the messiness of toddlerhood and saw that it actually might help Ben cope, their mutual anxiety abated. She didn't always have to have the exact sippy cup he wanted at that moment. She could go out for an evening with friends despite his fervent protests. As both survived these disruptions, his sleep improved, and he began to enjoy preschool and make friends. The process of mismatch and repair allowed them to form healthier boundaries while their trust of each other and of themselves grew.

We can take the lessons learned from this story and apply them to all of our relationships throughout our lives. Like Sarah's anxious strivings to meet Ben's every need, strivings for perfection in our adult relationships can create anxiety and prevent growth.

OPENING SPACE FOR IMPERFECTION

The board members of Brian's company had been working for months on a vexing problem. At meeting after meeting, they sat around the table in the conference room hashing out different solutions. Several individual members had strong ideas of what needed to be done and appeared unwilling to budge. The process was stuck. Many began to dread the gatherings. After one of the meetings, Brian's friend Clarissa, who sat on the board as a community member and ran a local dance school, took him aside and said, "Why don't you hold the meeting at my studio?" She suggested that instead of jumping right into the discussion about what to do, they should take some time at the beginning for each member to check in and talk about their day. "Lay some ground rules about simply listening without interrupting just for that part." Brian took her advice. When the group arrived, they were offered an array of seating options, including beanbag chairs, yoga balls, and folding chairs. Some chose to sit on the floor. The disordered arrangement itself relieved the pressure to articulate fully formed solutions. For the listening exercise, Clarissa asked them all to get up, walk around the room, and choose partners. Each member of the pair then took three minutes to share something positive and negative about the past week with their partner. The listening partner was instructed not to interrupt or offer any advice. They all discovered that this behavior called for great discipline. When they started to discuss the company's problem, Clarissa proved to be a tough taskmaster, as she set limits on their inclination to interrupt one another with solutions. Carrying over their experience from the listening exercise, the board members began to pause and take time to reflect on what their colleague had said before voicing their own perspectives. Sitting in a circle rather than at a table and meeting in a space so different from their regular workplace relieved the pressure on each individual member to come up with the correct answer, the perfect solution. Each could acknowledge that the other members of the group might also be right. They were energized by the process itself, and new ideas began to flow. Soon they came up with a cohesive, coherent plan to move forward. Opening up space and time for the messy process of working through a problem led to meaningful solutions.

A story of two friends offers another example. Sofia and Isabel had met in second grade. While each had very different experiences growing up, they shared an easy friendship for many years and remained friends even when Sofia moved across the country. They liked the same music, traveled well together, and in general found comfort in each other's company. Then they had children. Profoundly different approaches to parenting created the first rift in an otherwise smooth relationship. The divide grew along with their children's development, and around the time their kids entered elementary school, Sofia came to visit from the West Coast, and the two of them had an explosive argument that led to a complete breakdown in their friendship. Neither could recall exactly what happened, but they stopped talking to each other. As they lived on opposite sides of the country, it was relatively easy to go about their day-to-day lives as if it didn't matter. But as the years passed, the loss took its toll. They each made tentative attempts at reconciliation, but their phone conversations felt tense and awkward. The breakthrough came when Sofia returned to her childhood home on the East Coast for a family gathering that coincided with a break in Isabel's work. They decided to meet for a weekend and go hiking. The expanse of time allowed them to finally get into the mess of what had happened. The act of walking together calmed their bodies sufficiently to allow them to engage in emotionally charged talk. The regular, rhythmic movement helped them listen, and each finally took in the perspective of the other. They repaired the mismatch, gaining new levels of understanding of themselves and of each other. In the years afterward, as their own kids turned into young adults, they made a point to share a day of walking and talking when Sofia came east for annual visits. They were able to be present in each other's lives in deeper and more meaningful ways.

Working through mismatch to repair, in the moment and over years, allows us to grow and change. As both of these stories show, new meanings emerge when we create a space to listen to others' perspectives. And as we explore further in chapter 9, it's not simply a question of finding the right words. To create meaning at all levels of experience, including movement and sensation, we need to bring our bodies into the process.

A DEVELOPMENTAL VIEW

At the same time as D. W. Winnicott was consolidating his observations into a clinical theory in London, T. Berry Brazelton, then a young pediatrician in Cambridge, Massachusetts, was forming his own theories about imperfection. He noticed that young children tended to fall apart right before they made a developmental leap. In the introduction to his book *Touchpoints*, a model of caring for children and families founded in decades of clinical observations, he wrote: "Just before a surge in growth in any line of development, the child's behavior seems to fall apart. Parents can no longer count on past accomplishments. The child often regresses in several areas and becomes difficult to understand. Parents lose their own balance and become alarmed." But when such disorganization was viewed as an expected and necessary precursor for a new level of growth and developmental accomplishment, he saw that parents could take the opportunity to gain a greater understanding of their child rather than becoming "locked into a struggle."

Ellen felt that she was failing as a mother. After a brief period of a few months when it seemed that her infant son, Noah, had settled into a regular sleep pattern, it all fell apart. He was up multiple times a night in an incomprehensible, unpredictable pattern. She looked at Facebook photos of her friends with babies and saw no sign of the kind of profound fatigue and unraveling she was experiencing, which exacerbated her feelings of inadequacy. She tried many different approaches: She held and rocked Noah every time he awoke. She let him cry himself to sleep. She limited his nursing to only the beginning of the night, letting her husband do a bottle feeding when Noah awoke at two and four a.m. But as sleep deprivation clouded her thinking, she felt herself descend into feelings of hopelessness.

Then Noah took his first steps. Almost in parallel with his newly acquired mastery of upright mobility, his sleep began to improve. The time between night wakings lengthened. The methods Ellen had used to support his sleep in his early months began to work again. As Ellen in turn was more rested, the fog of depression that had begun to creep in receded.

T. Berry Brazelton showed a profound empathy for both parent and child. He not only appreciated the child's experience of disorder but saw how parents wrestled with many complex feelings as they adapted to their new identity. Parents who have unrealistic expectations, who struggle to understand their child's behavior and communication, are not bad parents. They are bewildered. A sense of inadequacy and guilt may cloud their view. Anxiety may lead them to try to control their child's behavior, as reflected by parents' frequent pleas to a pediatrician to "tell me what to do *now* to manage [X]."

While Brazelton's *Touchpoints* model is used primarily in work with children and families, the frame it offers for thinking about moments of disorder in childhood holds true for moments of disorder throughout everyone's life. It incorporates the fundamental principle of open dynamic systems theory we discussed in chapter 1 — that disorder itself provides the energy that fuels forward growth and development.

A CULTURE OF PERFECTIONISM

The expectation of perfection, for both oneself and one's relationships, pervades modern culture as a whole. We see a growing intolerance of mess. A Google search for the term *perfectionism* reveals a slew of articles with titles such as "Young People Drowning in a Rising Tide of Perfectionism" that reference research studies documenting evidence of this phenomenon. A measure of perfectionism called the Multidimensional Perfectionism Scale was developed and standardized by psychologists Paul Hewitt and Gordon Flett in the early 1990s and is widely used in social science research. One study demonstrated a 33 percent increase in perfectionism in British, Canadian, and American college students between 1986 and 2016. The study's lead author told the *New York Times,* "Millennials feel pressure to perfect themselves partly out of social media use that leads them to compare themselves to others." (See chapter 7 for more on this topic.) Parenting expert Katie Hurley described the "perfect girl syndrome," exemplified by a girl of nine, Gracie, who "had her whole life planned out and wasn't willing to deal with any missteps along the way."

This drive for perfection appears to be fueling the struggles of a generation of adults diagnosed with mental illness. Developers of the perfectionism scale have found over decades of research that perfectionism correlates with depression, anxiety, eating disorders, and other emotional problems. The abundance of how-to books and magazines and blog posts filled with advice and quick fixes reinforces the sense that things would be perfect if only we had the right answer; blog posts receiving the most hits offer "Six Steps to the Perfect Marriage" and "Ten Tips for

Raising a Resilient Child." But the expectation that there is a right way to achieve success, an expert who can tell us what to do in any number of situations, encourages an illusion that we can circumvent messiness in interactions with others. Books and articles offering "practical, useful tips" may actually reinforce the expectation of perfection that creates anxiety and impairs growth. There are countless right ways to address any problem, but they are unique and specific to particular relationships between people. The answer lies within the relationship itself.

The discussion after a talk we gave to an audience of professionals who worked with families and young children bore out this perspective. Pediatricians, nurses, lactation consultants, home visitors, and early-intervention specialists revealed the pressures they felt to tell their patients or clients "what to do." Many recognized that imparting expertise to parents might undermine the parents' natural authority and keep them from developing confidence *together with their child* in their capacity to cope.

On a large scale, this culture of advice cuts short the repair process. That is not to say that anyone needs to go it alone. Working through difficult moments in the setting of relationships in which you feel heard and supported promotes health and well-being more effectively than a rubric of tips or how-tos.

During the question-and-answer period after another presentation, this one for a group of mothers of young children, Claudia experienced the full force of parental expectation to provide "the right answer" to any number of parenting challenges. Instead of doing that, she kept listening to the stories and encouraged these mothers to trust themselves to know what to do in any given moment. She emphasized that they would make mistakes but that these very mistakes would lead them in the direction of healthy growth and change.

One mother wanted to know what to do when her three-year-old daughter threw her shoes across the room. "Should I set a limit? Should I ask her about her feelings?" Claudia helped this mother to consider what might happen if she accepted the uncertainty of the situation. What if she decided in that moment to firmly set a limit and her daughter completely disintegrated? She might be misjudging her daughter's ability to hold herself together. Recognizing that her daughter was tired and over-whelmed by feelings she couldn't handle, she might have to change course and instead offer comfort and containment. Or what if she tried to talk about her daughter's feelings but the little girl continued to fall apart? She would then see that what her daughter really needed at that moment was a firm limit. When they figured it out together, sharing the experience of repairing the mismatch, their relationship could grow, and they would have a deepening sense of trust and confidence from having gotten through a tough moment together.

Winnicott used the term *holding environment* to describe an environment of safe, secure relationships in which the full range of experiences were accepted, contained, and understood. The original concept refers to the way a mother offers her full physical and emotional presence to her developing child. However, the phrase is widely used by Winnicott and others to describe a variety of environments composed of both individuals and communities. The concept of the holding environment offers an alternative to people's reliance on expert advice. When they feel held in relationships, they can work through, rather than avoid, disruption and discord.

What makes someone feel or not feel held in a relationship? If mismatch and repair feed the soul and if messiness is necessary for growth and intimacy, what prevents people from letting themselves be in the mess? In the stories so far in this book, development derailed and relationships became stuck in an environment in which uncertainty did not feel safe. In contrast, in each story a sense of safety to invite discord led to opportunity for growth and healing. In the following chapter, we explore how you know in both your body and your mind that you are safe to make a mess.

3

FEELING SAFE TO MAKE A MESS

ELENA'S WORLD SEEMED TO unravel around the time her daughter, Flora, was born. First, the beloved family cat died. Then her mother-in-law was diagnosed with cancer. While the prognosis was good, treatment would require her husband, Sam, to travel. He already worked long hours running his own business and would now be stressed and less available. She agonized over how to discuss it all with her three-year-old son, Matteo. His life had just been disrupted by the arrival of his baby sister; how could any of them handle the pain of loss, the uncertainty of illness, and the messiness that accompanies both? Best to smooth it over. But when Matteo's difficult behavior escalated and repeated episodes of being sent to his room only made the problem worse, Elena could see that this smoothing over of the chaos, the figurative closing the door on the mess, was not working. Only when her mother came to stay with them for several weeks did she feel safe enough to begin to acknowledge and then take steps to repair the disruptions in their lives. She decided to delay starting a social work degree program for another six months so she could be more present with her family. She enrolled in mommy-and-me dance classes with Matteo, who had already shown a passion for movement and music. Her mother's calming presence proved critical for Elena to feel safe to work through the mess of difficult feelings the whole family experienced during that complicated transition.

What drives us to try to smooth over life's inevitable disconnections? We may fear that a crack in the system will lead the whole thing to break down. We need to feel safe and confident that when things fall apart, we will be able to put the pieces back together.

We saw in chapter 1 that for Eric's parents, who had lived through the Holocaust, a rigid avoidance of difficult feelings felt necessary for their very survival. They needed everything to be "fine." Their bodies had developed a heightened sensitivity in response to a real threat. When people feel threatened, their bodies may, in a way that can be beyond their conscious control, prevent them from connecting. Your thinking brain may tell you that a situation is safe while your body experiences threat.

HOW WE SENSE SAFETY

Let's look more closely at the process by which our bodies make meaning of our environment as safe or unsafe. Research using the still-face paradigm reveals that infants make meaning of an experience as threatening well before the development of the parts of the brain responsible for conscious thought in the form of words. We saw this happen when we studied a video of a six-month-old with his mother. We had not noticed it watching them together in real time, but when we played the video in slow motion and analyzed it frame by frame, the nature of the interaction was unmistakable.

The mother bends down to nuzzle the infant. The baby grabs her hair and won't let go. The mother yells "Ow!" and pulls back with an angry grimace. He communicates in his response that his mother's expression is more than just surprising or unfamiliar — it has specific meaning. The infant apprehends danger. Her automatic reaction, though it lasts less than a second, frightens him. He ducks. He brings his hands up in front of his face, partially turns away in his chair, then looks at his mother from under his raised hands.

While he is not yet able to think in words, this infant already has the capacity to attribute intention to another person's behavior. He believes something dangerous is about to occur, and he organizes a defensive reaction to protect himself. His mother almost immediately realizes it too, and she quickly tries to overcome the rupture and change his experience. At first, he stays hidden behind his hands, but he begins to smile. As they happily reengage, the experience of threat and its repair is now part of their sense of each other and of themselves. They both know they can overcome a big mismatch, even a scary one.

This interplay between mother and infant represents one of countless moments of mismatch and repair between parent and child that, as you have seen in the preceding chapters, support healthy growth and development. The infant uses the parts of the brain available to him to make meaning of the situation. The autonomic nervous system, well functioning at birth, is the first-responder meaning-making system for assessing the safety of the environment.

BEYOND FIGHT OR FLIGHT

The autonomic nervous system (ANS), with branches to every part of the body, takes in information about the external environment and adjusts the internal environment, all in a way that is out of conscious awareness. When we think of reactions to a dangerous situation, the well-known fight-or-flight response, controlled by the sympathetic branch of the ANS, typically comes to mind. Under the influence of the HPA (hypothalamic-pituitary-adrenal) axis, stress hormones are released, automatically engaging the body's motor system — your heart pounds; you breathe fast and heavy. But this simple explanation leaves out an important part of how people sense and react to danger.

In contrast to the sympathetic system, the parasympathetic system, which functions via the large, multibranch vagus nerve, keeps you still. It slows breathing and lowers heart rate and blood pressure. This stillness can serve to connect people. But in the face of overwhelming threat, it can also disconnect them.

The research of an important partner in our work, Stephen Porges, a neuroscientist at Indiana University, reveals how your physiologic state serves as a kind of gate, opening or closing the door to trust and engagement. It makes meaning of experience and influences your responses.

Porges refers to the way we assess the safety of a situation as *neuroception*. Prior to Porges's discoveries, scientists thought there were just two ways in which the nervous system functioned during interaction with the environment: If you felt safe, the parasympathetic system was active and you were calm and engaged. If you believed you were in danger, the sympathetic system, which controls the fight-or-flight response, became active.

But Porges identified a third way that the nervous system reacts, this one also under control of the parasympathetic system. The parasympathetic system, via the vagus nerve, sends two sets of fibers to each muscle and organ. One set of fibers, which he calls the *smart vagus* (also known as the *myelinated vagus*, a reference to the insulating sheath around the nerve fibers), is active when you are open to receive a hug, when you look into a person's eyes, when you listen and connect. Social engagement is a first level of response. When you sense danger, the second-level sympathetic fight-or-flight response kicks in. But there is a third level controlled by a different set of fibers of the parasympathetic system, what Porges calls the *primitive vagus* (also known as the *unmyelinated vagus* because it lacks the insulating sheath). These fibers take over in the face of inescapable overwhelming threat. The classic example is a mouse who, caught in the jaws of a cat, plays dead. The primitive vagus makes people still, but not in a way that invites connection. These three different ways in which your body makes meaning of the relative safety of the environment, what he calls the polyvagal theory, show that the two-part parasympathetic nervous system plays a major role in your assessment of and response to the safety of your environment. The functioning of this system is central to the ability to access social connection.

SAFETY IN FACE AND VOICE

With fibers going to the muscles of the face, middle ear, larynx, and heart, the smart and primitive vagus nerves are primary conductors of your sense of safety and your capacity or incapacity for social engagement. Porges writes, "Functionally the social engagement system emerges from a heart-face connection that coordinates the heart with the muscles of the face and head."

You are probably familiar with the concept of wearing your heart on your sleeve. But a more biologically accurate description, Porges showed, would be that you wear your heart on your face. Your availability for social connection is signaled on your face and in your voice. The exchange in the video described above shows the infant making meaning of danger from his mother's facial expression and the tone of her voice.

In *The Expression of the Emotions in Man and Animals*, which is perhaps as significant as *The Origin of Species* but less well known, Charles Darwin describes the highly intricate system of facial muscles and the similarly complex systems of muscles used to modulate tone and rhythm, or prosody, of voice that exist only in humans. Why do we have all of these muscles? We know if an interaction is safe, if people are available for connection, by reading the state of the autonomic nervous system on their faces and in their voices. We are practically seeing inside them.

The vagus regulates the muscles around the eyes — the orbicularis oculi — that function to convey an inviting expression that is often called *smiling eyes*. The smart fibers allow these muscles to move. But when you feel threatened, under the influence of the primitive vagus, these muscles may be still. Try smiling without using your eyes — it feels fake, disconnected. And while you might not be aware of it, when you engage with people who smile without using their eye muscles, you experience the smiles as fake.

Similarly, the vagus regulates the tiny muscles of the middle ear.

When the smart vagus is active, you hear the full range of sounds in music, in nature, and in the human voice. When you sense threat, when your primitive vagus takes the reins, these muscles are less mobile, with the result that sounds become distorted. The ticking of a clock, hardly noticeable when you feel calm, takes on an incessant, disruptive fingernails-on-a-chalkboard quality.

Neuroception explains the behavior of the infant in the video we described above. He does not consciously "think" that his mother is "angry." He does not have these concepts available to him yet. But he knows, through the meaning that his ANS makes of the situation, that her face and voice convey danger.

WHY WE NEED SOCIAL ENGAGEMENT

When you sense danger everywhere, the subsequent incessant flooding of stress hormones exerts harm on your brain and body. But the sympathetic nervous system is not the only way you can be harmed by the experience. The shutting down of the social engagement system can make you "heartsick," leading to illness and even death. The vagus nerve influences your immune system, heart rate, blood pressure, and internal organs. Loneliness can kill people by throwing this well-regulated system into chaos. Research demonstrates that loneliness increases the risk of heart disease, arthritis, and diabetes as well as emotional suffering and risk of suicide.

Social isolation and loneliness are not equivalent. The first is an objective measure of social connections and interactions; the second is a subjective perception of isolation. You can feel lonely even surrounded by people. Have you ever been at a social event where the people around you were laughing and engaging in easy banter while you looked on as a disconnected outsider? Loneliness in the company of other people has an exquisite painfulness, comparable to the experience of the infant in the still-face experiment whose mother is both present and absent.

Why might you feel lonely in the company of people? Something about that particular environment, for a range of reasons, does not feel safe. You make meaning of the situation as threatening. You struggle to make sense of the rapport among those you observe having fun. You feel disconnected and alone. A history of repeated lack of repair in important relationships may underlie this reaction. For people with relational histories rich in mismatch and repair, casual social interactions may seem effortless and harmless. But people who carry problematic meanings about social interaction, whether due to emotionally unavailable caregivers, intrusive caregivers who did not allow for any mismatch, or, at worst, abusive caregivers, may have an altogether different response. If you are in a roomful of people, social convention prevents you from running away or lashing out. If your body senses threat via neuroception, your primitive vagus takes over as a protective mechanism. This response, which occurs outside of conscious awareness, can create a kind of vicious cycle, as a history of unrepaired mismatch prevents you from accessing the healing power of social connection.

THE TRANSFORMATION OF PRINCE HARRY

When countless interactions have led someone to make meaning of the world as threatening, immersion in new interactions over time with cues of safety are needed to change those meanings. The change can be slow but profound.

When you watch Prince Harry today, with his warm, engaging smile and gentle voice full of compassion, you can see how Meghan Markle would have fallen in love with him in an instant. The expressiveness in the looks they exchanged throughout their wedding ceremony offers a study in the function of the myelinated, or smart, vagus — you can read the love and connection on their faces. But when you watch any of the multitude of media specials on the royal couple that preceded their wedding, especially the videos and photos from Harry's younger days, you can see that for a long time, the world did not feel safe for him. You can read the sense of threat on his face.

Harry's parents' marriage was unhappy from the moment it began. He was referred to as "the spare" in comparison with the heir, his older brother, William, who is ahead of him in line for the throne. In photos of Harry with his mother, Diana, we see from the open joyful smiles on their faces that she clearly offered him unconditional love. But tragically, she died the year after she and Charles divorced, when Harry was just twelve years old. In photos of Harry over the next twenty years, you see a kind of still, frozen face. He was in trouble, drinking excessively and engaging in reckless behavior.

If you look closely at the photos taken over the course of Harry's growing up, you can see the state of his autonomic nervous system displayed on his face. In one delightful picture from his early childhood, where he's on his mother's lap at an amusement-park ride, an openness to social engagement shines on both of their faces. In contrast, photos of his adolescence and young adulthood do not show the crinkling around his eyes that characterize photos of him with Diana or current photos. There is a stillness to his facial expression. Even in photos in which he is smiling, you do not find the warmth of engagement, the full range of emotional expressiveness that you see now. It appears that he was under the influence of the primitive vagus in response to a world that felt threatening, while now his smart vagus is fully online. In current interviews, you hear a lilting intonation in his voice that invites us in.

How did this transformation occur? The public display of Harry's life offers a glimpse of how he immersed himself in a brew of relationships that likely allowed him to move through the mess to embrace complexity and achieve an increased sense of coherence. What is more complex and coherent than a royal wedding? You see him playing soccer in Africa with children who had lost their parents to AIDS. He recognized in them the same kind of void he felt from the loss of his mother. His military service played a critical role in his development. He was able to join a unit in Iraq, to be "just one of the guys," which gave him an opportunity to be himself or, to use Winnicott's words, to discover his true self. It may be that these cumulative experiences gave him enough of a sense of coherence to engage in the difficult work of grieving the loss of his mother, which he publicly acknowledges he had not felt permission to do. While of course we do not know for certain, one can wonder if the counseling Harry sought to address his mother's death offered him a relationship in which to safely move through mismatch and repair.

An April 2017 article in the *Daily Telegraph* describes Prince Harry's interview with British journalist Bryony Gordon about his struggles to come to terms with his mother's death and his decision to seek counseling. "I can safely say that losing my mum at the age of 12, and therefore shutting down all of my emotions for the last 20 years, has had a quite serious effect on not only my personal life but my work as well."

With his brother and sister-in-law, he started the organization Heads Together to change the conversation about mental health and destigmatize mental health struggles. As described on their website, "Heads Together wants to help people feel much more comfortable with their everyday mental well-being and have the practical tools to support their friends and family."

Some of the media coverage of the new royal couple describes a bond they share over their work with children in Africa and their desire to use their fame to do good in the world. This explanation suggests that their love is based on ideas that can be captured in language. But multiple accounts reveal that partway through his first date with Meghan Markle, Harry asked, "What are you doing tomorrow?" and one can wonder if their connection is in a sense nonverbal. The neuroception of safety, which precedes words and conscious thoughts, might have had a significant role to play.

WHEN THE WORLD IS TOO LOUD

Perceiving the world as threatening may be the result of things that happen when we're young, as in Prince Harry's story. But qualities we are born with can also play a significant role. Babies have a wide range of reactions to sound, touch, and sensory experiences. Some infants like to be held; others are not cuddly and prefer to observe the world on their own terms. Some startle at the slightest sound while others sleep peacefully through anything. Some show wide-eyed alertness to any visual stimulus; some maintain focused attention on a human face. None of these variations is in and of itself "abnormal." But a child with heightened sensory sensitivity may in some settings experience the world as more threatening, or less safe, than other children do. While some children may find a social gathering fun, a child with a sensitive sensory system may interpret the situation in a different way: *There is too much going on. I am confused. I need to withdraw.*

Many people experience low-frequency sounds as threatening, which, according to Porges, has origins in an adaptive response by our ancestors to the growls of predators. A child with a particular variation in the parasympathetic system that causes him to perceive low-frequency sounds with a greater intensity may act in such a way as to protect himself and help to calm his nervous system. The classic lining up of toys or in-depth knowledge of every species of dinosaur may be a soothing activity in a world that feels overwhelming. While these behaviors serve an adaptive function for some children, they may be interpreted by adults who interact with them as signs of a disorder, and they may be labeled as having, for example, autism.

To describe the qualities a child brings to the world, people may say, "He's got a difficult temperament," or "She's slow to warm up." In the seminal research of Nancy Snidman and Jerome Kagan at Harvard begun in the 1980s, four-month-olds were identified as either high reactive or low reactive based on their responses to a range of sensory experiences — olfactory, visual, and auditory — at varying levels of intensity. In one series of observations, the infants heard a female voice speak three nonsense syllables at three loudness levels. The infants were then categorized by their crying and motor activity, including arching and arm and leg movements. Those considered high reactive were more likely to display facial expressions indicative of distress. Snidman and Kagan followed these children for years, obtaining a range of both behavioral and physiologic measures, and found that the categories of high reactive and low reactive mapped onto variations in temperament from toddlerhood through adolescence. The high-reactive infants became toddlers who were more likely to avoid new situations. As school-age children, they tended to be emotionally subdued and cautious. By their teenage years, the children in this group reported a more negative mood than their peers, with anxiety about the future. In contrast, those in the low-reactive group were least avoidant as toddlers and more emotionally spontaneous and sociable at later ages. What is called *temperament* may have origins in the meaning we make of our sensory experience.

When parents struggle to make sense of a child's behavior, the typical mismatch-repair process may be derailed. Alice and Bruce noticed Henry's exquisite sensitivity to sound from the moment he was born. When taking him out in the car with her, Alice learned to play the same repetitive, lilting popular children's song over and over in order to get through an outing in peace. Even a brief pause in the music would lead to frantic screaming from him that stopped equally quickly when the music resumed. As he grew into toddlerhood, this problem subsided but new ones arose. During one Fourth of July celebration, while Henry's sister, Emma, enjoyed the fireworks with Bruce, Alice ran with her screaming two-year-old to the safety of their car in the parking lot. Once the windows were closed and the sound of exploding fireworks was muffled, Henry's hysteria subsided.

At age three, rather than play with the other children in preschool, Henry preferred to run around in circles, sometimes displaying the massive meltdowns Bruce and Alice lived with on a daily basis. A teacher, observing this behavior, suggested he be evaluated for autism spectrum disorder.

From the perspective of the still-face paradigm, we can reframe the situation as a mismatch between Henry's biology and his environment. Henry's hypersensitivity led him to struggle with making meaning of his world through social engagement. The mismatch of his everyday experience, more intense and dramatic than that of a temperamentally "easy" child, called for a lot of effort on the part of his parents, teachers, and others in his social world to help him get to repair.

Henry went on to study music and become a professional oboist. With help from his parents, he found ways to navigate and manage his extreme sensitivity to sound. Henry's musical talent in fact might represent a flip side to his auditory hypersensitivity. An ability to discern individual notes and his perfect pitch led him to a natural solution to his problem. Before he could express in words that he was overwhelmed by certain sounds, meltdowns were the only way he could manage to convey his feelings. His neuroception of sounds as threatening became a kind of closed door, blocking him from access to meaning-making through social interaction. Only when he immersed himself in musical expression could he come fully into himself.

Porges describes how singing and playing a wind instrument both alter the structure and function of the middle ear. The threatening nature of low-frequency sounds is altered by engaging the muscles of the middle ear during the act of blowing on the instrument. A similar process is at work in what Porges calls a "neural exercise" of consciously taking slow, deep breaths to calm yourself. Both activities serve to bring the smart vagus online to open the door to social engagement.

Fortunately, Henry's natural creativity offered him an opportunity to make new meanings in the world. Until he went to college, Henry had few friends. He felt comfortable engaging in social relationships for the first time during the many hours a week he spent with the other members of his college orchestra, a time when his autonomic nervous system was transformed by the very act of playing his oboe. With the door to social engagement opened, he developed rich and rewarding friendships, first with his fellow musicians and then with a wider social network.

WHEN PARENTS BRING MEANINGS OF DANGER

Henry's nervous system created meanings of danger in response to certain kinds of sounds. Other variations in sensory processing, reactions to sights, touch, even to the position of one's body in space, may give rise to distorted meanings through a kind of chronic mismatch with the social environment. For people in these situations, the work of getting to repair is greater than it is for those without extreme sensitivities. Complicating the story is the fact that in every child's life, adults also bring meanings to the interaction, often carried from their own early relationships. If you are a parent who had relatively little experience of repair in your own childhood, you may make meaning of a situation, such as a screaming, out-of-control child, as threatening.

Henry's parents needed to be especially present to help their son make new meanings of his experience. Both Bruce and Alice drew on loving models of parenting from their own families of origin. Once a week, Alice had coffee with a group of mothers she had known since Henry was born. Bruce played piano every weekend with friends in a jazz quartet. Both parents had multiple experiences of being heard and supported, which served as sources of strength fueling their efforts to help their son feel safe with his own big feelings.

In Circle of Security, an evidence-based intervention developed to support parent-child relationships, parents learn to recognize how in their everyday interactions with their children they may bring meaning from past relationships. To demonstrate the notion that painful past memories can trigger us to feel threatened, the program employs what has become known by parents, therapists, and trainers as "shark music." Participants watch a film of an ocean at sunset with a soft melody as an accompanying soundtrack. Then they watch the scene again, this time with music similar to John Williams's brilliant theme from the movie *Jaws*.

Most likely Williams deliberately chose notes that create a feeling of dread in the opening scene even when the viewer is simply looking at an expanse of blue water. The reaction comes not from conscious thoughts, produced in the outer layer of the brain known as the cortex, but in the precortical sensory and autonomic nervous systems. We react to the *Jaws* theme not by thinking, *This music is from a scary movie*. The threat is contained in the sounds themselves. You make meaning of a situation as threatening without words or thoughts. In Circle of Security, the shark music comes to represent the way parents may feel threatened in their interactions with their child, making meaning of the experience in a way that is out of conscious awareness and that they cannot put into words.

The viral children's song "Baby Shark" adds an interesting twist to the relationship between music and meaning-making. In the opening notes, the song mimics the *Jaws* theme, but it quickly shifts to the light, captivating melody of the body of the song. The lyrics reflect this progression to safety, listing all the family members who go on a hunt (perhaps symbolizing the inherent dangers of the big outside world) and then concluding with "safe at last, doo-doo-doo-doo-doo-doo." As mystifying as the song's appeal may be to parents, children may be captivated by its reflection of the universal experience of moving from threat to safety.

When parenting itself feels threatening, your body may unconsciously override the sympathetic response, as neither fight nor flight is an option. The instinct to protect your children prevents you from either hurting or abandoning them. In these circumstances, the primitive vagus may take over. You may unconsciously present a still-face to your child, and this freezing of the social engagement system may in turn be perceived by your child as threatening.

Richard and Naema expected that clear limits and boundaries would characterize their parenting. They wished to be neither coddling and overly indulgent parents, as Naema's had been, nor strict authoritarians, like Richard's. They treated two-year-old Owen with respect, never using baby talk. In their view, all had been going well with this approach until one day when Owen was absorbed with a new Lego set he had received for his birthday, and Richard told him that it was time to leave the house. Owen threw himself on the floor and began kicking and screaming. Richard immediately swept him up off the floor and held him firmly as he flailed about, telling him in a firm yet gentle tone that he could not do that, that he might hurt himself or someone else.

From then on, Owen started having six or more tantrums a day. "Don't throw your food." Tantrum. "It's time for bed." Tantrum. It seemed that anything they said set him off. Each time they picked him up, held him, and told him in no uncertain terms that he had to stop behaving that way. The final straw came one day when Naema told him he couldn't have a cookie until he finished dinner, and he threw his entire plate on the floor, making a huge mess. What had become of their sweet and easygoing little boy?

Richard at first said he was bewildered by their son's sudden transformation. But when he and Naema consulted with a therapist, Richard revealed that he recognized himself in Owen. Identified from a young age by both parents and teachers as a "problem child," Richard was often in trouble. He had been sent home from kindergarten several times for hitting other children. His father had punished him with humiliating, often public, bare-bottom spankings. This went on for years.

Tantrums are a normal, healthy phenomenon. They occur when young children transition from feeling omnipotent in the first year to recognizing that they are relatively powerless. But for Richard, given the framework of his own childhood experiences, an out-of-control child represented terror and humiliation. His autonomic nervous system made meaning of Owen's typical and developmentally appropriate behavior as threatening. Those meanings had roots in Richard's early childhood. Rather than understanding why a toddler would have a tantrum and letting it run its course, he simply forbade it. He offered Owen no outlet for the normal frustration that a tantrum represents. Richard's social engagement system turned off when he was confronted by his toddler's tantrums. Naema's history was different, but as one of four siblings with few limits on their behavior, she had a pervasive feeling of emotional chaos that had also left her ill equipped to handle Owen's outbursts. She had no idea how to set limits in a way that would be helpful. In essence, Owen was on his own, with no adults to help him manage his big feelings. Richard and Naema needed to let Owen be a typical two-year-old. Both parents resisted engaging in the normal messiness that characterizes this developmental stage.

Insights from both the polyvagal theory and the still-face paradigm can help us imagine how this situation came about. Richard's dissociative response, triggered by the bodily memory of shame, fear, and pain, likely was transmitted not only by his behavior but also in the muscles of his face. Under stress, the smart vagus that regulates those muscles was incapacitated, giving way to more primitive functioning. Richard was presenting a still-face just at the moment when Owen felt most helpless and out of control. Though Richard was physically present with Owen, his face and voice were under the influence of the primitive neurologic response. This reaction was automatic and not under his conscious control. But Owen needed Richard to recognize his feelings of frustration and also set appropriate limits on his behavior. Sometimes tantrums need to run their course. By forbidding tantrums without appreciating Owen's legitimate feelings, Richard closed off Owen's way of communicating, since he had not yet developed language skills to explain those feelings. Owen's increasingly aggressive behavior might have been his two-year-old way of trying to communicate with his father.

This chronic lack of help from his father may have led Owen not to feel safe with his own big emotions. Richard needed to make new, less threatening meanings of his son's behavior in order to help his son feel safe. In part, these new meanings could take the form of words and thoughts. In psychotherapy, Richard could talk about his childhood and gain insights into the connection between his early experiences and the troubles he was having with Owen.

But to change the meanings embedded in Richard's body — in the reactions of his ANS — words and thoughts were not enough. And Owen, at the tender age of two, had also begun to create meaning in his ANS that his mess of feelings were not okay.

When the two took a parent-child martial arts class together, they learned a new "language" in which both could feel safe with their big feelings. Moving their bodies together through the choreographed mismatch and repair allowed them to find a new way of representing to themselves and to each other the inevitable miscommunications and misunderstandings. Richard learned to let the tantrums happen rather than squashing them, smoothing them over. And with this new approach, the frequency and intensity of the tantrums subsided.

With the opportunity to put words to his own experience and the chance to engage in a tussle in a safe and contained setting, Richard could respond to his son's behavior without activating his primitive vagus. When Owen expressed his relative helplessness in a normal way through a tantrum, Richard's availability as a safe haven was communicated in the expressive face he showed to his son.

Until they could let some messiness into their interaction,

Owen and his father repeatedly had mismatches without opportunity to repair. But through psychotherapy and the martial arts class and then Richard's newfound comfort with Owen's natural two-year-old tendency to make a mess, they could repair the mismatches, both big and small. Seeing the change in Owen and Richard's relationship and watching Owen's positive response, Naema learned that limits could be helpful but were much more effective with her and Richard's comforting and loving presence. As all of the family relationships flourished, with an increasing sense of trust, Owen in turn developed the ability to manage his big feelings without falling apart.

A DANCE OF NATURE AND NURTURE

The word *temperament* may suggest a definite inborn trait, like eye color. Similarly, a psychiatric diagnosis, such as autism, conveys the impression of a static problem intrinsic to the individual. But as we'll explore in depth in the following chapter, one's sense of the world as safe or threatening is not fixed. Perception can be transformed in the ongoing process of making meaning in relationships with other people.

Variation in sensory processing is an example of the child's contribution to the mismatch-repair process. These characteristics represent the nature side of the social engagement system. Life experience, the nurture side, contributes equally to one's interpretation of situations and relationships as safe or unsafe. Neither nature nor nurture alone is decisive; both interact in complex ways to shape the meaning we make of ourselves in the world.

While children are born with certain characteristics, and parents have experiences they bring to this new role, once parent and child have met, the child's contribution can't be separated out from the parent's. The development of each individual is intimately intertwined with his interactions in relationship with the other. For example, variations in the autonomic nervous system may lead a child to experience many forms of sensory input as overwhelming. In a protective way, his primitive vagus takes over. Children who carry the diagnosis of autism are known to have a narrower range of facial expressions. In turn, the adults who care for them become distressed as they struggle to reach the child, leading to a downward spiral of miscues and disconnections.

IT TAKES TWO TO TANGO

At a recent presentation of our work, a mother shared her technique for regulating herself when her two young boys didn't listen to her. After asking them for the second or third time to put on their shoes, she would begin to sing her request in an operatic voice. She not only defused the situation by doing something funny; she actually discovered her own neural exercise for calming the autonomic nervous system. Porges writes, "Singing requires slow exhalation, while controlling the muscles of the face and head to produce the modulated vocalizations we recognize as vocal music. The slow exhalations calm the autonomic state by increasing the impact of ventral [smart] vagal pathways on the heart." Her sons were startled out of their opposition, and rather than descending into a meltdown, they connected with her around the humor of the situation. This resourceful mother had discovered a way to calm her own big emotions, allowing her to be present to help her boys manage theirs.

When we look again at the video of the mother whose son pulled her hair, we see how both parent and infant had a significant part in the way the interaction played out. He initially disengaged in response to the experience of threat, and she, recognizing how she'd frightened him, made a great effort to engage him. It was as if he were presenting a mini-still-face to her. Following microseconds of mismatch, they found each other and reconnected in joy.

Both this video clip and the interaction between the opera-singing mother and her boys are examples of how the ability to manage emotions and behavior, commonly termed *self-regulation*, grows in relationships. Being close with others and being able to handle yourself emerge out of the same process: countless moment-to-moment interactions through which partners change and grow. As we'll explore in the following chapter, the exchange of individual meanings, goals, and intentions that makes up the process of mutual regulation is how we create new meanings together. Creating shared meanings is the most powerful neural exercise of all. An understanding of how this process works between infants and their caregivers can guide us in navigating all kinds of relationships in our adult lives.

4

STOPPING THE BLAME GAME

IN HIS MUSICAL *COMPANY*, Stephen Sondheim beautifully portrays the messiness of human relationships. The play's different married couples each express deep discord along with warmth and closeness, but the main character, Bobby, remains safely outside the fray. Toward the end of the play Bobby finally understands what he's been missing out on, and when he sings "Being Alive," he celebrates how being in the mess is to be fully alive. When you accept that you will never be completely in sync with another person, you open yourself to intimacy. Embracing the inevitably muddled, untidy nature of moment-to-moment interactions, creating space to be alone together with others, offers a path to meaningful engagement in the world.

You need to have a solid sense of yourself — to self-regulate — in order to be open to intimacy with others. Self-regulation is different from self-control, a relatively cold term that implies a need to rein in intense feelings. Self-regulation refers to an ability to engage in the world and experience a full range of emotions without falling apart. When you lose someone close to you, you need to grieve, to have profound feelings of sadness, but without losing your ability to function. Similarly, anger, a healthy part of intimate relationships, becomes a problem if, in a rage, you completely lose your sense of yourself and your partner. And you want to be able to feel intense pleasure without getting lost. While sex is one obvious example, people can also feel deep pleasure when they are alone. A child fully absorbed in imaginary play or an adult sitting in a dark theater watching a performance that speaks to them in a deep way may each experience a powerful sense of joy that comes with being fully oneself.

The sense of self grows out of interactions in the earliest intimate relationships of parent and infant. But even if your earliest relationships did not afford you the experience of mismatch and repair that build the capacity for intimacy and self-reliance, you can always learn new ways of being in relationships. New opportunities for moment-to-moment interactions can change your sense of yourself in the world. In the film *Alive and Kicking*, we meet a number of people who appear lost and alone but who find themselves through swing dancing. They step on each other's toes, argue over dance steps, and navigate the disappointment of losing a competition. Muddling through together, they find joy in belonging to this new community, a beautiful example of combining mutual and self-regulation. The act of dancing, together with the music itself, can help you feel calm in your body. And the regulation you experience in this activity comes as much through your interactions with your partner as from your own movement.

When parents are calmly present during times of play, they help their children achieve both self-reliance and intimacy. But under many circumstances, such "quality time" is elusive. Parents who work long hours and come home exhausted at the end of the day wonder why meltdowns always occur just when they are trying to get dinner ready. Consider the story of Lola and her mother, Simone.

After a long, difficult day dealing with dysfunctional office dynamics, Simone would come home to her three-year-old daughter, Lola, who would insist on imaginary play, overwhelming Simone's already taxed brain. Simone's inability to meet her daughter's demands led to explosive meltdowns that hijacked their evenings as Simone struggled to meet both her own needs and her daughter's.

Simone initially interpreted Lola's end-of-the-day tantrums as her daughter willfully "making my life difficult." When her mother didn't understand what Lola wanted right away, she would make a literal mess of toys in the living room as she tried harder and harder, in vain, to get her mother to engage with her in play. Simone would then yell at her for failing to clean up one activity before going on to another. Their mutual anger and frustration set the stage for unrepaired mismatch as each made meaning of the other in a way that precluded connection.

But when Simone paused and took some time to make sense of Lola's behavior, she understood that her daughter had missed her. She saw that Lola's meltdowns were perhaps a consequence of the strain of holding it together all day. The disappointment of her mother being physically present yet still unavailable for play was too much for Lola to handle.

Simone made a beautiful adaptation to this daily dilemma. She discovered that coloring together, with Lola sitting on her lap, offered them a chance to connect while at the same time engaging in an activity that was calming for both. They could be comfortably together and alone.

THE CAPACITY TO BE ALONE

The summer her two young-adult children each set off on a vacation with a significant other, Claire felt a shift within herself unlike what she'd experienced with other milestones. She recalled a morning long ago. Up at dawn, she sat on the sofa sipping coffee and watched her infant son, Ezra, asleep in his bassinet while her three-year-old daughter, Rachel, played an elaborate game of tea party with her dolls. All three were peacefully alone together.

Between the peaceful childhood scene and that summer lay years of ordinary struggles. She and her husband, Jared, had worked through many a difficult time together with each child, from disappointment around a canceled playdate to rejection from a much-desired college to their grandfather's death. Claire knew that more lay ahead, but she let herself fully feel the joy of this moment. She saw how those struggles — the messiness — had given her children a solid sense of themselves in the world and in turn opened them to opportunities for intimacy.

These two capacities, comfort with one's own self and openness to intimacy, are closely linked. The capacity to be alone grows out of relationships with others, while the ability to be intimate with others is rooted in the capacity to be alone.

Many of us feel pressure not only to achieve perfect attunement in our relationships but also to be available for interaction every moment. We need to always be playing with our kids or ready to give advice to a struggling friend or partner. *Serve and return,* a term used in the world of child development, reflects the idea that emotional growth is rooted in interaction. But in the tennis game of life, not every serve is returned. In order to feel comfortable in your own skin, you need some space to figure things out, to work through a problem.

This ability, it turns out, is a developmental process beginning in infancy. Claire held her newborn infants in her arms and spent the early days and weeks fully preoccupied with caring for them; in the years that followed, she "failed" to meet their every need, letting her children develop the ability to be comfortably alone. She did not need to engage with them constantly for them to know she was there. And eventually, she did not need to be there at all for them to have confidence to be out in the world.

In chapter 2 we discussed the concept of the good-enough mother developed by D. W. Winnicott. Less well known, but perhaps equally significant, is Winnicott's writing on the capacity to be alone as a developmental achievement. He described how, early in adult patients' therapy, moments of silence felt fraught with fear or anger. But after some time in analysis, as his patients developed a newly robust sense of self, they were able to comfortably sit in silence, and these moments felt calm and peaceful. The patient and the therapist could be alone together.

Listening to his patients' stories, Winnicott recognized that the capacity to be comfortable alone emerged from early parent-child relationships. He described the paradox that "the capacity to be alone is based on the experience of being alone with someone, and that without a sufficiency of this experience the capacity to be alone cannot develop." He added, "Maturity and the capacity to be alone implies that the individual has had good-enough mothering to build up a belief in a benign environment." As we saw in chapter 2, this "benign environment" includes children's repeated experience of successfully working through their parents' failures to meet their every need, enabling development of a sense of trust in themselves and others. These interactions become built into their personalities and ways of being in the world, holding them together when they are out on their own.

THE STILL-FACE PARADIGM:
ALONE AND TOGETHER

The ability to manage your behavior and emotions in your social world is essential to your health and well-being. The still-face paradigm reveals how the capacity for self-regulation is embedded in interactions in relationships. Intimacy and self-reliance are two sides of the same coin. Just as our research offers evidence of the clinical concept of the good-enough mother, our observations of parent-infant pairs in an experimental setting offers evidence supporting Winnicott's clinical observations about the development of the capacity to be alone.

We observed variation when we analyzed videotapes of parent-infant pairs in episodes of play and then in the still-face experiment. In those parent-infant pairs that displayed the typical pattern of mismatch and repair, the infants were generally able to self-regulate when confronted with the still-face situation. Left to manage distress on their own without the scaffolding of their mothers, these infants could hold themselves together sufficiently. They could organize their movements and behavior to signal to the mother: *Respond to me!*

Some infant-parent interactions were atypical, characterized by a lack of growth-promoting mismatch and repair due to either prolonged time to repair or, as with anxious, intrusive caregivers, little opportunity for repair. When these infants were confronted by the stress of the still-face situation, they turned to self-comforting, arching away, with a chaotic quality to their movements. While self-comforting can be adaptive, for these babies self-regulation seemed to take all of their energy, making them unavailable for connection. They shut out the world to regulate themselves. They turned inward, using all of their resources to hold themselves together. They had no energy for reconnecting.

The process of mismatch and repair gives the infant both a sense of himself and a sense of trust in his relationship with his caregiver. For that brief period when he loses his interactive partner, when he is, in a way, "alone," he can still hold himself together. He trusts that she will return. He trusts that he can make it, that he will be okay. But infants who did not have the typical experience of mismatch and repair had a more tenuous sense of self. Without the scaffolding of the interactive partner, they struggled to maintain a sense of coherence. They "knew" in their bodies they couldn't make it alone. Many of these infants completely fell apart or continued to rely on self-comfort and withdrawal even when the mothers became available for interaction again.

These variations occur at all ages. Couples therapist and author Sue Johnson found the still-face paradigm so deeply relevant to her clinical work with adult couples that she asked us to help create an adult still-face demonstration. Unlike the experiment we described in the introduction in which adults play the roles of baby and parent, this video presents a role-play of an adult couple. While the volunteers were coached in their respective parts, as they got into the role-play, they took off on their own, improvising in a natural way.

In the video, a man and a woman sit facing each other, having a heated disagreement. The man says, "I don't want to visit your relatives. They do not like me. They don't even notice me." In the middle of the conversation, the man shuts down, presenting a face that lacks expressiveness and connection. Then he turns his body away and looks down at the floor, repeatedly blinking and almost closing his eyes. Like the infant in the original still-face video, his partner falls apart. The agitation in her voice rises and her whole body strains toward him, her movements tense and frantic. After urgently trying, and failing, to connect by using words, she begins to cry, which appears to jolt him back. His face regains an expressive quality as he turns toward her, and his voice is gentler. He tells her, "I see you're upset and it's not you." He explains how her family intimidates him by asking questions about his career. He tells her that it is important to him that they continue talking together. She looks up at him and he meets her gaze. Their expressions soften as they reconnect.

Johnson writes on her blog:

> The dance between infant and mum and two adult lovers is made up of the same emotions — the same needs and moves. Any love relationship is a dance of connection and disconnection — of reaching and, if there is no response, of protesting, turning away, emotional meltdown, and, if we can manage it — repair and reconnection.

Johnson observes that in everyday life, partners in a couple are usually completely unaware of the effects of their still-face behavior. She writes:

> We find, in all our studies of helping couples repair their relationship, that adult lovers simply have NO idea about the alarm and pain that they deliver when they simply shut their lover out and become unreachable. These folks are often trying to avoid a fight, but in fact this disconnection turns up the heat and triggers frantic, and often negative, attempts by the other partner to get them to respond.

Bringing this process into awareness, noticing the still-face behavior both in yourself and your partner as well as the reactions the behavior precipitates, can help set a troubled relationship on a path of healing. When you get caught up in your own distress, you become unavailable for connection and may inadvertently give your partner a "still-face," triggering a downward spiral of missed cues and miscommunication. At such moments, you need to pause, breathe, and find a way to calm yourself enough to think clearly. When you can take in the other person's perspective, you can find a way to repair and come together.

FINDING BALANCE FOR THE CHILD INSIDE

When Amir was in elementary school, his parents' marriage began to break down. A seemingly innocuous comment by his mother might cause his father to explode. After speaking in a harsh derogatory tone, he would storm out of the room. While Amir's mother remained physically present with her son during these blowups, she disappeared emotionally. With both parents suddenly absent, Amir felt lost; the world no longer made sense. The moment-to-moment mismatch and repair with both parents was replaced by a prolonged period of mismatch without repair. These battles generally occurred at the end of the day, and the following morning as Amir got ready for school, his parents would appear to be fine and everything would seem close to normal again. Amir would feel a tentative, temporary sense of calm.

Eventually Amir's parents divorced, and the exposure to unpredictable and frightening confrontations ended. On a day-to-day basis he felt more or less okay. He went to college, got a good job, and got married. One evening after a stressful day at work, as Amir was sharing an important story, his husband, Leon, distractedly looked at the mail. Filled with an inexplicable rage, Amir flew off the handle and ran out, slamming the door behind him. Other unintended mismatches produced similar dramatic, out-of-proportion reactions.

As a child, Amir had experienced a recurring loss of moment-to-moment meaning-making, which led to an intermittent loss of his sense of self. The repeated prolonged periods of unrepaired mismatch that occurred as he lay awake in bed listening to his parents fighting, his brain and body bathed in the stress hormone cortisol, altered his body's stress response. His husband's inattention evoked that same lost feeling he'd had when his parents, preoccupied by their own distress, disconnected from him. The response to Leon occurred not in his conscious thought but in his body.

While his dramatic exit did not help the situation that evening, Amir knew from years of achieving calm through physical activity that he needed to move in order to reconnect with his husband. Predictably, as he got to the end of the block, he felt his heart rate slow and his breathing become regular. He could see the exchange for what it was rather than as a catastrophe of lost love. When he once again felt himself in his body, he could go home and speak with Leon about the blowup.

Unlike Amir's parents, Leon responded to the mismatch and did not leave it unrepaired. But Leon also knew not to immediately jump in to fix the problem. He could wait, giving his husband time and space to calm himself. He understood that the anger was not about him. Not that Leon didn't feel annoyed by his husband's outsize reaction. He managed his feelings by putting on a favorite album and becoming absorbed in the music. When Amir returned home, Leon listened to him and took in his apology. Leon acknowledged that he could have been more mindful of Amir's feelings while he was sharing a significant event from his day. Together they were able to repair the disruption.

The physical act of walking down the block gave Amir the opportunity to literally feel himself in his own body. In this different relationship, he could work through and past these inevitable disruptions. As his sense of himself in the world grew and strengthened, his relationship with Leon deepened. Leon could trust Amir to return and reconnect; he could wait. And Amir could let go of the terror.

This scene between Amir and Leon could have played out in a number of different ways. For example, Leon, having a history of similar incidents with his husband, might have shared at the moment Amir became upset that he understood that the reaction had roots in Amir's childhood. This response might have helped Amir calm down, averting his need to storm out of the house. Just as plausibly, Leon offering an interpretation in that moment, when Amir was already agitated about the events of the day, might have made the situation worse. The two would then have needed to reset and find a different way to reconnect. Indeed, either of those ways might have been as good as what actually took place. The critical factor was that they paused and gave space to each other to find their own way to calm themselves, and then they calmed each other. Such is the moment-to-moment experience of building strong relationships that starts in our earliest interactions as infants.

There is no specific road map for navigating a mismatch to a repair. Sometimes simply taking a few deep breaths creates sufficient space and time to be able to hear each other's point of view. Walking and listening to music are two of many self-calming strategies you can draw upon. Once you yourself feel regulated, you can listen better.

MAKING MEANING TOGETHER AND ALONE

Educator and child development researcher J. Ronald Lally uses the term *social womb* to describe the way the newborn infant continues to grow and develop in the context of social interaction after birth. Though uniquely helpless, completely dependent on caregivers, a newborn infant has a capacity for complex social interaction not found in any other living creature. At just a few hours of age, infants will turn to a voice, follow a face, and signal through body movements if they are ready to play or if they are overwhelmed and prefer to be swaddled and rest.

And from the beginning, their survival depends on the responses of caregivers to not only their physical needs but also their emotional signals. Winnicott's term *holding environment* captures this idea. The caregivers' ability to tolerate and contain the infants' distress helps them make sense of and learn to manage their experiences. *Contain* does not mean to control or eliminate feeling; rather, it refers to the caregiver's ability to let the baby have big feelings without falling apart. Even though holding a baby may seem to be simply a physical act, it is the caregiver's emotional presence that is important to the baby. A scene by a lake on a hot and sunny afternoon described in *Keeping Your Child in Mind* captures the active quality of both the physical and emotional aspects of holding:

> One mother was trying to tie a hat onto her young infant's head. He was clearly not happy about it. As she held the hat on and secured the strings under his chin, his fussing escalated to an all-out scream. She cooed and talked, reflecting his distress but with a soothing inflection in her voice. In her calm way she communicated with him that she recognized that he was upset, but was confident that he could survive this minor disruption to his day.

This simple interaction exemplifies the concept of the holding environment in which babies learn to regulate their feelings. Physically caring for her baby while also acknowledging his emotional experience, this mother helped him modulate feelings that seemed unmanageable. In one of our still-face experiments, we found that a mother simply placing her hands on her baby's hip when he was held in a car seat reduced the infant's stress and negative emotions.

Each of us needs an interactive partner to help us make sense of and manage ourselves in the world. When you can't make meaning of a situation, your sense of self is threatened. Your survival depends on co-creation of meaning. Over your life span, your ability to approach novel situations with a general sense of well-being and a sense of agency reflects a history of countless repaired mismatches in your earliest relationships.

We observed a very early instance of co-creation of meaning in one of our videotaped mother-infant interactions. A six-month-old is working to grab a toy just out of reach. When he fails, he becomes angry and upset. He looks away, sucking on his thumb. Calmed for a moment, he again reaches for the toy but again fails and again becomes upset. His mother watches briefly, a neutral yet focused expression on her face, before talking to him in a soothing voice. The infant calms down, becomes quiet, and, showing a facial expression fully concentrated on the object, once more reaches for the toy. The mother brings the toy just within the infant's reach. The infant successfully grabs the toy, explores it, and smiles: *I did it!*

The mother does not simply give the toy to the infant. She notices and supports and scaffolds his emotional experience, helping to transform a negative feeling into a positive one. An important aspect of this interaction is that the infant has his own repertoire of behaviors to calm himself. He is not completely dependent on his mother. This essential capacity for self-regulation emerges out of the moment-to-moment mutual regulation in this early relationship. This baby and his mother together have learned not only that he can be upset without falling apart but also that if he gets himself together, he can enlist the help of others to achieve his goals.

Children who have made meaning that the world is safe and manageable are gradually able to discover new meanings both on their own and in relationships with new people. These meanings give them the energy to explore more new experiences with hopeful curiosity. In this situation, self-regulation and interactive regulation are in balance. You can modulate your behavior and emotions in your interaction with another person whose behavior and emotions exert influence on you in an ongoing way. We call this process *mutual regulation*. When self-regulation becomes the predominant goal, a situation we explore in depth in chapter 8, it sets the stage for difficulties. Excessive self-regulation at the expense of regulation in interaction with another person is a pattern we have observed in infants of depressed mothers. These babies are preoccupied with self-comfort and self-directed regulatory behaviors. They turn away, rock their whole bodies, or suck on their fingers. They turn to themselves·when they do not get sufficient scaffolding from their caregivers. Similarly, their mothers regulate themselves by slouching and averting their gaze, appearing to withdraw into themselves. They are less available for interactive regulation with their infants. Rather than regulating each other, infant and parent affect each other in a pattern of mutual dysregulation. Both give up on working through the discord. They just shut themselves off.

WHY REGULATION MATTERS

Self-regulation begins at birth and continues throughout development as children learn to put words to feelings. In preschoolers

and school-age children, in addition to emotional and body regulation, self-regulation encompasses *executive function*, an
umbrella term used to describe the abilities of attention, flexible
thinking, and impulse control that are central to learning and
social interaction. Self-regulation is not a trait a person either
has or lacks. It emerges in a developmental process.

And as we've seen, self-regulation does not develop exclu-
sively from within. The capacity for self-regulation emerges
through interactions with others. Current research in our lab
offers a close-up look at the process of co-regulation. This
research is ongoing, and we have plans for a similar experimental design with parents of preterm infants and parents with
depression. Many research studies of stress involve multiple risk
factors, so it is difficult to identify the impact of the specific
stress on the relationship. For this experiment, the hypothesis
was that stress, independent of other factors, disturbs the mother
and, in turn, her interaction with her infant.

In the experiment, we divide mothers and babies into two
groups. In each case, the mother first plays with her infant face-
to-face. After that, the mother listens to either a recording of
several infants crying (none of them her own) or a recording of
an infant cooing (also not her own) for two minutes while the
research assistant plays with her actual baby. The baby does not
hear the recording and does not see the mother listening. The
mother then plays with her own baby again.

We analyzed the tapes of this second play episode for negative emotions and found that the babies whose mothers had
heard the recorded cries were much more likely to behave in a
distressed way than the babies whose mothers had heard the
coos. Surprisingly, when we analyzed the mothers' facial expres-

sions, vocalizations, touching, and distance from the infants, we did not find differences in the two groups' behaviors. It appeared that the infants were detecting that their mothers were upset, which disrupted their behavior, but as researchers, we couldn't see or hear the signals from the mothers. The infants were more sensitive than our coding system!

In other words, the infant's behavior and the mother's behavior are intimately intertwined. In this process of co-regulation, the baby's mood affects the mother, and the mother's mood affects the baby. In the experiment, the crying the mother heard was not that of her own baby, but we can imagine that hearing her own baby's cry would be significantly more stressful. When there are problematic patterns of interaction that we seek to change, we need to look at the relationship. When the interaction shifts from one of mutual regulation to mutual dysregulation, the problem is no more the fault of the parent than it is the fault of the child.

Three-year-old Luke had advanced verbal skills, and he noticed everything. If a vacuum cleaner was turned on down the hall, he would stop his play and say, "What's that?" If a truck went by, he'd run to the window to look and then, distracted from whatever he'd been doing, he would offer commentary on the qualities of the truck. When he played at home with his parents, Don and Kahli, this behavior was fun and interesting for everyone. But when they enrolled him in preschool, Luke began to struggle. He had frequent meltdowns. One day, as the children were changing from one activity to another, a particularly noisy and confusing moment of the morning, Luke managed to run out the door. When the terrified teacher caught him, she loudly reprimanded him as a result of her own fears, and his distress at the intensity of sensory input overwhelmed him. He fell to the ground screaming and managed to kick her in the chest. Kahli had to come and pick him up from school. At first, shocked and embarrassed, she spoke harshly to him. "Why did you do that?" she asked him when they got home, her shrill voice communicating a sense of outrage. Of course, he didn't know why he'd done it. His father sent him to his room alone, no questions asked.

For Kahli, the episode conjured up memories of her father's verbally abusive behavior during her own childhood. Given his mother's past experiences, Luke was a master at pushing her buttons. When their anger and strict limits only aggravated the problem, Don and Kahli began to fight with each other in an ugly blaming game. At school, Luke became increasingly impulsive, refusing to sit in circle time and instead running around the room. Luke and his parents were stuck in interactions characterized by unrepaired mismatch.

Six months into the school year, a teacher raised the possibility that Luke might have attention deficit hyperactivity disorder (ADHD). Don and Kahli were mobilized into action. A friend who specialized in behavior problems in young children recommended they see an occupational therapist. With the therapist, the couple took time to look closely at what precipitated Luke's behavior and recognized his sensory sensitivities as a root cause of his impulsivity and inattention. But the environment of harsh reprimands and marital conflict had also played a significant role. Research offers evidence that genes associated with behaviors of impulsivity and inattention may be expressed only in an environment characterized by stress and unresolved conflict. In situations relatively free of stress and conflict, they are not turned on.

Don and Kahli were both worried about their son. As soon as they started talking about him, their anxiety would escalate and before they knew it, they were yelling at each other. Armed with new insights about the meaning of Luke's behavior, they developed ways to quell their agitation and reassure each other that Luke would be okay. Kahli in particular needed to be mindful of how Luke provoked her. Seeing her husband as an ally rather than an opponent, she could accept his help when he suggested he handle a situation that had especially upset her. Kahli and Don stopped the blame game of finding fault in each other. They took time to pause, take a deep breath, and listen to each other. Appreciating Luke's unique experience of the world helped Don and Kahli be more tolerant. With his parents less reactive, Luke was no longer so impulsive. These changes created an environment at home that was more suited to Luke's intensity.

Further supporting positive growth in the family, they came to recognize the value of his sensitivity, including his artistic creativity and his ability to appreciate other people's emotional states. They recognized in him a budding capacity for empathy. Don and Kahli worked with his teachers to address situations in the classroom that might lead him to become overwhelmed. The occupational therapist offered strategies, such as taking breaks for a walk down the hall, to help Luke feel calm in the face of intense sensory stimulation. Luke's sense of himself in the world changed as he learned to control his strong reactions.

Luke's disruptive behavior was neither his nor his parents' fault. Rather, they had all been affecting one another in ways that exacerbated Luke's difficulty with regulating his attention and overtaxed his parents' own self-regulatory capacities.

WHY BLAMING MAKES NO SENSE

No matter what we label a particular set of behaviors and no matter what their original cause was, the lesson we learn from the still-face research is that the quality of interaction affects all types of behavior in all relationships. The behavior of a child with problems of inattention, hyperactivity, or both affects each parent and the relationship between the parents, and the parents' behavior affects the child. And each moment of interaction affects what comes next. The same is true for any behavior in any relationship at any stage of development throughout our lives.

The ability to regulate attention develops early. Consider the example of diaper changing, a seemingly mundane event that takes place with a baby multiple times a day. Many mothers and fathers in a natural way narrate the events for their baby. "Here comes the cold wipe!" a mother warns the baby in a reassuring voice. "I'm getting the diaper cream on the other table," a father explains, giving the baby a sense of his continued presence when he is temporarily out of view. These typical mismatches, the cold wipe and the parent who disappears, are quickly repaired. But a caregiver who is preoccupied by something else, be it other children, fatigue, or depression, may not be able to hold the infant's attention through the interaction. Certainly, we all have variations in our ability to be present for mundane tasks like diaper changing. But when a caregiver is mostly distracted and preoccupied, the baby's capacity to pay attention may be affected.

In their research on the long-term effects of postpartum depression on child development, our colleagues Lynne Murray and Peter Cooper at the University of Reading in Great Britain show that as soon as infants begin to engage with the world around them, the quality of face-to-face interaction affects the development of attention. Certainly, infants come into the world with a great variation in activity level and quality of attention, but these variations do not predict the course of development; it is the quality of parent-infant interaction that is predictive of the infant's ability to pay attention and process information in the wider social world. Parents with depression often struggle to sustain face-to-face interaction and engage in play, and their children are more likely to have behavioral difficulties later in infancy. The failure of co-regulation disrupts the infant's emotional state and it disrupts the infant's attention.

Though it is not the parents' fault that troubles from their own life may interfere with their ability to respond to a child in the way that is needed, it is their responsibility to address these issues, at least enough so that they can have a clear view of their child. Guilt is an experience that comes naturally with the job of being a parent. But "I'm guilty" can also mean "I'm responsible." What would happen if we replaced the word *fault* with the word *responsibility*? When we take responsibility, we generally feel empowered. When relationships become derailed, whether between a parent and a child, romantic partners, work colleagues, siblings, or friends, rather than assign blame, we need to recognize how each person in the pair has a role to play. We may need to seek and accept help (which, as we explore in chapter 9, can take many forms) in order to play our roles differently.

IT'S ALL ABOUT RELATIONSHIPS

A wise colleague pointed out that we would not treat a plant that is struggling to grow without considering the context of light, space, soil, and water. The environment is critical to a plant's health. A large body of research, represented in the Pulitzer Prize–winning novel *The Overstory*, shows that even trees have relationships. They communicate with one another, which facilitates growth in significant ways. A recent *New York Times* article titled "How to Become a Plant Parent" illustrates this point. The author describes a process of adjustment when you first bring your plant home. The advice she offers about how to water and repot your plant in keeping with its growth conjures up a kind of mismatch-repair image. "Experts say to go up only one size higher than your previous pot size," so if your plant came in an eight-inch pot, move it into a ten-inch one. "Using a pot that's too large might encourage you to water more, which will not be healthy for your plant," the author writes. She even identifies the inevitability of mismatch when she notes, "The biggest obstacle to being a successful plant parent will be overwatering. Yes, it will happen to you."

A friend who acknowledged her inability to have even a semblance of a garden said, "It takes all my energy just to grow my children." Analogous to parenting plants, parenting children depends on the qualities of each child as well as on the "environment," which consists primarily of relationships rather than sunlight and water.

The mismatch-repair process provides the energy to nurture and grow relationships. While our earliest relationships lay the groundwork, our full range of relationships, with parents, siblings, friends, colleagues, romantic partners, continue to shape our sense of ourselves in the world. In every exchange, we change each other.

Often people blame themselves — or others — for the problems in their lives. We've learned from the still-face research that in the ongoing effort to make sense of oneself in the world, blame is irrelevant and meaningless. When you find yourself stuck in a pattern of unrepaired mismatch, you may want to take a deep breath and ask yourself a simple question: Is there a way in which the other person is right?

In this chapter we have examined how microscopic moment-to-moment everyday disruption and repair build the capacity for self-regulation and intimacy. In the next chapter we show how this model derived from the still-face research informs our understanding of major life disruptions. The way you manage the everyday stresses of mismatch and repair becomes the basis for how you manage big stresses. If you learn to trust that you will get through a difficult time, you'll approach struggle with a sense of hope and agency. In contrast, if you've had a lack of opportunity for interactive mismatch and repair, you may rely excessively on self-comforting behaviors to hold yourself together, turning inward, away from social connection. You may fall apart in times of crisis.

5

RESILIENCE RECONSIDERED

WE TYPICALLY THINK OF resilience as the ability to overcome extraordinary odds, what we might call Adversity, with a capital A. A home destroyed in a tornado, a sexual assault, a severe accident — these are all (we hope) onetime events that result in a wide range of impacts. Why does one person move through and then past a traumatic experience while another's life is disrupted and derailed? Two women's experiences of being widowed exemplify this contrast.

At age seventy, Carol was on her own following the sudden death of her husband, Alan, from a stroke. She grieved his loss terribly, sometimes awakening during the night only to be reminded of Alan's shocking absence. During the day she kept busy and engaged in fulfilling activities, but the middle-of-the-night quiet conjured up the pain anew. She wept into her pillow as she allowed herself to feel the depth of loss. Wrapping herself in a blanket of grief, she could fully mourn her husband's death. The process itself released energy for her to set about building a new life. She traveled, took classes at a local university, and met new friends.

Soon after Carol lost her husband, her friend Bonnie, who, like Carol, had had a long and stable marriage, was also widowed. But in contrast to Carol's, Bonnie's life seemed to shrink as she descended to an unshakable depression. She couldn't bear the upheaval that grieving and starting a new life entailed. Following Dan's death, she lived in a low-level simmer of despair without fully mourning him. She was irritable and short with her friends, so she was unable to find comfort in these relationships. Fearing that she would fall apart if she let herself fully experience Dan's loss, she clung to a fragile sense of coherence by following a rigid daily routine, staying close to home, declining invitations from family and friends.

We describe Carol as resilient, while Bonnie, faced with a similar adverse experience, struggled to move forward. Part of Carol's resilience lay in knowing she would not always feel so deeply sad. This confidence was something Carol had developed over time, and she certainly didn't recognize it in the midst of her initial grief. But it supported her both emotionally and physically as she began to heal. This core sense of hope in the future, out of her conscious awareness, had come from a lifetime of strong healthy relationships beginning when she was very young. But Bonnie lacked such confidence. Both she and Dan had come from troubled homes. They had reached a comfortable equilibrium in their marriage, but they avoided emotional engagement in their wider social world. They had never had children, relying completely on each other for support. Now on her own, Bonnie was at a loss as to how to move forward.

RESILIENCE IS ROOTED IN DEVELOPMENT

Resilience is neither a trait you are born with nor one that you acquire in the face of catastrophe. Rather, resilience develops when you muddle through the inevitable countless mismatches that occur in relationships with people you love, beginning in early infancy. We use the word *quotidian* or *everyday* resilience to describe this developmental process. Resilience is woven into the fabric of your being in hundreds of thousands of moments over time.

As you survive the microscopic moment-to-moment stress of navigating a complex social environment, you develop a core sense that you can move through a difficult time, large or small, to arrive at a place of greater strength and understanding. Resilience builds as you realize you have the ability to navigate the mismatches. It is a muscle that grows from the repair of mismatch starting with your earliest relationships and continuing throughout your life.

The microscopic process of disruption begins in infancy and may take the form of a mother's engaging glance met by her baby's downward gaze or a father's loud vocalization precipitating the baby's startle reaction and cry. Repair follows in the form of mutual gaze along with an engaged smile and a softening of the voice as a parent holds and rocks the infant. When things go well, the disruption and subsequent repair occur in proportion to babies' growing ability to manage themselves in the world.

A nursing mother, distracted by a phone call during a feeding, may leave her screaming baby in the bassinet. But then she returns. She speaks gently and resumes the feeding. The infant, in surviving the stress of waiting, achieves a greater level of developmental organization. A toddler who calms down after an explosive tantrum with a parent who remains emotionally present but does not try to stop the meltdown develops a confidence in the ability to handle big feelings without falling apart. Parents of a preschooler with a new baby brother support their child in being "in the mess" of feelings of anger and loss while setting limits on behavior. In surviving this disruption, the child develops a deeper capacity to manage big emotions as well as a growing love for a sibling. Parents of school-age children learning to navigate increasingly complex social relationships may guide and support them. Rather than call a friend's mother to complain about a moment of discord, parents scaffold a child with encouragement while providing space to try to work it out. As adolescents move through the drama of separation and self-discovery, the disruptions become proportionally intense. In this phase, analogous to the toddler phase, parents who stay calm and present while also setting limits facilitate an angry teenager's complex transition to adulthood.

Psychoanalyst Erik Erikson described the Eight Ages of Man in his model of development. Each stage is characterized by a contrast between two ends of a spectrum of possibility. For example, he described the toddler period as "autonomy vs. shame and doubt." The dichotomy he offered for the stage of development Carol and Bonnie were navigating when they were widowed was "ego integrity (a solid sense of self) vs. despair." By the time the women reached their seventies, each had a unique way of being in the world formed by a lifetime of experiences. But what was it about these experiences that led to hope and resilience in one case and a sense of hopelessness or even despair in the other?

FROM GOOD STRESS TO UGLY STRESS

Researchers at the Center on the Developing Child at Harvard University, under the leadership of pediatrician Jack Shonkoff, have developed a framework for understanding a range of stresses in a child's life. According to this frame, *positive stress* is a kind of everyday stress accompanied by a brief elevation of heart rate and transient elevation of stress hormones. *Tolerable stress* is a serious, temporary stress response buffered by supportive relationships. *Toxic stress* is a "prolonged activation of the stress-response system in the absence of a safe, secure caregiving relationship."

While this terminology has gotten a lot of attention, we prefer to capture the range of a child's experience with a different set of terms: *the good, the bad, and the ugly. Good stress* is what happens in typical everyday interactions, what we have seen in our videotaped interactions as moment-to-moment mismatch and repair. *Bad stress* is the stress represented in the still-face experiment by the caregiver's sudden inexplicable absence. In the prototype experiment with a healthy mother-infant pair, the infant, having accumulated experience of overcoming micro-stresses, easily overcomes the bad stress in the repair episode of the experiment. *Ugly stress* occurs when the infant has missed out on the opportunity for repeated experiences of repair, as in situations of emotional neglect, and thus cannot handle any sort of bigger, stressful event. The meaning the infant makes of the experience determines the level of stress.

Bad stress is tolerable exactly because of the positive, or good, stress. When an infant has amassed accumulated doses of positive stress followed by repair in moment-to-moment interactions, he is prepared to handle the tolerable stress of a major life disruption. In a developmental process, the relationship is safe and secure exactly because the infant has developed trust in the process of moving through mismatch and repair with his caregiver.

Children growing up with insufficient experience of mismatch and repair are at a disadvantage for developing coping mechanisms to regulate their physiological, behavioral, and emotional reactions. We use the term *regulatory scaffolding* to describe the developmental process by which resilience grows out of interactive repair of the micro-stresses that happen during short-lived, rapidly occurring mismatches. The caregiver provides "good-enough" scaffolding to give the child the experience of overcoming a challenge, ensuring there is neither too long a period to repair nor too close a match with no room for repair.

RELATIONSHIPS AS BUFFERS: HOW EARLY EXPERIENCES GET UNDER OUR SKIN

The Adverse Childhood Experiences (ACE) study, which began in 1995 as a collaboration between the Centers for Disease Control and Kaiser Permanente, a large California-based HMO, had its origins in the exploration of the causes of obesity. Doctors were surprised to find that one of the greatest predictors of adult obesity was a history of childhood sexual abuse. Decades of subsequent research have examined a number of relatively common adverse childhood experiences, including parental mental illness, marital conflict and divorce, and substance abuse, as well as more ugly stressors, such as emotional and physical neglect, domestic violence, parental incarceration, and physical and sexual abuse.

Epidemiologic studies — that is, studies that look at whole populations rather than individual people — have demonstrated a link between the number of adverse childhood experiences and a wide range of negative long-term outcomes. These include physical health problems, such as diabetes, heart disease, and asthma, and also problems of social and emotional health, such as depression and alcoholism. Rather than identifying a specific cause of a specific problem, these studies offer evidence of associations between health effects and possible causes. The question remains: What is the mechanism by which these early experiences get under our skin or into the body and brain? How does childhood adversity cause long-term health problems?

Our research findings together with the Adverse Childhood Experiences study suggest that we can understand the full range of adverse childhood experiences as derailments of buffering interactive regulation. ACEs represent relational poverty with a lack of opportunity to experience repair.

As we saw in the preceding chapter, the ability to have big feelings without falling apart as well as the ability to form close relationships with others grows from the co-regulation you experience in moment-to-moment interactions in your earliest relationships. Those relationships can either buffer you from adverse experiences or amplify their effects. You then carry that way of being in the world forward into the future. The experience changes your brain and body, organizing the way you function in new relationships throughout your life with friends, teachers, siblings, and romantic partners. The effects of early experience may be amplified even more if similar patterns of interactions occur in subsequent relationships. Even if the situations of adversity are no longer present, when you become stressed, your capacity for self-regulation may regress as a result of these early disruptions.

The capacity of relationships to buffer adversity can be influenced by risk factors within an individual or within an environment. A good way to think of risk here is as something that depletes your store of energy. Poverty, for example, is an environmental risk factor. The experience of poverty draws energy from caregivers, making them less available to buffer a child from stress. Risk factors may also come from within the child. For example, a child who is born with intense reactivity to sound, as we saw with Henry in chapter 3, may cry more and have more difficulty settling than a child without this sensitivity. Caring for a distressed infant requires significantly greater energy than caring for a sleeping or quietly alert infant. Anything that negatively affects the caregiver's ability to engage in mutual regulation in the early weeks and months, when the child's brain is most rapidly growing, may affect the child's emerging resilience.

Mutual regulation in typical developing parent-infant pairs is usually successful, and the inevitable failures are quickly repaired. The caregiver can buffer the child from disruptive events that exceed the child's resources and from the disruptive effects of the caregiver's own limitations. However, caregivers whose energy for self-regulation is depleted by dealing with external events, such as poverty or community violence, or internal events, such as depression and anxiety, may not only fail to buffer the child from stress but actually transmit the stress of the disruption to the infant. Put another way, a distraught adult cannot calm an upset child and can agitate a calm child. Cumulative instances of repair and buffering over time stimulate infants to expand their own capacity for coping and resilience, whereas chronic failure of repair diminishes the infants' resources and induces helplessness and fragility.

RELATIONSHIPS BUFFER ADVERSITY

When Rebecca's sister, Lisa, fell into the grip of opioid addiction, her overwhelming need for the drug compromised her ability to care for her infant son, Ian. He would sit alone and unattended for hours in his playpen. Unpredictably irritable, Lisa would frequently lash out. Rebecca's efforts at helping her sister get treatment and sustain recovery were unsuccessful. The pull of the drug proved too powerful for the whole family. When Ian entered toddlerhood and acted in a typical toddler way — for instance, refusing to put on his shoes — Lisa, unable to manage her emotions in the midst of this devastating disorder, would on occasion slap him across the face. One day Ian appeared at day care with a bruise on his cheek. His teacher called child protective services, and Rebecca and her husband, Paul, childless at the time, offered to take their nephew in. When it appeared that Lisa was traveling farther down the destructive path of addiction, she relinquished her parental rights, and the adoption was finalized shortly after Ian's third birthday.

Rebecca and Paul, though distraught about Lisa, were thrilled by the unexpected opportunity to become parents. They could offer Ian a loving home. After a brief honeymoon period of peace and calm, Ian, feeling safe for the first time, began to act out. The cumulative losses of his early life had taken their toll. He began to exhibit what Rebecca described to their pediatrician as "explosive" behavior. Intense tantrums filled their days. Behavior management strategies proved ineffective. Magazine articles they read led them to wonder if he might have bipolar disorder. But then they had the good fortune to catch an episode of *60 Minutes* featuring Oprah Winfrey interviewing child psychiatrist Bruce Perry of the ChildTrauma Academy in Houston, Texas; after seeing it, they knew what direction their growing family needed to take.

Perry, who travels the world teaching techniques of trauma-informed care to educators, therapists, social workers, and foster-care agencies, explained in his interview with Oprah how people needed to understand what had happened to a child before they attempted to change the child's behavior. The brain is wired during a baby's early relationships, and when those relationships are chaotic, the wiring of the brain is affected. Perry contrasted "relational poverty" with "relational health," explaining how immersing the child in a whole new set of relationships, what he called a "therapeutic web," was needed to change that wiring.

Perry's model fits with the model we have developed using the still-face paradigm. As we have seen, the capacity for self-regulation is laid down in the process of co-regulation. In Ian's story, early scaffolding might have been compromised by his biological mother's substance abuse. This is not to blame her; it is to recognize that parents need to be able to be present to offer their child moment-to-moment repair of disruption so they can move forward together in a healthy direction.

We can understand the term *adversity* as anything that depletes caregivers' resources and prevents them from being present to regulate both their own and their infants' psychological state. Substance use, domestic violence, parental mental illness, marital conflict, and divorce exert their harmful effects and impede the development of resilience by depriving the child of the scaffolding that would otherwise be offered by interactive coping through mismatch and repair.

Unfamiliar with the impact Ian's early life experiences had had on him, Rebecca and Paul interpreted his behavior as "difficult," using words such as *oppositional* and *defiant*. Armed with new insights from Dr. Perry, they could find a different interpretation. They understood it was not simply a question of eliminating the problematic behavior or symptom with behavior management or medication.

By immersing Ian in a new relational milieu and offering him countless new experiences — not only with them but also in a neighborhood play group, with a family therapist, in a school setting with small classes, and in a range of supportive relationships (they even got him a dog) — they could change the path of his development and set him in a new and healthy direction. And Rebecca and Paul, whose resources were continually drained by Lisa's ongoing battle with opioid addiction and her erratic involvement in their lives, had to find their own "therapeutic web" in order to be the parents Ian needed.

Rebecca joined a knitting club. In the weekly gatherings, where the rhythmic clicking of the needles calmed her addled nerves, she drew on friendships with her fellow knitters to help her work through life's everyday mismatches, from a dropped stitch to a call from a teacher that Ian was having a bad day.

If Rebecca and Paul had continued to manage Ian's behavior without recognizing its meaning rooted in his early life experiences, Ian and the whole family might have gotten stuck in tormented patterns of struggle.

RESILIENCE AND TIME

When you find yourself overwhelmed by strong emotions and unable to calm down, time may lose its meaning. Along with your inability to think clearly comes a conviction that you will be in this terrible moment forever. Children whose brains develop in an environment of chaos can very quickly lose their sense of time, even if they move to a new environment rich in loving relationships, when faced with a small stress, such as being asked to clean up their toys. Promises of rewards for a change in behavior or threats of punishments for failing to calm down become meaningless.

Addressing this aspect of time, D. W. Winnicott used the lovely phrase *going on being* to capture the way we hold on to a coherent sense of self in the face of stress and disruption, an experience that develops in the earliest interactions between a parent and infant. Winnicott formulated the idea in terms of actual minutes. He described how when the mother is away for "x + y minutes" the baby can hold on to her image. But when she is gone for "x + y + z minutes," the baby is unable to hold on to that image, and from the infant's perspective, it is as if she no longer exists. This experience of "x + y + z" Winnicott called *trauma* (what we would call the *ugly*), and it can produce in the baby an "unthinkable anxiety" that he himself no longer exists.

The anxiety Winnicott refers to is the profoundly disturbing loss of an emerging sense of self. For example, Ian had an extreme stress reaction when another child stood too close to him in the lunch line at school. His body went into fight-or-flight mode and he shoved her. The teacher told him that he might be sent home if he did not calm down, but her words likely held no meaning for him. The intensity of his distress kept his mind firmly rooted in the here and now, unable to imagine a future time. At that moment, as Ian's teacher was standing over him and speaking in a harsh, reprimanding voice, his basic feeling that *I am Ian* might very well have faded away. This loss of sense of self is the unthinkable anxiety to which Winnicott refers.

Winnicott's ideas grew out of his careful observations in his clinical work. The significance of his concept of going on being is supported by evidence not only in emotional experiences but also in human biology. We have observed in our lab that the longer the interval from mismatch to repair, the higher the reactivity of the infant's stress hormone cortisol levels and the slower its decline. This research demonstrates that quicker repair of mismatching states in early mother-infant interaction is linked to better stress regulation in infants.

As we described in chapter 3, the stress response is moderated, via the autonomic nervous system (ANS), by the hypothalamic-pituitary-adrenal (HPA) system, which releases the stress hormone cortisol into the bloodstream. Its role is to supply adequate energy to cope with whatever danger or threat has caused the stress. Briefly elevated cortisol levels may help a person cope in the here and now, but chronically elevated levels have the potential for negative effects later in life, including difficulty regulating future stressors, suppressed immune function, and development of stress-related problems such as anxiety. In the case of a mismatch when the time to repair is prolonged beyond a child's ability to manage, the levels of cortisol rise. Stress can be cumulative, and the next encounter with stress may be distorted by the higher level of cortisol.

A highly reactive stress-response system leads to elevated

quantities of cortisol that can exert long-term damaging effects on the body and brain. The literal number of microseconds between mismatch and repair is what characterizes an experience as good, bad, or ugly. Wait too long and the good becomes bad, then ugly. But reduce the wait time to zero and the good disappears. Adverse childhood experiences, with lack of mismatch and repair, deprive children of the opportunity to learn to manage their behavior and emotions in relationships with people close to them. Consequently, they may quickly become overwhelmed by big feelings and lose their sense of time. They develop a sense of *I am stuck in this feeling* or *I cannot cope* or *I am helpless and fragile.*

Accumulated experiences of moving from mismatch to repair lead to a sense of going on being in the face of extreme distress. This is the essence of resilience. People can experience big, difficult feelings and hold on to the knowledge that at some future time, things will be better, as Carol did after her husband died. Without this cumulative experience of everyday resilience people may become easily unhinged by big emotions. They may, like Bonnie, fail to see their way into the future. Carol could hold on to her sense of self despite major loss. Bonnie experienced such a deep feeling of agitation that it threatened her ability to believe she would go on being. Her anxiety might well have been of the "unthinkable" kind, with her fear of falling apart preventing her from experiencing new ways of being in the world without her husband. Carol lived into her nineties, while Bonnie, sadly, experienced a gradual decline in health and died several years after her husband.

When people can imagine a different future — see their way forward, knowing that, as bad as things are, there will be a time when things will be better — they can find the courage to move through adversity. But those who have not had the experience of successfully moving from mismatch to repair, from disconnection to connection, from being alone to being together, may become stuck in a moment of time. When they feel angry, they will always be angry. When they feel sad, they will always feel sad. They will never feel different. The moment becomes a kind of forever, which is the essence of hopelessness.

Runners training for a marathon do not run marathon distances daily. Instead, they run a specific distance each day and increase the distance over the course of weeks. The training that develops a runner's stamina is analogous to the coping strategies developed in the infant-parent interaction. Endurance and resilience emerge out of the sheer number of miles you put in or the number of repaired interactions you experience. Resilience is built out of these moments. By working through the multitude of micro-stresses, we develop the resilience to handle big stresses.

As we explore in depth in chapter 9, this recognition of the developmental origins of resilience points to the value of creative activities, specifically those that involve relationships with other people, to move toward healing and resilience. Repetitive activities such as dance, drumming, or martial arts provide the kinds of experiences that support both self-regulation and your ability to be close with others. A yoga class offers movement that helps you feel calm and regulated. Equally important, your relationship with your instructor and your casual conversation with fellow yogis at the beginning and end of class may contribute to an increased sense of well-being and a new way of navigating in the world.

In today's quick-fix society, people tend to expect one answer that solves the problem, and if that fails, they move on to another. But resilience develops through countless experiences of mismatch and repair, so when you find yourself struggling, you need opportunities for new, different moment-to-moment interactions. Finding these opportunities takes a relational milieu, patience, and time.

EVERYDAY TRAUMA ACROSS GENERATIONS

Our understanding of resilience as emerging from countless experiences of mismatch and repair leads us to question how the increasingly ubiquitous word *trauma* is used. The trouble with the word *trauma* is that it is made to refer to a onetime event, while the vulnerability of trauma lies in its repetition. Sure, there are onetime traumatic events, but typically what makes an experience into a trauma is a backdrop of ugly, or unrepaired, mismatch. Just as the word *everyday* describes resilience, many experiences that are put under the umbrella term *trauma* are of the everyday kind. Frank and Lindsey's story offers an example.

When Frank was young and committed some typical childhood transgression, such as having a meltdown at a large family gathering, his father would shame him by sending him to sit on the bottom basement step, sometimes for hours at a time. As an adult, when Frank sought help from a therapist in coping with his increasingly explosive relationship with his twelve-year-old daughter, Lindsey, he did not use the word *trauma* to describe his own childhood. The emotional abuse from his father was an everyday experience woven into the story of his life.

But when Frank spent time thinking about his response to his daughter's emerging adolescent self, he realized that, in moments of conflict with her, he was flooded by the stress of his own memories, and he was shutting down. Normally a thoughtful and empathetic person, he simply told Lindsey to cut it out. In the setting of a consultation with a therapist, he recognized that he was emotionally absent during these moments, which were increasing in frequency. They wondered together if Lindsey was testing him, perhaps looking for a more appropriate response that would help her manage this emotionally fraught developmental stage.

Once Frank became aware of this process, he was more able to be present with Lindsey. Rather than react without thinking, he could pause, take a breath, and consider her perspective. He could tolerate her preteen tantrums and understand them in the context of her emerging sense of identity. Soon the frequency and intensity of their confrontations returned to a level typical for Lindsey's developmental stage. Frank, greatly relieved, once again found himself enjoying his daughter.

What Frank had experienced as a child might be termed *quotidian* or *everyday* trauma. It was not watching a relative get shot or having his house washed away in an avalanche. It was repeatedly looking for reassurance and containment and instead experiencing isolation and humiliation, a chronic unrepaired mismatch. Frank repeated this cycle of emotional abandonment with Lindsey when her behavior evoked this memory. When this dynamic was brought into his conscious awareness, he was able to offer his own young daughter the opportunity for repair and set their relationship on a healthier path.

GETTING OUT OF RUTS

Countless moment-to-moment interactions over the course of development are like raindrops that shape the landscape of your sense of yourself, both alone and in relation to others. An experience becomes traumatic when a person remains committed to a fixed meaning and stays stuck in a pattern of disconnection and miscommunication.

Two-year-old Mason and his parents, Mark and Tim, were stuck in just such a rut. Born eight weeks premature, Mason had had what his early-intervention specialist described as an "immature regulatory system." In day-to-day life this meant, among other things, that he had challenges maintaining sleep. When Mason fell asleep on Tim's chest, Tim would spend up to thirty minutes making tiny slow movements in an effort to transfer Mason to his bassinet without waking him. If Tim moved quickly, Mason instantly awoke with a total body startle. While it took more energy for Mark and Tim to care for him than they had anticipated, they supported each other and, recognizing Mason's vulnerability, rose to the task.

At six months, Mason had a choking episode. Tim thought he was having a seizure and called an ambulance. His own mother had a seizure disorder and he had witnessed frightening episodes as a child. Now he feared Mason would die. The doctors reassured him that it was not a seizure and that Mason was fine, but Tim remained shaken to the core. Although both Mark and Tim had initially been opposed to co-sleeping, Tim was now convinced that Mason needed to be in their bed. Mark reluctantly agreed.

Mason grew into a bright active toddler. However, when he

was stressed, his sensitive regulatory system would show itself. A sudden loud noise, such as a garage door opening, could disrupt his play; his whole body would startle and he'd collapse in hysterical tears. He remained in his parents' bed and continued to rely on the containment provided by Tim's body to organize his more vulnerable nervous system. His body did not know how to relax to sleep without his father next to him.

But after two years of disrupted sleep, Mark, who worked full-time while Tim stayed home with Mason, had had enough. He and Tim fought. He accused Tim of keeping Mason in the bed for his own needs. Mark felt pressure from his own parents, who disapproved of co-sleeping and had given them a beautiful and as yet unused crib. The whole family was stuck in a rut.

The one thing they agreed on was that the sleep situation needed to change. They first consulted parenting experts who advised them to simply go cold turkey and put Mason in his own room to sleep. But Tim recognized that if these patterns of interaction had developed over time, they needed to be changed over time. Tim and Mark needed to help Mason feel calm in his body without his father's physical presence. And Tim needed to address his deep-seated fears of losing Mason, which were linked to his own childhood experience of helplessly watching his mother's seizures. Mark and Tim also needed to address the conflict in their relationship over co-sleeping, which in turn was influenced by Mark's relationship with his own family.

While Tim did not think in terms of meaning-making, he knew instinctively that beyond deciding what to do, they needed to gradually create new ways of being together around bedtime. Initially Mark resisted. But Tim convinced him that this important transition in their family called for time and careful attention.

In consultation with an infant-parent mental health special-ist, they worked to change the patterns of going to sleep and staying asleep. Conflicts arose. Some nights went smoothly, while other nights Mason cried for hours as Mark paced around with him, finally helping him to calm down by reading him a book. For a few weeks, no one slept much. They allowed them-selves to be in a confusing and uncertain time as they figured things out.

Based on his own upbringing, Mark had expected that par-enting would be neat and orderly. But when Tim was called away for a few days and Mark suddenly became the primary caretaker, he quickly came to appreciate that real life with his young son was actually quite messy. An abstract set of rules did not make sense.

After a period that felt rather haphazard and disorganized, the whole family's experience around sleep shifted. Mason grew to trust that his parents were there even when he was not lying on top of Tim. His body learned how to be calm without his father's physical contact. Gradually, they transitioned him to sleeping in his own room. Sleep deprivation and chronic fatigue faded away. The sense of competence and efficacy on the part of both Mason and his parents together with Mason's newfound ability to sleep through the night led to new levels of growth and connection. Through the messy experience of creating new meanings around sleep, Mason learned that his relationship with his parents was responsive, flexible, and consistent.

Changing meaning for two-year-old Mason was relatively easy, although it still took thoughtfulness and effort. But one could imagine a different path. As we explore in chapter 8, when you remain stuck in fixed meaning, the impact can be amplified in relationships and experiences over time. Imagine if Mason's parents had been so distracted by their own distress and burdened by the conflict in their own relationship that, instead of gradually teaching him the new rules of the game of going to sleep, they had put him in his room and shut the door while they fought. These relationships would have become represented in Mason's mind and body in a different way. Those representations would then have been carried forward in new relationships, distorting meaning over time, perhaps through toddlerhood, school age, and even into his adult relationships.

The "game" of going to sleep is one way you learn to be in a relationship with others. While people might not use that word, throughout our lives we engage in countless such games, in our families, with friends, and in the workplace. In the following chapter we show how the games people play as children, whether a real game, such as peekaboo, or a game of saying goodbye to a parent leaving for work, stay inside them as adults. Games throughout development and throughout our adult lives help us to understand ourselves in the context of our own specific cultures and communities. Each new game we learn, through the ongoing process of mismatch and repair, builds a sense of belonging.

6

GAMES WE PLAY: LEARNING TO BELONG

PICTURE TWO BROTHERS, FIVE-YEAR-OLD Roland and eighteen-month-old Austin. Roland is teaching his younger brother a game he has invented that involves running across the room, jumping on a cushion, and running back. This teaching lies not in explanation or even demonstration but rather in repetition, complete with the inevitable mistakes. The game goes on for close to an hour. When Austin initially doesn't jump on the cushion but instead sits on it, Roland bends over in frustration, grasping his head in his hands. But in a flash he is up and at it again. When, after many more tries, Austin jumps on the cushion and runs back across the room, the boys collapse in fits of laughter as they enjoy the pure pleasure of connecting. After each round, as Austin comes closer to grasping the rules of the game, the joyful repetition not only allows him to deepen his connection with Roland but also reinforces for both boys that coming apart will be followed by coming together. The rhythm of the game, including the moments when Austin doesn't do it right, offers him the opportunity to learn *This is how we do things.*

We often consider culture as ingrained in language, but a young child makes meaning of his world and becomes part of his particular culture well before he has the capacity for language. Culture is embedded in the multitude of systems — sensory, movement, hormonal, autonomic, genetic, and epigenetic — we use to engage with the world. Roland is not teaching his brother with words. The whole bodily experience of playing together, the running, falling, collapsing to the floor, even the stress of not getting it, is teaching Austin not only the game itself but also how to belong.

In the broadest sense, culture is a set of shared activities, values, goals, and practices — that is, a common way of being in the world. Development is a lifelong process through which each of us learns to belong to a number of different groups, including, but certainly not limited to, professional, religious, geographic — even the changing culture of a growing family.

As two young people shift from the giddy excitement of the game of early courtship to the more serious rules of living together, planning a future, and raising children, each needs to learn the culture of the other's family of origin. What elements of those cultures will they bring to their new family? Some aspects require a rather simple process.

Jayden, like his father and three brothers, had an encyclopedic knowledge of statistics about baseball, basketball, and, Jayden's favorite, soccer. In Kiara's family, music was the common language. Her father would regularly quiz her on the composer of a particular piece of jazz playing in the background. Kiara was as ignorant about baseball players as Jayden was about Miles Davis.

Once she laughed at him and inadvertently hurt his feelings when he said he had never heard of Dizzy Gillespie. She apologized and then, rather than ribbing him about his lack of knowledge, she took on the project of introducing him to a wide range of musical genres. They soon discovered several new bands they both liked. Attending concerts together became a favorite activity. For his part, Jayden at first excluded Kiara from outings to sports events with his friends. When she grew frustrated when he decided to go to a soccer tournament instead of spending a free Sunday with her, he took time to teach her about the sport. Soon, attending soccer matches became another one of their favorite shared activities.

But some of the cultural differences ran deeper. Kiara, an only child, struggled to embrace the casual playfulness of Jayden's large family. She had grown up with a model of one-on-one interaction of serious engagement. She felt comfortable sitting at a table for hours discussing big ideas. The backyard Thanksgiving football game with Jayden's family, followed by a rush to fill your plate before the favorite dishes were gone, made Kiara feel anxious and awkward. When Jayden went to Thanksgiving dinner with his in-laws, his palms sweated and his body twitched restlessly as the family sat debating for hours on a range of subjects. For their relationship to grow, Kiara and Jayden needed to be in the mess of complicated feelings that the other's family engendered.

In part, they processed these feelings separately, with their own friends and family members. But they also developed a routine of going for a run together during or after family gatherings. The physical exertion calmed them sufficiently so they could listen to each other rather than be reactive and defensive in the

emotionally charged conversations the events inevitably provoked.

The complexity grew when they had their first child. Both
brought clear ideas of things they wished to emulate and things
they wished to avoid from their families of origin. Kiara valued
the intellectual curiosity of her family but not its emotional distance. She wanted her children to grow up with a sense of inclu-
sion she learned from Jayden's family. Jayden valued his close
relationship with his siblings but wanted to avoid passing on the
burden of obligation that he often experienced. Rigid expectations of behavior in relation to family events, even as he and his
siblings grew into adulthood with families and responsibilities of
their own, felt forced and disingenuous.

Together Jayden and Kiara needed to create a new set of
rules for the new family culture they made together. But creating new rules is far from easy. The culture of your family of origin is embedded in your body, not only in conscious thought.
Making the shift to a new one is, of necessity, messy and filled
with discord. Engaging in the conflict creates the energy to shift
to a new way of being with another person in the world. You
need to be in the fight. Then, by finding a way to repair discord,
you and your partner achieve new levels of coherence as a new
family unit. When you carry this expectation, you can save yourself a lot of trouble and perhaps even save a marriage that has
gotten off track.

NECESSARY PLAY

Human newborns know none of the rules of the world into
which they are born. They have to learn how things work in a

context for which they are not preadapted and which they cannot anticipate. They need to learn culturally specific ways of being with others. How does this happen?

D. W. Winnicott recognized the essential role of play in development. In an essay, he wrote: "It is in playing and only in playing that the individual child or adult is able to be creative and to use the whole personality, and it is only in being creative that the individual discovers the self." He was not recommending an outing to the toy store. Rather, he was referring to play as a spontaneous, loosely organized behavior with no specified objective or consequence.

Why is play so powerful? Playing a game engages movements, emotions, memory, a sense of timing and contingency, agency, and attention. These different systems, through the games we play together, constantly gain energy and information. They make up the infant's emerging sense of self and organize and guide his behavior as he interacts with the world of people and things.

New meanings become part of all of us through the countless games we play. In the games we engage in and invent as we get older, we gather and process information that forms the scaffolding of our social selves. An infant's process of belonging has a lot to teach us about how we succeed and where we might stumble in learning to belong, whether it's playing on a sports team, joining another family, learning a new job, or living in a different country.

Young people learning to dance the Cupid Shuffle at a college orientation party are making meaning in their new social environment in a way similar to the infant in his family. While it starts with stumbles and missteps and awkward rhythms, the students gradually get in sync with one another. That accomplishment is all the more pleasurable because of the initial mismatch, as it leads to the joy of connecting in shared meaning.

In the game of peekaboo, at first, parents have to play both sides of the game; the babies, who have no idea what's going on, will react with all kinds of behaviors, many of them unrelated to the game. They look away when they should be looking toward the parents or they pull at their shoes or look at their hands. What they are doing is messy, variable, unstable, and disorganized. But with repetitions over time, they pay more attention and can anticipate the coming *boo*. Some of the messiness begins to smooth out.

With more repetitions, babies start to control some of the pace of the game. They begin to signal the timing of the *boo* by using their hands to cover their faces. Eventually they start to be the peekaboo-ers. They have learned both roles in the game. Sequences and rhythms emerge as they adjust their reactions in response to their play partners' movements. The ability to guess their partners' intention grows. And on it goes through endless repetitions until an infant has fully incorporated the game and both players are in sync.

Infants cannot teach themselves the game of peekaboo. They depend on older children or adults to scaffold their experience. The same goes for learning all the other ways of being in the world. They learn the game — the routine — of getting a bath, being changed, eating, going to sleep. Each of these games is repeated countless times over days, weeks, and months. Each has a form that is individualized and involves learning with a particular partner.

A successful history with a specific person via interchanges such as those in repeated peekaboo games leads the infant to an inner knowledge that *We can repair mismatches.* This knowledge is not in words, as he does not yet have language, but it is very powerful. It contributes to the baby's developing sense of trust, safety, and security. Through the accumulation of successful repairs, infants come to know implicitly that their dysregulated emotional states and the sense that something is wrong can be transformed into a positive state and an accompanying feeling that things are right.

The game of peekaboo nicely represents the comings and goings, disruptions and repair, of life. In typical play, again and again, the game builds up an infant's sense of what Winnicott termed *going on being.*

In a series of experiments using the still-face paradigm, we explored the role of games in making meaning well before the parts of the brain responsible for abstract thought have developed. To assess the way relationships become represented in the brain and mind before babies have language, we identified games during face-to-face play between infants and their mothers that could easily be identified as unique to them as a dyad. It might be a particular touching game or an exchange of vocalizations or a canonical game such as This Little Piggy. During the still-face episode of the experiment we looked to answer the question, Will the baby make use of the game to elicit his mother's attention? The study examines what's called *relational memory:* how we develop memory of a specific way of being with another person.

In one dramatic iteration of the experiment, a mother claps her hands while singing joyfully, " 'If you're happy and you know it clap your hands!' " She takes her infant son's hands in hers and claps them together to teach him the rules. The experimenter then instructs the mother to hold a still-face. The baby has no words to make sense of his mother's unusual behavior, but he wants to connect with her. He looks down at his right hand. Slowly, seemingly with effort, he raises it from its position at his side. Then he brings his left hand across his chest to meet his right in a gentle clap. At that moment the still-face portion ends and his mother joyfully reaches out with a warm smile and holds his two joined hands — the result of his miraculous effort — in her own hands.

At nine months, this baby is not capable of thinking, *I play this game with my mother, so I will clap my hands to bring her back.* His immature brain has not yet developed the capacity for language. But while he lacks the ability to think in words and certainly does not know the lyrics to the song, one could say that the music of his relationship with his mother lives in his body and brain. He can get the motor neurons running from his cortex through the brain stem and down the spinal cord to connect with the muscles of his hands and arms to move them in a specific way in an effort to evoke a response from his mother. These movements are not orchestrated by the layer of the brain responsible for language and symbolic thought; these parts of the brain are not yet fully developed. The motivation to connect is located in the deeper brain structures.

We see in this baby a sense of agency, the ability to affect his environment to produce a positive experience. But that sense is present not in the form of words and thoughts. It has been incorporated into his brain through movement of his body in play with his mother. In a similar way, relationships become represented through the countless games children play in interaction with their caregivers as they grow and develop.

THE GAME OF GREETING: A CULTURAL VARIATION

In the 1970s a group of us traveled to southwestern Kenya to study the parent-infant relationships among the Gusii, a Bantu-speaking agricultural tribe in the densely populated highlands of the country. The project, sponsored by the National Science Foundation, was led by Robert LeVine, an anthropologist who had studied the Gusii's belief system as a graduate student. He and his colleagues had started using observational techniques to study different cultures. While five-minute observations were themselves revolutionary back then, we planned to observe interactions of children with adults for whole days and videotape different interactions. In the expanse of time we spent with the group, they got used to us and our presence faded into the background.

There, mutual gaze has a very different meaning than it does in Western culture. The power of gaze in interpersonal relationships is apparent in the elaborate Gusii belief system built on concepts of the evil eye and the danger people feel at being seen at vulnerable periods of life. We were interested in observing how infants learned the rules of the game of greeting within this cultural context.

Among the Gusii, the mutual greeting between mothers and infants differs markedly from the exuberant greetings of their North American counterparts. Gusii mother-infant greetings may or may not involve eye contact, and the emotional tone of interchange between parent and infant has a more sober quality. The child does not look at the adult, and neither of them shows big excitement or emotion. They also do not engage in face-to-face play the way adults and infants do in the United States. American parents are conversational and treat their infants as interactive partners. When our research group asked the Gusii mothers to do face-to-face play with their infants, the mothers looked at us like we were silly. But they did oblige!

Frame-by-frame analysis of videotaped interactions revealed that the mothers looked away from their infants just as their infants made eye contact and smiled, exactly the opposite pattern from that seen in most interactions of Western mothers and their infants. In response to their mothers turning away, the Gusii infants looked away and their smiles vanished; they actually seemed to deflate. An infant's initial gaze and smile conveyed *I want to interact* but was mismatched by his mother's nonverbally expressed *I don't* or, more accurately, *Not that way*.

Why do the mothers in this community turn away like this? Gusii mothers do not tend to reciprocate their infants' big smiles because the mothers' greeting is already sculpted into a culture-specific form that precludes such exuberance; direct gaze and high levels of affect violate cultural norms.

But then how do mother-infant pairs in this community become coordinated and what does their coordination look like? Our hypothesis was that infants and caregivers discovered and co-created a form of interaction that conformed to culturally appropriate ("natural") ways of being together. As with infants learning social games, Gusii infants achieve the culturally appropriate Gusii greeting in a bootstrapping bit-by-bit process in the

context of caregiving relationships. Over time and countless interactions, the infants select a set of behaviors with meanings that
conform to the sober Gusii greeting. Through continuous repetitions, Gusii infants learn to belong to their unique culture.

The Gusii game of greeting is one of a myriad of examples
that demonstrate just how radically different ways of being are for
individuals in different cultures. We might note that were a North
American mother to turn away like a Gusii mother, clinicians
would likely raise concerns about the mother and the mother-
infant relationship. We can only guess what a Gusii clinician
would think of a Gusii mother engaging in an American-style
exuberant exchange, but no doubt the Gusii clinician would see it
as abnormal. The point is that despite the remarkable differences
between the Gusii and Western greetings, both are assembled in
caregiver-infant pairs via a repeated selective process of mismatch
and repair. Over time, this process brings greater complexity and
coherence to the parent-child relationship, and each pattern is
growth-promoting for infants within their own cultural context.

SOCIAL GAMES GROW OUR BRAINS AND MINDS

Relationships become represented through the games people
play throughout development. A recent conference on the science of representation with the title Duality's End presented
contemporary research on the brain/mind distinction. A rapidly
growing body of knowledge reveals that the distinction between
mind (mental processes both in and out of awareness) and brain
(neural structures that hold these processes) is artificial.

People typically think of relationships as represented by conscious thought and words. For example, you use language to describe your relationship with your parents as close or filled with conflict or in more complex ways. A person might say something like "My mother worked a lot and was often emotionally distant but at times she gave me her full attention." This sentence is a verbal representation of a relationship. But as we have seen, relationships are embedded in many other systems besides conscious thought. Social experience, through the countless interactive games people play, becomes the content of the brain and body. Teammates in a soccer game who coordinate to execute a goal with patterns of interaction embedded in movement of their bodies, with minimal to no exchange of words, offer an example of how representation of relationships occurs in the whole organism.

As we explore in chapter 8, aberrant games that make up relationships, such as interactions with a depressed or fear-inducing parent, are learned in the same manner as all social games, using systems in the brain and body both in and out of awareness. The impact can be amplified in relationships and experiences over time.

When Ilana and Andrew began couples therapy, Ilana recognized that she brought unhealthy interactions from her relationship with her mother into her interactions with her husband. But changing these interactions was quite another thing from recognizing them. Simply having the words and thoughts was not sufficient. She and the therapist had come up with a kind of "case formulation" or narrative explanation for why she tended to react in certain ways, but stopping to conjure up the words and ideas from therapy to deal with a problematic exchange with Andrew in real time took too long. She complained to their therapist that "conversation is too fast." In addition to talking about their relationship in psychotherapy, the couple needed to find new ways to interact that did not involve verbal explanation. Ballroom-dance lessons played a critical role in helping Ilana and Andrew learn new ways of relating that did not call for conscious thought. They muddled through as they learned the steps, laughing at their mistakes. Eventually they moved together in sync with the music, and their relationship grew strong.

When you are learning the game of tennis, first you learn how to hold a racket, serve, and keep your eye on the ball. But once you have learned the game, you do not think about the rules. They become automatic, embedded in your body and brain. Tennis, like the game of greeting, is an example of what's called *implicit relational knowing*, which refers to patterns of interaction that occur regularly between two people but happen out of their conscious awareness. The term was developed by the Boston Change Process Study Group — "the Playpen," as its members call it — a number of psychoanalysts and infant researchers that have included Ed, Lou Sander, Alexandra Harrison, and Dan Stern, among others. The group meets regularly to discuss how infant-parent relationships relate to adult psychoanalysis. Jerome Bruner used to tell a fable of an ant captured by a centipede to demonstrate the concept of implicit knowledge. Recognizing that he was about to be eaten, the ant asked the centipede to answer one question. The centipede agreed. The ant asked, "How does your twenty-third leg know what your fifty-seventh leg is doing?" The centipede, thinking about the answer, became frozen and immobile. The ant walked away.

If you have been holding a tennis racket wrong for years, you need to work through many mistakes to learn a new grip. But if you had to stop and think through the new grip with every single stroke, you would not be able to play. The movements need to be automatic; in a sense, nonverbal. Similarly, changing an unhealthy relationship requires not only language-based understanding but also movement through the messiness of day-to-day interaction to grow a new way of being together. This is true in our work lives too.

GAMES IN THE WORKPLACE

When you start a new job, learning the rules of the game takes time and inevitably involves making mistakes. Some work cultures invite employees to learn from mistakes and then move forward. When Elliot, a recent college graduate, started a new position on the tech crew of a theater company, he was terrified that he'd screw up. After he'd been on the job a week and a half, his fears were realized. He and Phil, another member of the crew, were moving a piece of furniture that was part of a set of a new show; they'd strapped it into the truck and were on their way from the storage building to the theater when suddenly the large cabinet began to slide. Phil stopped the truck and Elliot ran around to try to keep it from slipping, but his weight failed to match the momentum of the heavy object, and in seconds it fell off the truck. Terrified, they inspected the damage. A panel had been dislodged and lay on the ground a few feet away. The wood on one side had a small dent. Relieved the cabinet had not shattered completely, they reloaded it and drove to the set. Reluctantly, they told their boss what had happened. "You did what?" he said. But then he caught himself and added, "Did it more than once myself." He shrugged it off as a relatively minor mishap.

From that moment on, Elliot felt part of the team. Through surviving the mistake, together with another member of the team, and getting to the other side of the experience, he felt a greater sense of belonging to the culture of theater techies. His investment in the work and his sense of competence increased. He took on more responsibility, enhancing the effectiveness of the team as a whole.

In work environments, we typically encounter a range of tolerance for mismatch and repair. Some colleagues leave little room for the back-and-forth exchange of ideas, while others show more comfort with the process of working through problems. Immersing yourself in relationships with the latter may help you manage relationships with the former. But when rigidity comes from the top, the workplace culture may not invite belonging.

Seth looked forward to joining his longtime friend Arthur in a new business venture. Arthur held a leadership position at a company that was looking to expand into the field in which Seth had considerable expertise, and Arthur recruited his friend to join their efforts. Some misgivings lingered in the back of Seth's mind at the prospect of having his friend as his boss, but he pushed them aside in his eagerness to engage in the growth of new ideas and opportunities.

But soon Seth learned that while he and Arthur had been playing Ultimate Frisbee during their free time, enjoying the forgiving environment among teammates that was typical of their relationship, Arthur had been learning different rules in his workplace. The head of the company, Arthur's immediate boss, though short in stature, had a towering managerial style. His every comment and gesture communicated that he was above them all. He discouraged open dialogue and discord. His was the last word. This rigidly hierarchical culture pervaded the environment. Now that Arthur had someone beneath him, even though it was his friend, he adopted the same style.

For a time, it seemed that it would be possible for Seth and Arthur to work together, for their relationship to tolerate some give-and-take. But a change in the company — a vice president's sudden and unexpected departure — destabilized the whole organization, and the rigidity that had taken over their relationship came out in full force. Arthur needed to control Seth's every move. Eventually Seth concluded that he could not grow in this organization's culture. He left the job, moved away, and eventually found a more suitable workplace where he could comfortably engage his own creativity. What Seth saw clearly and Arthur did not was that a work culture characterized by rigid thinking, one that resists the messiness of discord, will fail to grow. His perception was accurate; several years later, Seth learned that the company had closed down.

PLAYING FROM THE START

At the college graduation of their oldest son, Max, Gabriella and Stefan shared a sentimental memory as they sat in the audience awaiting the ceremony. Before Max was born, both had been busy chefs, regularly working fourteen-hour days. Gabriella recalled coming home from the hospital, laying Max down on the bed, turning to Stefan, and asking, "Now what?"

For new parents, the experience of learning to connect and

communicate with a new being for whom they are completely responsible can feel like a challenging task. T. Berry Brazelton, who was often referred to by parents and professionals alike as "the baby whisperer," saw this anxiety again and again in his decades of practicing pediatrics. He heard parents-to-be fretting and worrying, "How will I know what kind of person my baby is?"

In an interview shortly before his death at the age of ninety-nine, Brazelton answered the question. "As soon as they played with the baby, they knew." While practicing general pediatrics and raising his own children, Brazelton grew to appreciate through the countless interactions with newborns and parents that each baby comes into the world with a unique set of qualities and ways of communicating. In the interview, he describes the Neonatal Behavioral Assessment Scale (NBAS), which he designed to organize ways of playfully observing newborns, as "my greatest contribution." The NBAS offers the opportunity for playfulness that in ideal circumstances accompanies people getting to know each other. For example, he saw parents delight in observing their baby make early crawling movements while lying on his stomach. "He's so strong!" they would exclaim. When their sleeping baby diminished his reaction to the sound of a rattle, becoming still and quiet after two or three shakes, they marveled at their baby's capacity to protect his sleep.

Drawing on the NBAS, educator J. Kevin Nugent and colleagues at the Brazelton Institute at Boston Children's Hospital developed the Newborn Behavioral Observations (NBO) system. Unlike the NBAS, which is designed to evaluate a baby, the NBO is used as a clinical tool for building healthy relationships from birth. Not a test, it offers a way to organize the parents' observations about a baby side by side with caregivers. Items modeled on those in Brazelton's original toiletry kit are used for demonstrating a stance of curiosity and a process of messy, playful openness. These observations can be integrated into the work of maternity nurses, pediatricians, lactation consultants, early-intervention practitioners, and a wide range of others who interface with new families. Siblings and other family members can also be brought into the process.

For Dara and Carlos, the days and weeks before the birth of their second child were filled not with joyful excitement but with fear and dread as their three-year-old son, Ronan, voiced his unambivalent anger about his new sibling's imminent arrival. Extremely close with his mother, Ronan had difficulty with even the slightest separation. His parents could not imagine how they would manage to fit a new baby into what felt like set patterns of interaction established as a threesome.

When the maternity nurse Gladys entered Dara's room during Ronan's first visit to the hospital to see his mom and baby brother, Ray, she found him glued to his mother's side. A pained expression twisted his tear-covered face. Carlos looked on from a chair in the corner in tense anticipation as Dara held Ronan close. Ray had been sleeping in his bassinet in the room, and Gladys rolled it to the bedside, speaking both to Ronan and to the newborn. Ray woke up, and Gladys brought out a bright red ball. The ball was one of the "orienting items" used to demonstrate how, at even a few hours of age, many babies show preferences for specific objects, voices, and human faces. When Gladys demonstrated for Ronan how Ray followed the red ball with intense interest, Ronan relaxed. With a curious expression, he inched away from his mother. Gladys then brought out a small rattle, used to show a newborn's ability to listen and orient to sound, and held it out to Ronan. "Do you want to help me?" she asked. Tentatively, Ronan left his mother's side and made his way to the bassinet. Looking down at this new person in his life, with Gladys's coaching, he gently shook the rattle. When Ray turned toward the sound, Ronan's face was transformed by a joyful grin. For the first time in months, both Dara and Carlos breathed easily. In that moment they saw an opening and a possibility of a way forward to a harmonious family of four.

This process of open observation offers an opportunity to bring the idea of play, with its inherent mismatch and repair, into parent-infant and sibling relationships right from birth. Many parents today are burdened by an expectation of perfection. When clinicians can protect time to listen to parents and their newborn babies, they can convey the idea that there is no "right" way, and caregiver and infant will figure things out together.

Playing with a newborn, whose neurological system is immature and prone to disorganization, calls for time and attention. Stressed parents may not be available to play in this way. That stress can come from many sources. The stress of a fussy baby, the everyday challenges of navigating demands of work and raising children, often without the support of extended family, are frequent causes. Stress may come from fraught relationships among family members. It may come from the strains of poverty and single parenthood. Parents deal with these stresses in different ways. Some ways are adaptive and others may lead to a downward spiral of disconnection.

Many parents now turn to phone or computer screens, both for themselves and for their children, to relieve that stress. We suggest that screen time is not objectively good or bad. What matters is how screens, and all forms of technology, affect relationships. What happens between a parent and child around allowing or not allowing screen time? Might turning to a screen help you regulate when a social interaction has left you feeling overwhelmed? When does that help become problematic because it allows avoidance of social interaction? In the following chapter we explore the ways technology has changed the games people play, not only as parents but in all aspects of their lives. We consider how the still-face research helps makes sense of both the positive and negative impacts of technology and how to reduce its negative effects.

7

TECHNOLOGY AND THE STILL-FACE PARADIGM

IT HAS BECOME A common concern that the addictive nature of social media combined with the cell phone's portability and social acceptance are creating an epidemic of distracted parenting. Some even refer to ADHD as a deficit of parental attention. Many people who have heard or read about the still-face paradigm wonder if the escalation of cell phone use is re-creating a persistent still-face experience for developing children. But the parent in the still-face episode of the experiment is not distracted. She is there and yet not there. The brief period represents to the infant an incomprehensible loss, and he struggles to make meaning of the situation.

In her acclaimed book *Reclaiming Conversation*, Sherry Turkle references a small study made up of anecdotal observations of the behavior of parents eating with young children in fast-food restaurants. Researchers found that "across the board, the adults paid more attention to their phones than to their children." The children either became passive and detached or began to act out in an effort to get their parents' attention. Turkle accurately describes the situation as the child competing with the cell phone. She writes, "We see children learning that no matter what they do, they will not win adults away from technology." Then she draws on the still-face paradigm to explain the significance of the child's experience: "Infants deprived of eye contact and facing a parent's 'still face' become agitated, then withdrawn, then depressed." Although we appreciate the reference to our research, we do want to point out that the infant in the original experiment does *not* become depressed. Moreover, the situation of a child with a parent using the phone is fundamentally different. Because her parent is unavailable, the child is deprived of face-to-face interaction. But the parent does *not* have a still-face.

How might children make meaning of a parent on a cell phone? They see a parent paying attention to something other than themselves. The experience is similar to when a parent comes home from a long day at work and starts to make dinner instead of sitting on the floor and playing. Even parents talking on old-fashioned phones show on their faces and in their voices that they are paying attention to something other than their children. Parents who raised children before the age of cell phones recall that the moment they picked up the receiver, their children, who had been happily playing on their own, had a sudden need for their full attention. As with current technology, many children experienced their parent paying attention to something other than themselves as a deprivation.

Understanding how the still-face paradigm is *different* from a parent on a cell phone may offer insight into the social problem we are facing with escalating technology use. A parent using a cell phone is distracted, not absent. The cell phone is ubiquitous and compelling, although other than that, the situation is not really different from a parent talking on an old-fashioned phone. But the way children make meaning of the parent on the cell phone is rooted in a history of moment-to-moment interactions from their earliest development.

The reaction someone has to an interactive partner on a cell phone is embedded in relational history. While one person might simply temporarily find something else to do, another might react with annoyance. Yet another might experience a partner using a cell phone as an abandonment and have a total emotional collapse, as we saw with Jennifer in chapter 1. The still-face paradigm illuminates these variations. A person who has a robust history of navigating the typical clarifications and readjustments of moment-to-moment interaction is less likely to exhibit the dysregulation and disorganization that some of the children in the fast-food restaurant showed. In contrast, for a person who's had scant opportunity to repair, the cell phone can produce sadness, anxiety, or extreme anger. People lacking in opportunity to move through mismatch to repair rely on continual connection to hold themselves together. Without it, they may become overwhelmed with feelings they cannot manage.

Individual relational histories determine the degree of stress you experience from the disconnect produced by a partner's inattention, whether it's due to looking at a cell phone, looking at the mail, or doing any of a variety of things that may call your interactive partner away. If you then turn to your own device to calm your feelings of distress at that lost connection, you enter a vicious cycle. Your use of the cell phone then produces further disconnection, not only raising your anxiety but also depriving you of the calming effects of face-to-face engagement described in chapter 3. The anxiety produced by the disconnect keeps leading you back to the screen.

It is the pervasive relational stress, not the device per se, that is the primary problem. What stresses were those mothers who were observed in the fast-food restaurants experiencing? The researchers Turkle cites may in fact have been witnessing a long-standing pattern of problematic interactions between parent and child that had been years in the making. An overwhelmed parent, perhaps caring for a newborn and other children with minimal support, might have limited resources for engaging in the moment-to-moment interaction her young infant requires. When growing children lack well-developed self-regulation abilities, they become more difficult to care for, with excessive tantrums and unpredictable sleep patterns. Sleep deprivation and constant battles might further stress parents, who then become increasingly emotionally unavailable, exacerbating young children's difficulty managing their own behavior and emotions. The stress of parenting an out-of-control child can send a parent fleeing to technology, both for herself and her child. (Of course, at times, a parent simply needs to be on the phone.) The cell phone use is not the cause of the problem but rather the result of this history of moment-to-moment interaction characterized by unrepaired mismatch. As we explore in detail in chapter 9, the solution to the problem of technology lies not in admonitions for limited use but in just what Turkle advocates: immersion in real face-to-face interactions.

AUTISM AND TECHNOLOGY

In May of 2017 the French newspaper *Le Monde* published an article suggesting a connection between the rise in autism and cell phone use by parents. It presented a hypothesis that toddlers were experiencing frequent still-face interactions with parents who shifted attention from their children to look at their electronic devices. Turkle alluded to this issue too in her book, suggesting that parents were concerned about a connection between cell phone use and Asperger's syndrome (that condition and other related developmental problems are now collectively referred to as autism spectrum disorder).

The cell phone–autism link can be debunked simply by the fact that the exponential rise in autism diagnoses preceded the current epidemic of cell phone use. But the question offers an opportunity to consider the way cell phone use and behaviors associated with autism might be linked. As we described in chapter 4, we need to look not only at the behavior of the parent and child separately but also at how they affect and change each other in moment-to-moment interactions, what we call the *mutual regulation model.*

A child with sensory sensitivities or other neurobiological vulnerabilities may adapt by going to great lengths to shut out the outside world. Children who have challenges with socializing may naturally gravitate to the smoothed-out passive engagement offered by screens, which don't demand a response. Parents may then turn to their own phones to calm themselves from the extreme stress of working to connect with these children. Further complicating the situation, parents under stress may convey that stress to their children, who increasingly turn to technology to self-regulate and reduce stress and anxiety.

At age two, Billy knew every word to every song of the Disney movie *Aladdin.* When he and his big sister watched it together, he would act out the songs, his body movements almost perfectly in sync with the cartoon characters'. This quirky habit was one of the delightful aspects of his obsession with screens. But as he got older and couldn't be separated from his Game Boy on family vacations, his parents, Stella and Jim, began to worry. Their efforts to limit its use resulted in explosive meltdowns, especially when the family was out for dinner in a restaurant; Billy's tantrum threatened to disrupt the meal not only for them but also for all the other customers. So, in an effort to salvage the experience for Billy's big sister, they often relented, enduring the judgmental glares of the other diners for both the disruption and the parents' failure to set limits on his screen use.

A therapist suggested Billy might be on the autism spectrum, which helped Stella and Jim recognize his social media use as a symptom of his difficulties. But rather than confronting the problem only through screen prohibition, they also made efforts to expose Billy to ways of being in the social world that he could tolerate. When they went to a toy store, a sensory-overload experience for any child, Billy found comfort in the section of toy musical instruments. Stella began to use music in a more deliberate way to help him organize himself when he appeared on the verge of unraveling, and she found ways to listen to music with him at other times as well. She found that classical music in particular helped him calm down. They took a music class together. As soon as he could hold a small guitar, she signed him up for lessons. In third grade he joined the school band.

Billy's love of music expanded to art in middle school when he developed a close relationship with a beloved and talented art teacher. His colorful images often depicted young children playing together. Using his artistic talents to address his childhood social awkwardness helped him to make meaning of his early experience. Years later, he put his artistic talents to use as a graphic designer, continuing to paint in the calm space of his home studio. Over time his social anxiety abated. On his own, he gradually lessened his use of screens as he gained access to the more rewarding experience of human social interaction.

In Billy's story we can understand technology use not as the cause but rather as an effect of his difficulties. Video games offered Billy relief from the overwhelming onslaught of stimulation from the social world. Stella and Jim had both each other and a large support system to help them through the messiness of interacting with their hard-to-reach son. Without such a network, each parent might have retreated to the cell phone as an interactive partner, leading to a downward spiral of disconnection. The three-dimensional messiness of actual interaction, while complex and challenging, allows people to change through the process of mismatch and repair. When they flee to the smooth two-dimensional surfaces of cell phones, they lose that experience. They can become stuck and fail to grow.

ANXIETY, DEPRESSION, AND SOCIAL MEDIA

While an association clearly exists between problematic cell phone use and stress, depression, and anxiety, there is little evidence that cell phone use causes these problems. As with behaviors associated with autism, it could well be that the phone is the response rather than the cause. In a *New York Times* article addressing the role of new technology in the current epidemic of anxiety in young people, Tracy Dennis-Tiwary, professor of psychology at Hunter College, wrote: "When we're anxious, we gravitate toward experiences that dull the present anxious moment. Enter mobile devices, the perfect escape into a two-dimensional half-life, one that teenagers can make sense of."

Research also demonstrates a clear connection between low self-esteem and high levels of social media use. However, as psychologist Erin Vogel is quick to point out, it's not clear whether social media use causes low self-esteem or if individuals with low self-esteem gravitate to social media. In her research, Vogel aims to untangle this question.

On social media, people display the positive aspects of their lives. We don't see photos of exhausted parents with unruly hair and spit-up on their clothes or couples sleeping in separate rooms after a blowout fight. These uniformly positive images may lead people looking at them to feel worse about themselves. Vogel designed an experiment to test this idea with college students in her lab at the University of California, San Francisco. She and her colleagues made social media profiles of supposedly real college students. They found a temporary drop in students' self-esteem after viewing just two or three profiles of attractive and physically fit individuals who had more comments and likes than they had.

This experiment suggests that social media plays a role in decreasing self-esteem. But as Vogel acknowledges, in this experiment the researchers were looking at one moment in time. What variation might we see if we were able to examine behavior according to the quality of relationships across development? A person with a fragile sense of self might be more significantly affected in response to these profiles than a person with a robust sense of self. In what can quickly become a downward spiral, the device is used to quell the distress produced by the continuous comparison with others that the ever-present technology engenders.

TECHNOLOGY USE AS SYMPTOM

In the preceding examples, we've seen that excessive use of technology can be understood not as the problem itself but as a symptom of an underlying problem. It serves an adaptive function. Only when we understand the function the behavior serves can we directly address the underlying issue. In other words, the behavior has a purpose. It has meaning. Parents observed in the fast-food restaurant, stressed by the challenges of parenting, used their cell phones to relieve that stress, inadvertently producing a descent into mutual dysregulation. Their children lost their interactive partners to the smooth two-dimensional surfaces, but they also lost the scaffolding that three-dimensional face-to-face interactions provide. Children with unusual social behavior — and their parents — may similarly be drawn to the illusion of connection the cell phone provides if there is a paucity of actual connection. When people struggle with a variety of emotional difficulties, technology use may serve a complex function. As the following story demonstrates, we need to understand the purpose of the behavior in order to change it.

WHEN TECHNOLOGY REPLACES REAL
RELATIONSHIPS

Psychoanalyst Danielle Knafo offers a case study on the link between technology and perfectionism in contemporary society that we addressed in chapter 2. She describes a session with her patient Jack, a man in his late forties. In their first three meetings he'd shared with her that his parents had a deeply troubled marriage. Jack described his father's submissive relationship with his mother and his wish to avoid a similar situation. At the same time, he acknowledged his desire for an intimate relationship. Jack had already had two failed marriages. During his fourth session, he told Dr. Knafo about his new relationship with Maya. Knafo writes:

> With Maya, he seemed to have found a way to answer his needs without feeling compromised. She was a special woman, one who somehow understood the disappointments of his past relationships and his daily stresses, one who made love with him whenever he wanted to, one who was perfectly compliant.
>
> Jack stared at me intently and said, almost in a whisper, "My Maya, she's a real doll, Doc."
>
> I watched him laugh, rocking from side to side and bringing his hands out from under his knees to lightly slap them. Then something dawned on me. No, it couldn't be, could it?
>
> "Yeah, she's a real doll," he repeated, his laughter beginning to die down. "Literally."

A wish to avoid the mess of relationships is not new. In the early 1940s the Mills Brothers song "Paper Doll" held the number-one position on the singles chart for twelve weeks; its lyrics speak of a wished-for paper doll that, unlike a real girl, who might leave after a quarrel, would always be reliably waiting at home. But the technology that allows the fantasy of perfection to flourish is new. Faced with this unfamiliar situation with her patient Jack, Knafo began researching the phenomenon of love dolls. Modern dolls are a far cry from the inflatable companions of earlier times. Knafo learned about RealDoll, produced by a multimillion-dollar company that sold dolls for as much as ten thousand dollars each. The contemporary incarnation of the blowup doll is anatomically correct and feels like real flesh.

Knafo worked with Jack in psychoanalysis, eventually helping him to transition to a relationship with a real person. She writes, "At times he spoke of Maya with nostalgia, recalling a period when life seemed easier, less messy, and more under his control." Yet with Dr. Knafo, Jack came to understand the impact of his early life experience, and by the time they were done working together, he was ready for a human relationship with all its inherent imperfection.

After her experience with Jack, in the course of her research on the subject of high-tech dolls, Knafo discovered the phenomenon of high-end "fake babies." This new market, which appeared in the late 1990s, allowed for a pseudo-experience of parenting. Knafo considered the role of loss in the motivation for a customer to buy a Reborn, the name given to the newborn-baby doll. New technology allowed the doll to feel warm to the touch and even look like it was breathing and crying. Knafo wondered if mothering the doll might "address concealment of trauma of a lost child, or the inability to have children, or even the inability to connect with a real child." She encountered a doll artist who said she had found her calling in making these dolls after seven miscarriages.

For mothers struggling with the unbearable loss of a child, the doll might offer a temporary solution. Just as Jack's attachment to RealDoll Maya was a symptom of his difficulty with real intimacy, the attachment to a Reborn can be understood as a symptom of blocked mourning. The idea that miscarriages deserve time and space for mourning is relatively new. The work of mourning a lost child is never done. Both of these uses of dolls illustrate how symptoms serve an adaptive function; the behavior has meaning. We need to understand that meaning in order to eliminate the symptom and so move forward to healing.

As we saw in chapter 5, resilience, the ability to recover in the face of adversity, comes from the experience of countless moments of mismatch and repair. The smoothness of the screen's two-dimensional surface limits the experience of mutual clarifications, corrections, and adjustments that leads to trust, social competence, and an increasingly complex sense of ourselves in relationships in the world.

Over the course of Jack's relationship with Dr. Knafo, together they came to understand the meaning of Jack's preference for a doll over a human connection. Had Dr. Knafo simply tried to discourage him from using the doll without learning the underlying meaning of the behavior, he might not have found his way to more real and satisfying human relationships. When we eliminate a symptom without recognizing its function, we fail to address the underlying problem. If we understand the problem of technology and social media overuse as a symptom, we see that simple admonitions to limit time and find good content are not sufficient. Our overreliance on technology and social media may be a symptom of a social and cultural movement away from the normal messiness of human relationships. If so, only immersion in relationships can provide the solution.

This idea of symptoms as adaptations has relevance not only to our understanding of overreliance on technology but also to the way we understand and treat all forms of emotional distress. In the following chapter, we explore how behaviors in the context of troubled relationships and emotional pain often serve a purpose. Rather than simply aiming to eliminate them, we need to learn their purpose. What we call "symptoms" serve as communication that the balance between self-regulation and interactive regulation is off-kilter. We need to be able to calm ourselves while also accessing the calming influence of others.

8

WHEN MEANING GOES AWRY

WE ALL FEEL LOST at times. Our sense of emotional well-being may falter or even collapse. Understanding how our earliest experiences become part of us, as elucidated by insights from the still-face paradigm, can guide us in a direction of healing and growth at six months, sixteen years, or sixty years. We struggle to heal by connecting with others when our earliest relationships distort our ability to see the people in front of us.

We learned from the still-face paradigm that very young infants have the ability to adapt to a difficult situation. But paradoxically, that very adaptation can be problematic. Infants of depressed mothers who turn inward to protect themselves from their caregivers' emotional unavailability are prevented from engaging in other relationships that might offer an alternative experience. They miss out on new opportunities for growth through mismatch and repair.

Throughout our lives we may adopt behaviors and ways of interacting that protect us from emotional pain in the moment but that in the long run get in the way of building strong relationships. We all do this to some degree. It is not abnormal or atypical. But understanding how it happens can help us to change when we feel stuck in relationships that are not moving forward in healthy ways.

Bernie was growing frustrated. He knew that almost every member of the group he ran for young men in recovery from opioid addiction had had a deeply troubled childhood. The language of ACEs, or adverse childhood experiences, had begun to make inroads in the world of addiction treatment, with increasing recognition that early experiences played a significant role on the path to substance abuse. Yet week after week, group discussions remained concrete as the men addressed the difficulties of navigating life with daily trips for medication-assisted treatment, their frustration over encounters with child protective services as they tried to get visits with their children, and countless other current challenges. Not that these weren't valid concerns. But Bernie felt that they were just skimming the surface. Each group member fed off the others in what often seemed like an endless list of grievances that left little room for reflection. Bernie's decades of experience as a therapist had taught him that only when his clients experienced feelings connected to their troubles did they begin to change their behavior. The group was stuck in a fixed, rigid rhythm.

Then he had an idea. He knew about the classic still-face video on YouTube but felt watching it would be too upsetting for the group, so instead he shared with them a post from a parenting blog about "present but absent parenting." The blog's author spoke to the way a child in such an environment could feel lonely even in a houseful of people, and Bernie felt it captured the experience conveyed by the still-face video. He read the piece aloud with the group. They had developed enough of a sense of trust and safety with one another that this simple intervention brought about a major shift. At first they related the article to their experiences as fathers, sharing guilt over their inconsistent presence in their children's lives. But then, after a pause in the conversation, one young man said, "That was me." His voice cracked and then tears began to flow as he spoke about being a "mistake," growing up in a home where his parents hardly noticed him. As the group listened, he let himself be fully in the pain of the moment, connecting his grief over his lost relationship with his own parents to his profound love for his infant daughter. He took a big chance. He risked an unrepaired mismatch, but he trusted that he could connect with Bernie and the others. From that moment forward, the dynamic of the group shifted as others took similar risks and opened up about their feelings. They began to see one another as the complex individuals they were, each with his own story. The label of *addiction* took a back seat to meaningful communication. Through their relationships with Bernie and with one another, together they took a significant step forward on the path to recovery.

LOSING IT

The still-face experiment offers insight into the early experience of that young man in the group. In the video we described in the introduction, as well as in countless other versions of the experiment, we see how the baby's interaction with her mother appears to literally hold her together. When the baby loses the scaffolding of her mother, her body becomes disorganized; she flails about, her arms and legs moving randomly. It is as if this small person's structure is collapsing, the glue dissolving. One can stand to watch the video only because the quick return of her mother leads to an almost immediate restoration of the child's coherence, what Winnicott called *going on being*. The baby's emerging sense of self, the very notion that *I am*, depends on the reliable return of her mother.

But what if a mother does not reliably return? For the infant who has no way to understand her absence, his sense of his own existence is threatened. Winnicott described this experience using the rather old-fashioned word *madness*. He wrote: "Madness here simply means a *break-up* of what may exist at the time of a *personal continuity of existence*."

Thinking about madness from a relational perspective can take us inside the experience of profound emotional distress. Substance abuse is but one of many problematic paths a person may take in the wake of the chronic unrepaired mismatches that characterize adverse childhood experiences. Understanding the developmental origins of such paths can point us in the direction of healing. People in the throes of emotional distress may say, "I'm losing it." Losing what? The still-face research teaches that without the scaffolding of relationships, a person may lose his very sense of self. Meaning, coping, and resilience emerge from the messy process of mismatch and repair. When these experiences are lacking, people may flounder. They may close themselves off from others with anxious rigidity or descend into hopelessness.

Suicide might be described as an ultimate failure of going on being. In the spring of 2018, the suicides of two public figures, Kate Spade and Anthony Bourdain, brought considerable attention to the subject. In a *New York Times* article, psychiatrist Richard Friedman wondered why there had been a decline in deaths from heart disease and HIV over the past several decades but a rise in the rate of suicide. He suggested that the lack of progress in suicide prevention was due to a lack of funding for research. He wrote: "The simple reason suicide has been neglected for so long is stigma. It is a human behavior that terrifies most people. Suicide is wrongly seen as a character or moral flaw — or even a sinful act. It is viewed as something shameful that must be hidden."

The terror and shame Friedman spoke of capture well the feelings that accompany a complete failure to make meaning, when one's sense of one's own existence falters.

In a compelling and meticulously argued article titled "Suicide in the Age of Prozac," journalist Robert Whitaker tries to make sense of the rise in suicide rates over many decades despite advances in treatment, especially antidepressant medication. While Friedman views suicide as a medical problem, Whitaker views it differently:

> It was in the late 1990s that the [American Suicide] Foundation came to be led by academic psychiatrists and pharmaceutical company executives. The Foundation promoted a narrative that conceptualized suicide within a medical context.... Yet suicide rates have risen since that time, which provides reason to ask whether this medicalized approach has been counterproductive.

While the subject of suicide is vast and beyond the scope of this book, the differing views of Whitaker and Friedman provide a point of entry into developmental and relational understanding of emotional suffering. The still-face paradigm offers a different perspective from the medical model. As we have seen, emotional well-being and emotional distress both grow out of variations in the repeated moment-to-moment exchanges that make each of us who we are. On one end of the spectrum, robust interactions of mismatch and repair lead a person to experience the world as safe and filled with people who can be trusted. At the other extreme, if experience of repair is lacking, fear and mistrust inform a person's understanding of himself and the world around him. The two extremes help us make sense of the more typical experiences that fall somewhere in between. Rather than being fixed, the meanings you make in your earliest experience are continually changing in new relationships in an ongoing process of making meaning of yourself and the world as you grow and change.

We need not stigmatize emotional suffering to appreciate its complexity. Acknowledging developmental and relational context should not be shaming. People can miss out on the opportunity for mismatch and repair in different ways. In extreme situations, such as an infant in a foster family of ten who receives only infrequent attention from his caregivers and minimal opportunity for social interaction, the majority of mismatches may go unrepaired. More commonly, the time from mismatch to repair is overly long, with the duration of distress beyond the child's capacity to manage. This may happen when a caregiver is available emotionally only intermittently, which may result from a range of challenges, including depression, substance abuse, marital conflict, and feeling overwhelmed, exhausted, and alone.

Lack of opportunity for repair also results when mismatch is suppressed. Helicopter parents who won't permit their children to experience failure don't prepare them to move through stress to growth and resilience. The tiger mom or authoritarian parent who demands conformity to her goals and punishes mismatch also quashes a child's self-confidence when she leaves no room for error. An infant may avoid an overly intrusive parent as a way to adapt to a problematic situation. But if that way of relating extends to interactions with other people, avoidance of engagement with others may interfere in ongoing development, inhibiting the opportunity to grow through new relationships.

From Harlow's monkeys, who craved comfort over food, to the original still-face research with infants, to the still-face experiment with adults, to the stories in this book that are derived from clinical experience, we have seen again and again that emotional well-being is rooted in the quality of one's earliest relationships. Just as countless moments of repair give a person a core sense of hope (*I can overcome this*), the lack of opportunity for repair may leave someone with a core feeling of hopelessness (*Nothing will work*). The full range of emotional struggles everyone experiences fall along this spectrum of meaning-making. What is termed *depression* may in fact be an inability to see one's way past a difficult moment — *I am stuck here. Nothing will change.* What we term *anxiety* can also be seen as a rigid clinging to behavior that holds someone together when he feels his sense of self dissolving — *If I change, who knows what will happen?*

But do not despair. As we will explore in depth in the following chapters, your mind and brain are capable of significant change throughout your lifetime. The critical point is that your sense of yourself in the world emerges, grows, and changes in an ongoing developmental process. Your emotions grow out of your relational history. Even if you've had the most adverse set of early experiences, when you immerse yourself in new relationships with space for mismatch and repair, meanings of hopelessness can be transformed into meanings of hope.

A SHATTERED SENSE OF SELF

Parents leave their children all the time. In fact, a child's sense of himself and the world around him develops out of these natural comings and goings. *Mama, where are you? There you are.* These experiences form his core feeling of going on being. But a period of separation beyond the child's ability to manage precipitates an unbearable anxiety. For the child, having no way to make meaning of his mother's absence, it is as if she no longer exists. And if she no longer exists, the child's sense of his own existence falters. The experience goes beyond terror, sadness, or rage. It is a total negation, a sense that *There is no me.*

Even though Wyatt was fifty and had a successful career and two children of his own, when his elderly mother had a familiar response to a seemingly minor family conflict, Wyatt felt instantaneously transported back to his three-year-old self. Back then, following any kind of discord or disagreement between his parents, it was as if a veil of sadness fell over his mother, making her unreachable. As a child, Wyatt was terrified. Now this veil had once again fallen over his mother. As a young child, struggling to make meaning of his mother's intermittent emotional unavailability, Wyatt felt lost. As an adult, bolstered by relationships with his wife and teenage children, he could observe his reaction to his mother's behavior. Time, therapy, and a series of new relationships had offered him the opportunity to reinterpret his mother's intermittent emotional absence. Though unsettling and startling in its appearance after so many years, the behavior no longer precipitated the same inner panic and dissolving of his sense of self. He could contemplate the situation, including his own reaction, from a comfortable distance.

Wyatt recalled that as a child when his mother withdrew, he feared he had done something to hurt her. He felt a profound sense of disorientation. Lacking any other way to understand the experience, he had assumed that something about his behavior had caused his mother harm. An unshakable feeling of shame settled in that took decades to overcome. Without his mother emotionally present to interact with him, Wyatt was shaken to the core. His experience with his mother lived in his body. Recall the polyvagal theory we discussed in chapter 3. When Wyatt was a child, his body would shut down under the influence of the primitive vagus as he experienced a deep-seated sense of threat in the face of any messy social interaction. If he could harm his mother, what harm might he do out in the world? Throughout his childhood he was extremely shy and inhibited. He found it best to stay quiet and hidden.

When Wyatt had children, his mother shared enough of her story for Wyatt to make sense of both his own and his mother's experience. Their relationship continued to grow and change. Wyatt learned that his mother had had multiple miscarriages before Wyatt was born. In the world his mother lived in, there had not been time or space to grieve. Forums for parents experiencing pregnancy loss did not exist. As is not uncommon, the grief held her in its grip even after she had a healthy baby, showing itself during Wyatt's early months and years in behavior consistent with what today would be diagnosed as postpartum depression. His mother's sudden, inexplicable emotional absences created in Wyatt an intermittent failure of going on being.

The anguish of a child unable to reach her mother is captured in Kate and Anna McGarrigle's lyrics to "The Bike Song." The lyrics suggest a now adult child tied to a relationship of inexplicable disconnection. In the woman's voice in the song we hear the pain and longing together with an inability to comprehend. We can imagine this daughter confronting a form of still-face as she implores her mother to look at her when she is crying. She wonders what she needs to be to make her mother fall in love with her.

The emotional absence of Wyatt's mother represented an unmourned loss. Still stuck in the grief precipitated by her multiple miscarriages, she had held back from "falling in love" with her son, protecting herself from a sadness that felt unbearable. They remained isolated from each other with a thick wall of disconnection built of their distorted meanings lodged between them.

WHEN WE DON'T FEEL KNOWN

In adult relationships, we may feel that our partners do not see us for who we are, or we may find ourselves unable to listen to our partners when we project meaning onto their behavior that they did not intend. These patterns may originate in early experiences of not being seen.

For a child, the terrifying feeling that the self is dissolving may go hand in hand with an experience of not being seen. When Wyatt could look back at his childhood experience, he said of those moments when his mother was physically present but emotionally absent, "It was as if there was no me." What might get in the way of parents engaging in the messy process of getting to know their child? Perhaps, as for Wyatt's mother, there was a loss of a baby, and this new child was what might be termed a *replacement child*. Current online forums and other forms of support for this kind of loss use the gentler term *rainbow baby* to capture the joy and light of a healthy child born following the storm of a miscarriage or death of an infant. While the loss of a child is never resolved, if time and space are not made to mourn, the grief may get in the way, wreaking havoc on the relationship with the living child. As with Wyatt's mother, a kind of survival instinct kicks in. Rather than surrender to falling in love, a parent may guard against the feeling to protect herself from the real though unlikely possibility of another unbearable loss.

When parents have ongoing problematic relationships and are preoccupied by unresolved conflicts, either past or present, they may have difficulty seeing their child as his or her own person. Parents' preconceived notions often begin before their child is born. One mother whose partner intermittently threw her against the wall in anger throughout her pregnancy saw her unborn son as a brat, convinced that the painful kicking she felt indicated he was "just like his dad." Another mother described her own mother's chronic illness and rapidly declining health, which coincided with her pregnancy, with the words "She's been dying my whole life." In the next breath, she described her unborn daughter as *tenacious*, a term that could also represent her experience of her own mother's "clinging on" in a way that caused ongoing turmoil throughout her own development.

This kind of certainty, a parent's fixed idea of her child's identity before the two even meet, precludes curiosity about the child. The parent projects her own meanings onto the child's behavior. In contrast, if a parent takes a stance of uncertainty and an attitude of *Let's engage and I'll get to know you while you get to know me,* she allows space for her child to grow. The messiness of that process leads to increased coherence and complexity of babies' sense of self and their relationships with others and the world around them. This same stance of curiosity helps people in building healthy relationships in their adult lives.

Psychologist Alicia Lieberman of the University of California, San Francisco, makes use of the Newborn Behavioral Observations (NBO) system that we mentioned in chapter 6 to help new parents see the "real" baby. She views the set of observations as a relationship-building tool that encourages parents to be curious about their newborn child, writing, "This process of *discovering the infant* is used to strengthen the mother-infant relationship." She explains how the process of taking time to notice the baby's unique behaviors is particularly helpful for parents whose emotional states are stuck in other troubled relationships, making it difficult for them to pay attention to their infant's communications.

When parents continue to be preoccupied, the process of getting to know their infant may be derailed, with significant consequences. The negative impact on children's development when their parents struggle with postpartum depression is well known. These children have significantly more emotional, behavioral, and learning problems. How does this happen? What is the mechanism of this association? Our analysis of videotaped parent-infant interactions offers an answer to these questions.

We found that, overall, depressed mothers look away more and express more negative, angry, and sad affects than do non-depressed mothers. They engage in less play and use less motherese, the exaggerated inflection that parents use in speaking with their babies. Our research with infants of mothers struggling with postpartum depression demonstrates that as early as six months, infants have already learned a way to make meaning of their environment that is different from the meaning-making of infants of nondepressed mothers. In one video typical of these infant-mother pairs, rather than robust efforts to engage the mother we saw in the original experiment, the baby quickly turns inward. He sucks on his hand. His body appears to collapse as he slumps in his seat. He focuses his gaze on objects, like a chair or a light overhead, rather than on his mother.

Unlike babies who go to great lengths to engage their mothers, babies with depressed mothers learn early how to cope with withdrawn partners. They know from experience that pointing, crying, or cajoling likely won't work.

From this perspective, babies who find a way to deal with a caregiver's withdrawn behavior are not disturbed but incredibly resourceful! They use the tools they have to hold themselves together, or self-regulate. This kind of coping has an adaptive function. Rather than becoming completely unhinged, the baby works out a way to join with a depressed interactive partner, in a sense meeting her where she is. It's as if the baby is saying, *Okay, it's all right. I'll handle this myself.*

When we consider the alternative, the sense that the self is dissolving, we can understand the baby's behavior as quite adaptive. Psychoanalyst Melanie Klein used the powerful word *annihilation* to describe an experience that is the opposite of

Winnicott's *going on being*. Without this coping behavior, there could be more dire consequences. An infant who completely loses a sense of self lacks motivation to take in food for sustenance, leading to a potentially life-threatening failure to thrive.

WHEN LACK OF LOVE IS DEADLY

One classic study offers dramatic evidence that not only do our earliest relationships hold us together — they keep us alive. This extreme situation can help us make sense of more typical, less dramatic, but nonetheless devastating moments of emotional pain we inevitably experience as adults.

In the 1940s, when orphanages for young children still existed in the United States, high death rates in those institutions were attributed primarily to contagious diseases. But Austrian psychoanalyst René Spitz had a different hypothesis; he believed the deaths were due to a lack of a consistent caregiver or a lack of love. To test his theory, he observed groups of infants in two different institutions and followed them into toddlerhood. In both institutions, infants who were admitted shortly after birth received adequate nutrition, shelter, and medical care. But they differed in one significant way. In the institution he called Nursery, infants were cared for in a prison nursery by their incarcerated mothers. In the other, a hospital ward he called Foundlinghome, overworked nurses had to care for from eight to twelve children each. In Spitz's summary of his findings, he wrote that the children in Nursery developed into normal healthy toddlers, but the emotionally starved children of Foundlinghome did not thrive, and many of them never learned to speak, walk, or feed themselves. He went on to reveal the most shocking finding:

The most impressive evidence probably is a comparison of the mortality rates of the two institutions. In a five years' observation period during which we observed a total of 239 children, each for one year or more, "Nursery" did not lose a single child through death. In "Foundlinghome," on the other hand, 37 percent of the children died during the two years' observation period.

In these extreme circumstances, even when adequate nutrition is available, emotional deprivation may lead to physical starvation or even death. Spitz wrote that "such variations caused by psychosocial factors can literally become matters of life and death."

Critics of the study suggested that these groups had different genetic risk factors. Parents who would abandon their children, the argument went, passed on genes to their children that made them vulnerable to poor developmental outcomes. More recently, compelling research by child psychiatrist Charles Zeanah at Tulane University has refuted that notion. Along with colleagues Nathan Fox at the University of Maryland and Chuck Nelson at Harvard University, Zeanah had the opportunity to conduct a study in Romania comparing in-home foster care with institutional care in an orphanage.

In 1966, to counter a declining birth rate over the preceding decade, Communist leader Nicolae Ceaușescu authorized Decree 770, which severely restricted access to abortion and contraception. Women of childbearing age were required to see a gynecologist monthly, and hospital procedures were monitored by secret police. As a result, women had children they could not afford to care for. Large numbers of children were placed in orphanages.

Ceauşescu was overthrown in the Romanian revolution of 1989, but the new government maintained that orphanages offered an acceptable environment in which to raise children and therefore foster care was unnecessary. Zeanah and his colleagues were able to examine this assumption. Two groups of children were randomly assigned to either foster care or the orphanage. Zeanah and his colleagues studied the children over more than fifteen years.

In an article in *Forbes* tellingly titled "It's the Orphanages, Stupid!," journalist Maia Szalavitz described the results as "stunning." She wrote:

> Just as in Spitz' research, children who received parental love did much better than those raised in the best Romanian orphanages. The foster kids grew faster, had larger head sizes (a measure of brain development) and even IQs that were higher by nine points. These kids were happier and paid attention better than the kids who stayed behind at the orphanages.

Findings from the Romanian orphanage study further support the idea that forms of emotional suffering to which a psychiatric diagnosis may be attached are embedded in relationships. According to the same *Forbes* article, "52% of those who ever spent time in an orphanage developed some form of mental illness — compared to 22% of those without that experience. Children taken from orphanages and randomized to foster care had half the rate of conditions like anxiety and depression compared to those who remained institutionalized."

In situations of emotional neglect, all of the children's energy goes to holding themselves together in the absence of a caregiver to scaffold them. They fail to develop and may die, overwhelmed by the effort to manage their bodily functions on their own using only their limited capacity to self-regulate. Szalavitz referred to the work of Bruce Perry in her discussion of the problems inherent in growing up in an institution where the care was inconsistent and often impersonal. She quoted Perry as saying, "Typically the care of the infant is spread among multiple staff over multiple shifts, many of whom are just doing a job. The necessary sensory cues such as smile, touch, song and rocking required to stimulate normal growth and functioning of the infant's stress response and relational neural networks is just not provided in the patterns or quantities required for normal development."

Psychiatrist Bruce Perry emphasized time and repetition as central to the way babies make meaning of themselves in the world. The situation of the orphanage, while extreme, highlights the critical role of early relationships in building the capacity for self-regulation. Even in less extreme situations, when our ability to manage ourselves and be close with others falters, we need "time and repetition" in relationships to grow and change.

BRINGING OLD MEANINGS TO NEW RELATIONSHIPS

Symptoms that reflect emotional distress have meaning within the context of relationships. Anxiety may result from feelings of

vulnerability of one's sense of self. Rigid behaviors serve to maintain a sense of coherence. Feelings of sadness or hopelessness
may have roots in early experiences with a paucity of opportunity for repair. Behaviors such as irritability and social withdrawal
have a protective function. These early relational experiences
are carried forward in new relationships and continue to influence the developing sense of self.

Our colleague Tiffany Field, a researcher at the University
of Miami, found that infants of depressed mothers engage in
more negative patterns of interaction with an attentive, nondepressed adult and might even induce a negative emotional state
in that person. They bring their relational experiences with their
mothers to other relationships. Eventually, with the accumulation of failure, these infants develop a negative emotional core
characterized primarily by sadness and anger. That does not
mean they are always angry but that the sadness persists in the
background even in the face of events that provoke other emotions. They develop a view of their mothers as untrustworthy
and unresponsive and of themselves as ineffective and helpless.
The behaviors these infants acquire in order to adapt to their
mothers become automatic.

Field's study explains our observations that infants of depressed
mothers have less engaged and more negative interactions with
a friendly stranger than do infants of nondepressed mothers.
When research assistants in our lab played with the babies of
depressed mothers, they experienced a sense of frustration. After
struggling to engage the babies, they described their interactions
as "failures." But interestingly, they attributed the problem to
themselves, not to the babies. The research assistants, in a way
that was likely out of their awareness, took up a role in this

distorted game, communicating their frustration in the form of less joyful play. Their behavior, in turn, led to further disconnection. Over time in the interaction, the research assistants smiled less, touched less, and moved farther away, demonstrating how problematic interactions from infancy can be carried forward in time and into other relationships. This idea that people transfer experiences from early development to other relationships throughout their lives forms a central part of the healing action of psychoanalysis, a topic we'll address further in chapter 9. Patients transfer their feelings from troubled past relationships into the therapeutic relationship, where insight and understanding may loosen the grip of these problematic patterns. Therapists are mindful of their own reactions, or countertransference, using these responses to gain insight into the experiences of their patients in the wider social world.

The babies' behavior with our research assistants could be considered an early form of transference, and the research assistants' behavior could be viewed as a form of countertransference. The baby brings a pattern of interacting with a caregiver to this new interactive partner. When people are stuck in negative patterns of interaction as adults, often it is because they transfer patterns from other relationships, making it difficult to connect with the people in front of them.

In one particularly striking set of still-face experiments, we saw how infants can hold a kind of "memory" of interactions in their bodies. One group of infants was exposed to the still-face paradigm twice, two days apart. A second group of infants experienced the still-face paradigm only once, on the second day. Both groups were observed during a play period preceding the second day's still-face. We found that the babies in the first group had higher heart rates during the play episode, showing that they anticipated the stress of the still-face simply because the setting was the same. While they did not "remember" in the way adults think of memory, in terms of words and thoughts, their bodies remembered. It appears that these babies carried the meanings from the still-face into their play two days later. The physical space, with its specific combination of sensory impressions, meant stress. In contrast, the babies who had not experienced the still-face had normal heart rates as they engaged in stress-free play.

What if the still-face had been a slap or a sudden emotional absence? In chapter 6 we described the countless moment-to-moment games of changing, feeding, and going to sleep that become part of an infant's way of being in the world. But if these games involve being ignored or being hit or listening to screaming fights, those experiences too become part of the infant's physiology and way of responding to the world.

SYMPTOMS AS COPING

If a withdrawn, restricted, or rigid way of being in the world persists, it might map onto collections of behaviors we call depression or anxiety. But perhaps these behaviors have their origins in adaptation to a world that lacks purpose or has distorted meaning. Behaviors that represent ways of coping in the short term are not adaptive in the long run. They close people off from the normal messiness of social engagement that promotes healthy growth and development, leading to a downward spiral of disconnection.

Humans have a natural motivation to make meaning even

in the most adverse of circumstances. They will do whatever it takes to hold on to a sense of coherence, to avoid that unbearable anxiety of loss of sense of self. Babies hold themselves together enough to gain energy to move on to the next hour or day. They use the resources immediately available to them, even if in the long term those same behaviors may become problematic.

This way of thinking is echoed by psychoanalyst Robert Furman. He suggests an alternate way to understand behavior that is commonly called ADHD. He describes how, when children experience intolerable emotional distress, they have a range of options. They may withdraw into fantasy, which manifests as distractibility and inattention. The fantasy offers an escape. They may use actions rather than words with symptoms of impulsivity and hyperactivity. This behavior gives them a means to express feelings for which they lack words. These symptoms may in fact represent an adaptive response to an overwhelming experience.

Think of a young child lying in bed listening to parents screaming at each other and knowing that one of them might hurt the other. The thought *It's my fault* may give a sense of coherence to an incomprehensible situation. But it carries the long-term negative consequence of an internalized sense of shame. Interactions between an infant and a depressed parent may help that baby maintain a coherent sense of self but over time may lead to disengagement from other people and things. As Furman describes, and as the following story illustrates, hyperactivity and inattention can be understood as adaptive behaviors that children employ when they are struggling to make sense of their experiences.

Ten-year-old Maria arrived at the front door ready to leave

for school missing both a shoe and her backpack. Her parents, Juan and Veronica, laughed as they shared this story and others like it about their often-distracted daughter in consultation with a therapist. Juan had been just like Maria as a child. But their worries about her ran deep. After Maria looked at her passport in anticipation of a trip to visit her grandparents in Ecuador, she asked why hers looked different. Theirs each had a visa stamp but hers did not. The unusual questions suggested that she was beginning to figure things out on her own. Her parents struggled with how to explain that, in Veronica's words, they were "in the country illegally." Her parents went to great lengths to protect her from the news, with its incessant talk of the "problem" of undocumented immigrants, but undoubtedly she heard things at school. Her parents did not know how to discuss the fraught situation. After telling the therapist this story, Juan paused to consider the problem and then went on to share another major concern. Maria had suffered relentless bullying since she'd started second grade, coinciding with political shifts characterized by anti-immigrant rhetoric. One classmate had told her, "Our president doesn't like people with your color skin." Maria's teachers had recently recommended she see her pediatrician for an ADHD evaluation. Perhaps with a diagnosis, they said, Maria could get services to help her manage her distracted behavior. Juan was adamant. "There is nothing wrong with my daughter."

In this story, we see multiple layers of meaning of Maria's behavior. The certainty of a diagnosis, with an approach to treatment characterized by the management of her behavior, or "symptom," could get in the way of understanding the full complexity of her experience. Contributing to her behavior were a biological tendency for distractibility, the experience of bullying, and her very real worry about the possibility of deportation, a worry that at the moment Maria did not have language to express. The complexity of the story emerged not in standardized questionnaires used in an ADHD evaluation but in an expanse of time to listen with curiosity. Her inattentive behavior was imbued with multiple interlacing meanings.

Eliminating the symptoms that accompany emotional distress might provide short-term solutions, allowing, for instance, an impulsive child to sit at a desk or a depressed adult to get out of bed in the morning. But if these problematic behaviors serve an adaptive function, are actually a way of coping or holding oneself together, then if the relational and developmental context of these behaviors is not addressed, we should not be surprised if they reappear in different and sometimes more problematic forms.

EVERYTHING IS BIOLOGY

"But it's genetic" and "These are brain diseases," people might say. Once we recognize that our genes, brains, and bodies make meaning in relationships, the false duality of biology and experience, of nature and nurture, collapses. As we discussed in chapter 1, the growing field of epigenetics changes the way we think about nature versus nurture, showing us that rather than an either/or situation, experience influences the expression of genes. These epigenetically influenced genes, in turn, determine the structure and function of the brain.

Behavioral epigenetics specifically refers to the way environment, or life experience, influences gene expression and subsequent behavior and development. A child may be born with a particular gene for some problematic trait, but the expression of that gene, and so the effects of that gene on behavior, will vary according to the environment. Whether or not a given gene is expressed directly affects the developing structure and biochemistry of the brain. Thus, experience shapes genetic potential, and early life relationships are critical in influencing development of the brain.

For example, the 5-HTT gene affects the way the body responds to stress. It influences the structure and function of parts of the brain that play an essential role in emotional regulation. The S, for "short," variation of this gene is associated with depressive symptoms. But the expression, or effect on behavior, of this genetic variation is strongly affected by life experience. In the absence of significant stress, the gene is not turned on and so has no significant effect on the individual. Stressful life events, however, turn the gene on, altering the brain and significantly increasing the likelihood that the person will experience depression. In our lab we found that infants with the S-allele had a stronger negative reaction to the stress of the still-face experience than infants with the L-homozygous variation. These findings indicate that an individual with this genetic variation, the S-allele, is more vulnerable to the inevitable disconnections of typical interactions as well as to prolonged disconnections in environments where experience of repair is lacking.

Many people think of genetics as fixed and unchanging. And indeed, the genome, or sequence of base pairs of genes, does not change in response to the environment. Genetic diseases like cystic fibrosis and muscular dystrophy result from a change — a mutation — in a base pair in the genome. In contrast, the *epigenome*, or pattern of methylations and levels of gene expression, can change rapidly in response to the environment. Our bodies continually change gene expression in response to the environment without any change to the DNA sequence itself. For example, a study showed that daily mindfulness practice resulted in changes in gene expression that in turn led to faster recovery from stress.

Another study showed that a person with the S version of the 5-HTT gene is at increased risk for ADHD. But children with this gene variation who live in homes filled with conflict are more likely to actually be diagnosed with ADHD. To put it in a more positive way, the fact that you have the variation as part of your genotype doesn't mean you will have the characteristics of the ADHD diagnosis.

It may be helpful to recognize that while the constellation of behaviors associated with ADHD does tend to run in families, there is no one ADHD *gene*. This is a common misconception among parents and professionals alike. ADHD consists of a collection of behaviors that tend to go together and represent a problem of regulation of emotion, behavior, and attention. These behaviors emerge through the interactive process of making meaning throughout development, starting with people's earliest relationships.

Referring to emotional struggles as "brain disorders" leaves out the role of the meaning-making process in co-regulation of emotion and behavior. No one can understand the brain simply by looking at the brain. Through the process of epigenetics, genes make meaning of experiences in the context of relationships, changing the structure and function of the brain.

The good news is that you have the opportunity to rewire your brain over your entire life span. While the rewiring takes longer for older children and adults than it does for infants, the same changes we see in babies occur at all ages in experiences that offer the opportunity for repeated new interactions over time. Many studies offer evidence of brain changes with a variety of different types of psychotherapy. We can understand these results as demonstrating that new relationships with new opportunities to make new meanings can rewire the brain.

A video produced by the Harvard Center on the Developing Child refers to primary caregivers of infants and young children as "neuroarchitects." When you become an adult, a new team of neuroarchitects can help you build new meanings when you feel lost.

The still-face research teaches that when people's lives start out in problematic ways, these experiences exert their long-term effects when fixed meanings become stuck in their minds and bodies. The roots of these problems may run deep for those who grow up in an environment without ample opportunity for repair. A depressed mother or father, an extremely fussy baby, a marriage in trouble, or, at worst, a situation of abuse and neglect — these are all circumstances that can lead to fixed meanings of hopelessness.

People may carry these meanings of hopelessness forward into other relationships in their lives, with fear preventing them from being open to the kinds of relationships that allow for growth and change. When meanings have gone awry, we need to do more than just label and eliminate problematic behaviors and emotions. Acknowledging their developmental and relational origins leads us to a new model of healing.

9

HEALING IN A MOSAIC OF MOMENTS OVER TIME

FROM THE DAY HE was born, Simon struggled to fit in. The youngest of three, he cried incessantly, disrupting his previously calm, easygoing family. As he entered toddlerhood, his dramatic reactions to the world around him wreaked havoc on many a family outing. Not being first to press the elevator button could precipitate an all-out meltdown. In a kind of chain reaction, his own intense behavior followed by the less-than-positive response of his parents and siblings upset him even more. He couldn't take in their efforts to calm him and descended further into his own distress. In those early years, when his parents, Jacinda and Roman, sought an answer to the question "What's wrong with Simon?," many professionals wanted to call the problem autism, ADHD, or even depression. But his parents took a close friend's advice to be cautious and give Simon time to get it together, to make sense of himself in the world. It was a path that was far from easy. They listened carefully and tried a range of approaches to help Simon manage the intensity of his experience. Some worked; others did not. Sometimes they set firm limits, bearing the consequences of the disruption these limits inevitably produced. At other times, they went to great lengths to accommodate his inflexibility. Eventually, as he gained the ability to give words to his feelings, Simon learned to adapt and belong. Still, on occasion, he would descend into dark and brooding moments that worried Jacinda and Roman. They drew on support from family, friends, and a number of different therapists to navigate these challenges as Simon grew and developed.

An extremely bright and thoughtful child, Simon was the only one in his family to be accepted into a private high school on a full scholarship. On a whim, he joined the fencing team, an activity in which he had no experience. It was a decision that proved transformational. His natural skill and passion for the sport carried him through the typically tumultuous adolescent years. The physical and mental activity of fencing and the relationships with his coach and teammates provided countless opportunities for working through mismatch to repair. His parents' tolerance for the messiness, their willingness to make mistakes and work through the times when they didn't get it "right" throughout his childhood, had laid the foundation for a positive sense of himself that was now fortified by new relationships. While that core tendency of intense reactivity persisted, as did the occasional moments of darkness and brooding, Simon incorporated these qualities into his sense of himself in ways he could manage. He could recognize these moments as temporary and find his way out. Though he fenced in college, after he graduated, his busy work life precluded continued participation. He began playing Frisbee instead and joined an Ultimate Frisbee club. As his capacity to self-regulate grew, he was able to make new meanings in new relationships.

In contrast, Mona grew up in a family where messing up was not tolerated. When she committed a typical childhood transgression, such as resisting bedtime, she received a swift slap across her face from her father, which brought an abrupt and violent end to the mismatch. Rather than experiencing repair, she would cry herself to sleep.

As a mother herself, Mona was startled by the physical rush of intense rage she felt when her two-year-old son, Rashid, grabbed her glasses off her face or accidentally hit her with a toy. She knew in her conscious mind that this was typical toddler behavior. But calmly setting limits, as doctors and experts in a multitude of parenting magazines advised, was beyond her during these episodes. While able to keep herself from hitting him, she might smash a plate against the wall or collapse in tears. Though she understood the well-intentioned advice, in the heat of the moment, she found it impossible to stop and think about her reaction.

Mona knew that she wanted Rashid to have a different childhood experience than she'd had. As the reaction to her son was embedded in her body, it could only change by the creation of new meanings, and not just in the form of words and thoughts. Mona found those new meanings in a mosaic of experiences. Talk therapy was essential. However, as in the relationship between Eric and Dr. Olds in chapter 1, the moment-to-moment interactions with her therapist played a role as great as or greater than their conversations about the impact of her abusive relationship with her father on her parenting. In addition, her relationship with her wife, the expression of creativity through her career as an interior designer, and her aikido practice all brought room for mismatch followed by growth-promoting repair. Getting through all of this messing up allowed her to build new nonviolent meanings in her relationship with her son.

In these two stories, we see the extremes of influence of nature and nurture. Because of the qualities Simon was born with, his childhood was characterized by more unrepaired mismatch than his easygoing siblings experienced. For Mona, the paucity of repair resulted primarily from her parents' troubles. In each situation, distorted meanings of the world as an overwhelming and hopeless place might have been carried forward into new relationships, creating a knotted meshwork of difficulties. As we have seen, in reality, nature and nurture are intimately intertwined from the moment we engage in relationships with others. To be able to change for the long term, Simon and Mona needed something different: a new network of relationships and activities. None of the change was quick or easy. Over time, each developed a more full and complex sense of self.

THE HEALING PARADOX

When we suffer, whether with painful feelings within ourselves, difficulties in our relationships, or both, we may naturally seek a quick solution that smooths over the bumps. But when we look beyond the short term, we recognize that we need to do exactly the opposite. By immersing ourselves in a new set of interactions over time, with hundreds of thousands of moments of engaging with the mess, we create new meanings by moving through mismatch to repair. And as we have seen, the meanings we make of ourselves are not only in words and thoughts. New interactions need to bring in our bodies as well as our minds. Confronted with a problem of emotional struggles, we need to be creative. How inventive of Simon to find his way to fencing, an activity one could describe as organized, coherent nonviolent combat that, like all sports, demands dealing with and overcoming failure.

In his book *The Body Keeps Score*, psychiatrist Bessel van der Kolk of the Trauma Research Foundation offers a comprehensive overview of how stress lives in the body and how using the body can help a person to heal from extreme stress or trauma. Van der Kolk writes about an innovative theater program in Lenox, Massachusetts, called Shakespeare in the Courts that offers an example. In the program, teenagers found guilty of a variety of offenses are sentenced to six weeks, four afternoons a week, of intensive acting study. This experience gives vulnerable young people an opportunity to put words to their feelings, an important step on the road to managing themselves in a social world. Many come from chaotic home environments. Lacking consistently available caregivers, they have not previously learned how to describe their emotions, and one result is the impulsive behavior, literally doing without thinking, that got them in trouble. Van der Kolk describes how the director Kevin Coleman works with the teens. Coleman uses acting to help give language to their emotional experience. As van der Kolk explains, Coleman does not ask the kids how they feel, a question that invites judgment with words like *good* and *bad*. He wants them to be free to notice how they actually feel. In a sense, the theater program supports the teenagers' ability to listen to themselves, to find meaning in their own behavior. Van der Kolk writes:

Instead Coleman asks, "Did you notice any specific feelings that came up for you in that scene?" That way they learn to name emotional experiences: "I felt angry when he said that." "I felt scared when he looked at me." Becoming embodied, and for lack of a better word "en-languaged," helps the actors realize that they have many different emotions. The more they notice, the more curious they get.

In creating something, whether a piece of sculpture, a painting, or a book, you go through a lot of material that isn't quite right until you find your way to what you really want to communicate. When you anxiously strive to produce a fully formed idea from the start, you can become stuck, unable to create anything. In contrast, by embracing the mess, you find your own artistic voice. In the same way, when you seek to create yourself anew out of a history of distorted and troubled meanings, in new relationships, you need to move through countless imperfect interactions that aren't quite right.

In the Shakespeare in the Courts program, juvenile offenders all prepare their own performance pieces; it's part of the terms of the sentence. In rehearsal, these budding actors, like professional actors, inevitably mess up, forgetting a line, missing a cue. In running through a scene multiple times, they learn to breathe through errors on the way to a more seamless, though never perfect, performance.

LEARNING FROM WAR TRAUMA

Early relationships build the foundation of self-regulation and ability to be close with others, and these early experiences influence all relationships going forward into adulthood. When adults experience trauma, both the way they respond and the way they heal are affected by these early experiences. Consider the example of war trauma, from which the now common term *post-traumatic stress disorder,* or PTSD, has its origins.

Actor Stephan Wolfert performs a powerful one-man show he created called *Cry Havoc!* for a variety of audiences. At the beginning, he uses his own voice to create a sound that soon becomes clear to the audience as the *whoosh* of a train on a track, represented through the mechanical movements of his body. Gradually, words are linked to the sounds and movements, and a narrative starts to emerge.

Wolfert offers up a compelling tale of his life and of the healing that began when that train stopped in a small town where he discovered Shakespeare. After layers of adversity beginning in childhood, including abuse by his alcoholic father, his parents' domestic violence and subsequent divorce, a paralyzing sports injury, and years of war trauma and terrible loss, he went AWOL from the military. On a train ride through the middle of Montana, he spontaneously jumped off in a town where, as fate would have it, he happened upon a local theater production of *Richard III.* He was immediately captivated. This event proved to be the first step on a journey to develop a program using Shakespeare to heal war veterans struggling with combat trauma.

The tagline on Decruit.org, Wolfert's program's website, reads "Treating Trauma Through Shakespeare and Science." Wolfert recognized how the brains of veterans become wired for survival in combat but that the vets lacked the opportunity to rewire to adjust to civilian life. His story enriches our understanding of healing from trauma whether rooted in childhood, in our adult lives, or in both.

When Wolfert performed for our fellows in the University of Massachusetts Boston Infant-Parent Mental Health Program, he explained that for combat veterans, healing comes not primarily from Shakespeare's words but from the rhythm and the breath of reciting them. In a sense, Wolfert's performance enacts an infant's meaning-making through sensory experience and movement to conscious thought and language. When deep-seated meanings are out of awareness, they can wreak havoc on your current experience. Wolfert enables his audience to connect with their own more fundamental bodily meaning-making systems and bring those meanings into conscious awareness.

For Wolfert's audience, the experience of vicariously traveling with him on this journey can have a powerful transformative effect, just as watching the performance of *Richard III* had for him. In today's world, going to the theater is typically thought of as entertainment, not therapy. Wolfert's play and his story offer examples of finding creative avenues for healing.

A person's physiological stress system is altered when the process of mismatch and repair is derailed early in life. The experience lives in the body, and when someone is stressed as an adult, the body may respond in ways shaped by this early experience. Learning new patterns involves using both the mind and the body. If meanings were formed before language developed, then change calls for new meanings that are not based solely in language and conscious thought. In order to be in new relationships that break the unhealthy patterns of childhood, people need to learn, as Wolfert demonstrates, new ways to breathe.

In the film *Leave No Trace*, a war veteran travels with his daughter in an attempt to escape the demons that haunt his mind. We see him in a number of close encounters having seemingly ordinary experiences that we might not think of as *therapy* in the conventional meaning of that word but that could be therapeutic. These experiences might have offered him space to grapple with the messiness of interaction and provide occasions for growth-promoting repair. But for this man, they are just out of reach.

When forced by a social service agency from his place of safety in the forest and brought with his daughter to live on a farm, he asks if he might work with the horses. The farmer tells him that he is needed to harvest Christmas trees, work that requires him to be close to loud machinery. When he takes a moment alone in the stable and meets the gaze of one of the horses, we see his expression soften and his body relax into the potential healing power of connection that he has been seeking. But denied that opportunity, he decides to leave, taking his daughter with him. Along their increasingly treacherous journey he has other close encounters with creative opportunities for healing. A fellow veteran he meets generously shares his therapy dog, whose ability to sense tension and distress in his body offers him comfort. In another particularly dramatic moment, he watches his daughter handle a hive of bees without any protective gear after the beekeeper told her that she had earned their trust. One wonders if a safety net that included all of these relationships — with other veterans, horses, dogs, and even bees and beekeepers — might have helped this veteran change the distorted meanings created in his mind by the trauma of war. Perhaps such a mosaic of experiences would have enabled him to adjust to civilian life and rejoin society. Instead, he sees a life alone in the forest as his only option.

While this film is fiction, it is based on a true story, and many real-life creative opportunities for healing war trauma exist. All of them share in common an abundance of messiness of interaction and opportunity for repair, for building a sense of safety in relationships. In a particularly striking real-world example, veterans have found healing in relationships with neglected, abused, or abandoned parrots, many of whom have lived most of their lives alone in tiny cages. At Serenity Park, a bird sanctuary outside Los Angeles, the parrots live in an environment designed to duplicate their life in the wild. Lilly Love, a veteran with severe PTSD for whom conventional treatments had been unsuccessful, described her experience at Serenity Park in a *New York Times* article about this unusual healing relationship: "These forgotten great beams of light that have been pushed aside and marginalized. I see the trauma, the mutual trauma that I suffered and that these birds have suffered, and my heart just wants to go out and nurture and feed and take care of them, and doing that helps me deal with my trauma. All without words."

Distorted meanings children make in their early years are carried forward into the experience of trauma as adults, creating a tangled web. A recent study showed that female war veterans struggling with the physical pain of fibromyalgia frequently had histories of both military sexual trauma and childhood trauma. Women veterans with the highest rates of sexual trauma in the military also had the highest rates of childhood neglect and abuse. Sadly, they may have been seeking what they thought of as the safety offered by the organization of military life. This study offers an example of distorted meanings from childhood carried forward. The meanings that have origins in childhood are further distorted by trauma of combat and sexual assault during wartime. These meanings are then held in the body in postcombat life in the form of chronic pain syndromes.

An adult's response to trauma in any form is embedded in the early experience of adversity. Trauma reverberates in a continuum of experience across development. Whether due to the trauma of war, years of troubled relationships, or both, when you make meaning of the world as unsafe, of people as untrustworthy, of yourself as ineffective and powerless, any short-term treatment, while perhaps helpful in the moment, will understandably fail to change these meanings. Without a dramatic shift in patterns of interactions, new relationships continue to be distorted, providing fresh opportunity for trauma. Put more bluntly, it is not simply what happened when we were young that screws us up now. Along the way to growing up and into our adult lives, we continue to create new ways of being screwed up. Only when we have accumulated a whole new set of interactions, when we work through the inevitable moments of disconnection to again find connection, will we grow and change.

PSYCHOTHERAPY AS CONTROLLED DISCONNECTION

Psychotherapy can be understood as an opportunity to create new meanings. Research has shown that the value in a multitude of different forms of psychotherapy lies in the relationship between client and therapist. Central to all of these forms of therapy is the messiness of moment-to-moment interactions in a setting that offers a chance to engage in and struggle with multiple levels of meaning that make up the relational experience of the psychotherapy itself.

As we discussed in the preceding chapter, one founding principle of psychoanalysis is the concept of transference. Intense feelings from past relationships are brought to this new relationship with opportunity for reflection. If your early life was characterized by prolonged experience of a still-face without opportunity for repair, the moments of disconnection that occur within the therapeutic relationship are not only inevitable but necessary for healing.

In your relationships outside of psychotherapy, you might react to a still-face by shutting down, or dissociating, reactions that are typically out of awareness, or unconscious. But the safe setting of talk therapy helps to bring these reactions into awareness. In a moment of disconnect, you can process the experience. A therapist looks at her watch just as you share an important thought while in a heightened state of emotional distress. With the therapist, you can examine how the unexpected disconnection affects your body and mind in the moment. When you link these experiences with words, they lose their power.

Drawing on the polyvagal theory we described in chapter 3, if lack of opportunity for repair has left you experiencing your social world as threatening, your primitive vagal system has likely been overactive for years as a form of protection. The body says the world is dangerous, and this interpretation becomes a way of being in all situations. In a therapeutic setting, the quiet of the room, the reliability of the time, and even the rhythm, or prosody, of the therapist's voice allow the smart vagus to come online. With your social engagement system available, you can feel safe to navigate the normal messiness of human interaction in relationship with your therapist. The energy for growth that comes when you work through these "mistakes" can then help you engage in a multitude of other new relationships with new opportunities for repair.

Winnicott beautifully captured the notion that health lies in grappling with the messy experiences life naturally presents. He wrote: "We all hope that our patients will finish with us and forget us, and they will find living itself to be the therapy that makes sense." Psychotherapy is one circumscribed intervention that provides a new set of interactions in which to create new meanings, different from the problematic ones that lived in your body. These, in turn, carry forward into your new experiences and relationships.

HEALING IN NEW RELATIONSHIPS

New relationships form the essence of creative engagement as a path to healing. While first relationships provide the core ingredients, they are not permanently "baked into the cake." New ingredients in the form of new relationships allow for continued growth and creativity with complex elaboration of your sense of self.

Anil had struggled with feelings of depression for most of his adult life. His parents had been successful engineers in Iraq, but, experiencing a precarious sense of safety in their war-torn homeland, they had immigrated to the United States. Here, they owned a grocery store. Anil held all their hopes; they expected him to become an engineer and live their unfulfilled American dream. Anil had complied with their fantasy of his life in America. By all external measures, his life was a success. Only his wife, Lana, knew the deep unhappiness that plagued him.

Anil felt that in his childhood, his parents had not engaged with him or with each other when difficult moments arose. Years of lack of safety had left them with an understandable need to avoid uncertainty. When the time came for him to choose a career, Anil had followed his parents' path and become an engineer. His motivation had not been desire but a fear of indecision and a fear of disappointing his family. Exploring a different career path did not feel like an option when he was younger. Decades later, although he earned a good living for his family, his job felt deadening and he struggled with what was diagnosed as depression.

At the age of forty-five, with Lana's encouragement, Anil plunged into that disorganizing place of uncertainty. His true passion had always been composing musical scores. While he had played around with the craft, writing compositions to accompany their daughter's dance performances, he'd longed for an expanse of time to immerse himself in the process. He wrestled with the idea of letting go of his professional identity as an engineer. Unlike his parents, Lana stayed with him through the struggle rather than avoiding it. With her job as a health-care administrator, they could manage financially. Finally, he decided he would leave engineering and devote his life to composing.

Anil's relationship with Lana gave him the ability to handle the messiness of discovering himself anew, of embracing a more complex and coherent sense of himself. Over their years of marriage, they moved through many trials together. As two individuals who each brought a different way of seeing themselves and the world around them, they had countless experiences of working things out together. These experiences strengthened Anil's sense of agency and his confidence in his ability to make choices and discover his own meaning. While lack of mismatch and repair in Anil's childhood had led him to resist this type of exploration and anxiously cling to rigid expectation, his relationship with Lana helped him to find his way out of despair in middle age to hopeful creativity. Recognizing that success can take many forms, Lana, unlike Anil's parents, was able to tolerate the uncertainty of the new path he chose.

While early relationships shape us, throughout our lives we can change, creating new meanings in new relationships. If we carry meanings of anxiety, fear, and hopelessness from our childhoods into new adverse experiences we encounter throughout our lives, interactions in new relationships with space for mismatch and repair offer the path to healing.

The still-face research teaches us that therapy is not a one- or even two-dimensional solution. We need to let go of an expectation that the path to growth and healing will be smooth. Rather, the very rockiness, the unevenness of new roads we build going forward, leads us to a new view of ourselves and of the world. And not only psychotherapy but more everyday activities such as joining a martial arts studio, walking in nature with a friend, cooking for others, or taking a photography class are all ways of healing the mind and body by opening ourselves up to a mess of possibilities for connection and belonging.

10

FINDING HOPE IN UNCERTAINTY

IN OUR OPENING CHAPTERS we drew on the work of Stephen Hawking to demonstrate the role of error in the creation of life itself. In a brilliant essay entitled "The Dangers of Certainty," philosophy professor Simon Critchley offers a similar idea. Critchley describes Heisenberg's uncertainty principle, which states that the more precisely the position of a particle is determined, the less precisely its momentum can be known, and vice versa. The uncertainty principle demonstrates the limits of absolute knowledge in our physical world. Applying the uncertainty principle to the social world, Critchley writes: "We encounter other people across a gray area of negotiation and approximation. Such is the business of listening and the back and forth of conversation and social interaction."

Tolerating uncertainty in the gray area across which people communicate makes room for error. Without error, nothing changes and nothing new can be created. Tolerating uncertainty is not easy. It disrupts and unsettles all of us. Uncertainty may lead you to retreat to rigid thinking. But the fantasy of a neat and simple solution can limit growth and produce a deadening effect. And the opposite is also true: When you acknowledge what you don't know, plunging into and muddling through the limitless uncertainty, then you have the opportunity to discover creative solutions to complex problems. Staying with the unpredictability allows you to heal and grow.

Certainty may hamper your relationships if you transfer meaning from interactions in prior relationships. You struggle to connect when you bring feelings about other relationships into a place where they don't belong. If your early relationships did not have tolerance for typical misunderstandings and misinterpretations, you may react to your partner with certainty that you know what is right.

THE TYRANNY OF CERTAINTY

Certainty leads us away from growth and healing; worse, it can lead us to potentially dangerous and harmful places. Certainty and authoritarianism often go hand in hand. Tara Westover in *Educated*, a memoir about her troubled upbringing as a daughter of survivalists in the mountains of Idaho, tells a story of growing up in an environment characterized by authoritarian certainty. In one revealing example, her mother sustains a serious head injury in an early-morning car accident after her father insisted the family make a twelve-hour drive overnight. But because of her father's certainty about the evils of hospitals, he kept her at home instead of seeking medical attention. She remained in their dark basement for weeks, unable to tolerate light, and the long-term impact came in the form of chronic debilitating headaches, impaired memory, and inability to resume her work as a midwife. While neither of us knows the author personally, we wonder if the creative process of writing her memoir played a role in helping her leave behind the tyrannous certainty that characterized the circumstances in which she was raised.

In relationships that have gotten off course, we see individuals with a striking lack of curiosity. One or both partners communicate an absolute certitude. Leaving no room for doubt, they may be extraordinarily certain that they know, understand, and can speak for the experience of others without further discussion or question.

Nadia lived in an apartment five floors below her sister Olga's. They were close growing up as the family survived the pogroms of Russia in the late 1800s and immigrated to the United States. But when their brother Endre died, a fight over his belongings led to a rift between the sisters that remained unrepaired, with each one certain the other was wrong, until they both died in their nineties. Their children took sides and the whole family remained stuck in conflict in an effort to hold on to their entrenched positions.

Milton and his sister Delia seemed headed down a similar path. Locked in rage embedded in misunderstandings around the family business, they hardly spoke for many years. The discord remained unrepaired until Milton's young-adult son sought help for debilitating anxiety. The lessons he learned set in motion a cascade of events that proved healing for the whole family. In his own therapy he learned to pause and breathe when he felt overwhelmed with fear. He introduced this technique to his father, who applied it when his anger at Delia threatened to shut down his thinking. This shift created just enough open space that he could recognize that his sister had a different perspective; she wasn't necessarily right, but he understood that she had her own reasons for the views she held. This shift in his thinking was sufficient to allow him to approach his sister and begin to break down the wall between them. They started to play tennis, an activity they had enjoyed together as children. There were many errors as well as some great plays that felt just right. Through the hours of rhythmic back-and-forth, conveniently also an outlet for their aggression as they hit the ball with resounding thwacks, they started to again enjoy each other's company. The rift began to heal.

OPENING SPACE FOR UNCERTAINTY

As these two family stories show, people get stuck when they don't leave open space for mess and uncertainty. Brazelton demonstrated the value of uncertainty when one of the fellows he worked with told him about his encounters with the family of a newborn infant on two home visits. In the first visit, the home felt calm and organized. Impressive in their togetherness, the parents and baby appeared well groomed in neatly coordinated clothes. When he happily reported his findings, Dr. Brazelton was quiet and did not seem to share his colleague's joy. A week later, at the second visit, things had come apart. Mom was a mess. Dad looked like he had not slept for months. While the fellow was worried, when he recounted the story, Dr. Brazelton seemed relieved about the change. He said, "They have made space for the baby."

The literal mess reflected the inevitably messy and uncertain process of raising a human being. Uncertainty plays a critical role in the development of one's sense of self from the earliest months of life. As we've seen, after the stage of what Winnicott called primary maternal preoccupation, when the mother anticipates the helpless infant's every need, there comes an essential time when she cannot and should not do so. As a child gains increased competence and begins to develop into their own separate person, the mother will naturally be unsure of what her child needs. The good-enough mother is not perfect, and these very imperfections give her children space to grow into themselves.

The concepts of certainty and uncertainty have broad implications for how we raise our children. Authoritarian parenting, as in "my way or the highway," may be linked to difficulty with emotional regulation in children. Authoritative parenting, in contrast, is associated with children having a greater capacity for emotional regulation, flexible thinking, and social competence. An authoritative parenting stance encompasses respect for and curiosity about a child, together with containment of intense feelings and limits on behavior.

Parental authority is something that, in ideal circumstances, comes naturally with the job. It is not something that needs to be learned in books from experts. So what might cause parents to lose their natural authority? Stress is far and away the most common culprit. That stress might in part come from the child, if, for example, the child is a particularly "fussy" or dysregulated baby. It might come from the everyday challenges of managing a family and work in today's fast-paced culture, which parents often do without the support of extended family. It may come from more complex relational issues between parents, between siblings, between generations.

When infant-parent mental health therapists work with families of young children, they aim to help parents reconnect with their natural authority. By offering parents space and time to tell their story and by addressing the wide range of stresses in their lives, they help parents make sense of, or find meaning in, their children's behavior.

Parents often go to a pediatrician or other identified expert with an expectation of advice and judgment. Infant-parent mental health specialist Kaitlin Mulcahey, a former fellow in the Infant-Parent Mental Health Program who is now at Montclair State University, recently gave a talk to professionals who work with young children and parents in which she acknowledged the pressure for advice coming from both sides: parents come with an expectation of answers, and professionals come with the well-intentioned wish to help. Dr. Mulcahey described a simple technique she uses. When asked by a parent what to do about any given situation, she pauses and takes a slow, deep breath. She finds that into that small open space, a parent's own observations and creative solutions emerge. A parent might say of her fussy infant, "I noticed that she feels more relaxed when I hold her on my shoulder," or "I wonder if playing music will help her to feel more settled." The breath you take, whether as a professional, parent, lover, colleague, or friend, helps ease the anxiety that can come with the open-endedness of "just listening."

Some guidance about what to do may naturally enter into the conversation. But premature advice without full appreciation of the complexity of the situation can often lead to frustration and failure. In contrast, when a parent has that aha! moment of insight, the joy and pleasure that come from recognition and reconnection for both parent and child can be exhilarating.

Similarly, when people allow and work through moments of discord throughout their lives, they experience the surge of growth-promoting energy. That kind of joy may happen when a mother finally succeeds at putting her struggling infant to her breast to nurse, when parent and toddler effectively navigate an explosive tantrum, when sisters survive years of dramatic disruptions to be each other's maid of honor, when friends, spouses, and colleagues work through discord to reach new levels of intimacy. As we saw in chapter 4, your sense of self and your capacity for intimacy are two sides of the same coin. When the most intimate relationships offer space for uncertainty, with each repair, partners reach new levels of complexity and coherence and have greater tolerance for the new uncertainties that inevitably arise.

UNCERTAINTY FOSTERS EMPATHY AND HOPE

"I know how you feel" is a common well-intentioned yet sometimes jarring expression of sympathy. It stands in contrast to empathy, a kind of not-knowing. In her collection of essays *The Empathy Exams*, Leslie Jamison captures the quality of uncertainty in empathy. She writes: "Empathy requires inquiry as much as imagination. Empathy requires knowing you know nothing. Empathy means acknowledging a horizon of context that extends perpetually beyond what you can see." When we aim to imagine our way into other people's experiences while acknowledging we can't really know, we can join them.

How do you learn to listen in a way that is open to uncertainty? The core capacity to listen with curiosity, to tolerate uncertainty, comes from one's earliest experiences of being listened to. In rounds with Dr. Brazelton so many years ago, colleagues found his profound empathy for the newborn baby striking. He could observe and listen. He understood that this new person was someone he would get to know. He knew the baby had something to tell him, and he recognized he did not yet know what that was.

A new romance between two adults shares qualities with the falling in love between parent and newborn child. Winnicott's notion of primary maternal preoccupation could easily be used to describe how when adults fall in love, all-consuming passion fills their minds and lives completely, often to the exclusion of all other concerns. But as it is with mother and infant, that stage of pure devotion is inevitably temporary; real life quickly inserts itself.

Malik was going through a rough patch when he met Taylor. Living by himself in a city with which he was unfamiliar, he felt isolated and lonely. Instant attraction led to a honeymoon period of pure bliss, but as the two became closer, inevitable misunderstandings arose. Malik had virtually no experience moving through conflict. His father, himself raised by an abusive alcoholic father, was emotionally remote and disengaged. When Malik and Taylor stumbled in a moment of discord about where to spend the Thanksgiving holiday, Malik's instinct was to flee. But Taylor, as calm and centered as Malik was intense and explosive, encouraged him to stick it out. At first Malik interpreted Taylor's wish to be with her family as judgment about his own family. But Taylor had a completely different motivation: she was worried about her aging parents and felt pressure to spend time with them. When they listened and acknowledged each other's intentions, they were able to come to an understanding.

After this experience of working through mismatch to repair,

Malik learned to pause and breathe, to tolerate moments when Taylor didn't quite get what he was feeling. Together they moved through moments of uncertainty to a profound sense of connection and shared meaning. Their love for each other deepened and grew.

In his poignantly beautiful book *When Breath Becomes Air,* neurosurgeon Paul Kalanithi, who left his memoir unfinished when he died at age thirty-seven of metastatic lung cancer, wrote, "The word *hope* first appeared in English about a thousand years ago, denoting some combination of confidence and desire." This definition of *hope* applies as well in the context of relationships. *Confidence* reflects the experience of moving through mismatch to repair again and again, a process from which a sense emerges that the relationship will hold, a knowing that *We will get through this. Desire* adds the layer of intimacy and trust.

One could say that in his relationship with Taylor, Malik discovered hope. Unlike his early experiences, characterized by fear of any turbulence, in this new relationship, he saw that when people misunderstand each other, all is not lost. In fact, misunderstandings are necessary to access the repair that provides energy for growth and change. When two people move from misunderstanding to understanding, they connect with each other.

When you feel hopeless, lacking in experience of repair, clinging to certainty gets in the way of listening and leads to a downward spiral of rigidity and hopelessness. In contrast, when you experience the joy of moving through mismatch to repair, in a kind of positive feedback loop, your sense of hope opens you up to listen to others with curiosity, leading to further connection and growth. A core sense of hope, growing in relationships with space for mismatch and repair, gives people the courage to let go of certainty. When they have hope, they can open themselves to empathy and truly listen to each other. Then, together, they can come up with creative solutions to problems both large and small.

BUILDING NEW ROADS

At a recent presentation, a young woman asked an interesting question. After explaining that she had been raised by a seriously mentally ill mother and an emotionally absent father and thus had experienced years of unrepaired mismatch, she wondered, "Do I need to go back and repair those problems or can I start building new meanings from here?" The image came to mind of looking back on a path of cracks, potholes, and even closed roads. One could sense in this young woman pressure to address things from the past that she might not want to or even be able to bring to mind in her conscious thoughts.

The answer to the young woman's question is itself messy. New roads going forward will have their own cracks and potholes. For anyone to heal from adverse childhood experiences, repair must be now, ongoing in the present. The healing that you gain from immersion in new relationships gives you different meanings about yourself. These new meanings in turn inform the way you integrate your early life experiences into a new, more coherent sense of yourself in the world. Rather than holding on to fixed meanings of anger and hurt, you can make sense of those experiences in different ways. New meanings that you give to your troubled early life experiences open you to further healing through deeper and more messy connections in your current life.

Our decades of research with the still-face paradigm and our clinical practice have taught us that engagement in the world, being open to the messiness, offers endless new opportunity for repair — for building a new network of roads. Healing troubled old relationships becomes possible when people are given the opportunity to create new meanings in new relationships. If they did not have many of these reparatory opportunities in their earliest relationships, whether due to a prolonged period from mismatch to repair, multiple experiences of unrepaired mismatch, or paucity of mismatch, the possibility of creating new ways of being in the world, to make meaning anew, is always there.

Our culture, replete with advice, quick fixes, and simple answers to complex questions, places little value on tolerating uncertainty, on moving through disruption to repair, on the path to creativity. If you resist the disorganization that typically accompanies a developmental leap, you may become rigid and fearful. Holding on to certainty for dear life, afraid to make the leap, you miss out on opportunities for growth. The current epidemic of anxiety and depression, especially in young adults, may be due in part to an unrealistic expectation that struggle should be avoided at all costs. Many of us suffer from the illusion that neat and predictable is better. But resisting the inevitable disruption makes people unable to change and progress, to find something new.

Simple answers to complex problems may offer the comfort

of certainty up front. But in the long run, they prevent you from growing in healthy ways. Instead of remaining stuck in hopelessness, you can become unstuck by immersing yourself in movement through mismatch to repair. If you listen to others with curiosity — not always knowing the answer and not always getting it right — you can connect and rediscover hope.

11

THROUGH DISCORD TO
CONNECTION AND BELONGING

As HE WAS SPEAKING on the topic of Listening with Curiosity at a conference of educators, Anthony noticed a small child fidgeting in the lap of a woman in one of the front-row seats. Apparently this audience member had had babysitter troubles and needed to bring her young daughter along. When, to his surprise, he saw the child's tiny hand go up in the question-and-answer period, he took the opportunity to model the subject of the talk. In response to the little girl's question — "Can I have some more crayons?" — he paused, considered his options, then answered with a question of his own: "How many crayons do you have now?" Delighted to be included in the adult conversation, the girl spread her arms wide and exclaimed joyfully, "So many!" She returned to her coloring, apparently less interested in the answer to her question than in being permitted to join in the event and hearing the speaker's interest in her perspective.

To others in the audience, this three-year-old's question might have just seemed silly, a question that the lecturer could not possibly answer. Wasn't that up to her mother? How could he have crayons when he was up there giving a professional presentation to adults? But rather than responding dismissively or feeling pressure to come up with an answer, Anthony introduced a playful way of not knowing. He was curious not only about the little girl's perspective but also about her motivation in asking the question at all. Did she really want more crayons or did she just want to be included? When he matched her intention, her show of delight energized the whole audience, and they reacted with appreciative claps and laughter. Many remembered this moment better than anything he said in the talk as a lesson they might incorporate into their own work.

Dr. Brazelton's way of relating to newborns on rounds all those years ago, taking time with parents to listen to their baby's earliest communications, can point the way for introducing playful uncertainty into our everyday interactions. He recognized that parents and newborns do not automatically know each other's intentions. Dr. Brazelton created space for exploring the baby's intentions or, in our words, the meaning of the baby's behavior. Inspired by those rounds, we have seen again and again that creating a playful space when we do not know each other's intentions but move through countless misreadings and misinterpretations until we arrive at a place of mutual understanding forms the building blocks of healthy, strong relationships.

When you bump up against certainty in your partner, it creates an experience of not being seen, not unlike the baby who encounters the mother's inexplicably still face. In the experiment, the experience is fleeting. In actual social interactions, a stance of certainty cuts off the messy process of mismatch and repair. When you are stuck in a problematic interaction, you need to pause and take time to notice the other person's underlying intentions and motivations. Is your partner tired from a long, stressful day at work? Worrying about a sick friend? Is there some way in which your partner's perspective, although different from yours, may be right? Equally important is to consider your own intentions. Why are you insisting on a particular viewpoint? What meaning does the issue have for you beyond the immediate interaction? What meanings do you carry from other relationships in other times?

It may be that, both in your personal relationships and in your larger social world, you have lost the ability to play. When you invite play into your interactions, with the inherent uncertainty of not knowing the other person's perspective, you begin to truly see the other person. Many people in our world today feel unseen and unheard. If we can embrace the uncertainty of getting to know one another, from birth through old age, we can build a society where all of us feel recognized and feel like we belong.

LISTENING FROM BIRTH

A newborn's brain makes as many as one million connections per second as they learn to adapt to the outside world. In the earliest moment-to-moment interactions between parent and child, the baby's nascent sense of self, alongside the parents' new identities, begins to take shape. Relationships are formed and transformed. The normal disorganization in the first days after the birth of a baby, along with hormonal changes and the typical but largely unspoken feelings of terror, creates a particularly open space for change.

Brazelton's approach to being with a parent and a newborn is seen in the Newborn Behavioral Observations (NBO) system and in the clinical use of the NICU Network Neurobehavioral Scale (NNNS). Both use Brazelton's red ball, small rattle, and flashlight as tools for getting babies to tell their stories. Brazelton's approach and his tools offer a way to support parents' earliest efforts to get to know their infant. When we can protect time to listen to parent and baby together, we convey the idea that, in contrast to there being a "right way," they will figure things out together. The observations reveal how babies come into the world with their own ideas about what is right for them. When parent and child muddle through, they almost always come up with a better solution than the one an expert might impose.

For example, when researchers and clinicians use the tools to observe sleeping babies, they find that some shut out the rattle after one or two shakes, protecting their sleep, while others startle with every shake of the rattle, even after ten repetitions. These infants communicate their intense response to the world around them. Parents who are already sleep-deprived might slide into depression if they think that the easily disrupted sleep is their "fault." Observing the baby's behavior offers time and space to reinterpret the meaning. The baby's intention is not to say *You are a bad mother* but rather *I prefer a quiet space*. These new meanings may help parents to repair the mismatch. A soft voice, dim lights, and gentle music may calm the baby sufficiently to ease the sleep disruption. This repair in turn increases parents' confidence, energizing them to make the effort to support an easily unsettled baby. And so it goes, moment by moment, on the path to a strong relationship.

When nurses, doctors, and other practitioners make time to listen with parents to a newborn baby's communications, they are offering an opportunity for a new mother or father to express difficult feelings that might be in the way of seeing a child's true self. In the twenty minutes we spent with Mikayla in the hospital getting to know her newborn, Aaron, she shared her worry that her baby would be a "stranger." Haunted by the cultural image of perfect bonding at the moment of birth, she was fortunately able to express her fears. With these scary thoughts out in the open, they held less of a grip, giving her space to see what her baby was like. When we asked her what she had noticed about Aaron, she surprised herself by telling us, "He likes to be held up against my shoulder and he prefers to move around when he's lying down. He doesn't seem to like to be swaddled." Already she knew so much about her baby! When we saw Aaron and Mikayla in a visit a few weeks later, tears filled her eyes and her voice cracked as she said, "I can say to him 'I love you' and I know I really mean it."

Ambivalent feelings like those expressed by Mikayla are not uncommon in new parents. But when parents do not feel permitted to express them, the effect can be a downward spiral of missed cues and disconnection as they struggle with feelings of self-doubt and guilt. When these dark but normal feelings must be hidden because of shaming cultural prohibitions, they can exert their impact over time with distorted meaning-making in ongoing interactions.

If the meanings we make of ourselves in the world have their origins in our earliest relationships, it follows that to build healthy societies, we would do well to invest in relationships right from the start.

RIGHT FROM THE START

A community located as far west from the central hub of Boston as one can go and still be in Massachusetts has found creative ways to bring the idea of protecting open space for uncertainty to the community as a whole. In an initiative we have developed, funded by a variety of local organizations, a wide range of professionals who work with parents and infants learn to draw on Dr. Brazelton's observations of play to spotlight the tremendous capacity for connection babies have when they enter the world, each with their unique way of communicating. The program highlights the need to support mothers and fathers, enlisting their natural expertise during this major and often disorganizing transition to parenthood.

A meeting we held with maternity-unit nurses on a stormy November evening in 2016 at Fairview, a local hospital in rural South Berkshire County, marked the beginning of what would come to be known as the Hello It's Me Project. The project brings maternity nurses together with other practitioners who work with parents and infants in the early months of life.

All ten nurses who attend to the approximately two hundred deliveries per year squeezed into the small patient lounge. They eagerly shared their feelings of helplessness when they saw families who were clearly struggling, since the nurses had no choice but to send them home "on a wing and a prayer." They listened with rapt attention to the presentation and seemed intrigued by the idea of learning new ways to support parents and newborns.

On a spring weekend about six months later, when the weather shifted dramatically in the span of two days from snow to warm sunshine, these same nurses joined pediatricians, family medicine doctors, nurse-practitioners, early-intervention specialists, childcare providers, lactation consultants, and a range of others for a two-day training course focused on using observations of newborn behavior to open up a space for curiosity and uncertainty. While the medical model of care often puts the professional in the role of expert, we wanted to shift that mindset and mobilize parents' unique capacity to tune in to and respond to their newborns.

The Hello It's Me Project now extends north to Pittsfield and surrounding communities. The largest city in Berkshire County, Pittsfield offers a study in contrasts. A rich cultural community and a wealth of natural beauty sit side by side with poverty, violence, and a growing crisis of opioid addiction. Berkshire Medical Center, the local hospital with over seven hundred deliveries per year, has seen a dramatic increase in families in crisis, with a 300 percent rise in newborns with opioid withdrawal. Families from the full spectrum of socioeconomic backgrounds have struggled with generations of mental illness, substance abuse, or other adverse childhood experiences.

At the original weekend training, Patty, one of the nurses who had worked on the same unit for decades, shared that she had seen troubled family relationships passed from one generation to the next. "Now," she said, "I feel hopeful that the next generation may have a different path."

PLANTING SEEDS OF HOPE

The meanings we make of ourselves in the world as hopeful and capable of empathy or, in contrast, as hopeless, fearful, and closed off evolve in countless moment-to-moment interactions.

Clearly, the brief experience of a set of observations around the birth of a baby is not sufficient to change the life course of any child or family. It must be just the first of many of what our colleague Lou Sander termed *moments of meeting*.

Notice that Patty had used the word *hopeful* to describe her experience. In our first meeting in that hot, cramped lounge on the maternity unit, the mood had been decidedly hopeless. Fast-forward a year to another meeting, where the Fairview nurses excitedly discussed the presentation they would be giving at an upcoming national nursing conference. Far from feeling hopeless, they now had a structure for taking time to observe the baby together with her parents and other caregivers.

They described a mother, Bethany, who had been abandoned by the baby's father halfway through her pregnancy. In her grief and fears about single parenthood, she had not formed much connection to her developing baby. When he was born, she showed little interest in feeding him. Charlie was a quiet baby who was likely to fall asleep rather than scream to get his needs met. Their differences might have proved to be a mismatch with dire consequences. The nurses were alarmed by the real risk to this baby of failure to grow. They took time to show Bethany how Charlie turned a full ninety degrees to locate the sound of her voice. They shared their observation that she calmed his scattered movements simply by placing her hand on his chest. Upon recognizing with surprise and delight that "my baby knows me," Bethany began to set an alarm at night to wake herself to feed him.

Buoyed by the power of facilitating these moments of meeting, particularly with troubled and vulnerable families, the nurses brought renewed energy and hope to their work. In their presentation to their nursing colleagues at the national nursing conference, they captured the complex meaning of the process of uncertainty involved in taking time for open play. They saw mistakes as an inevitable and necessary part of caring for a new baby and described the intervention as *"a vehicle to empower parents and allow us to shift the focus from nurse to parents as the expert of their infant"* (italics theirs).

At another local conference we spoke at a year after the original training, the nurses on the Fairview maternity unit had an opportunity to watch the still-face video. When we visited the maternity unit several months after that, nurses told us how the still-face paradigm had brought about a second dramatic transformation in their work. They saw anew a baby's tremendous capacity for connection and the potential for devastation when that connection was lost.

Dr. Brazelton traveled to a number of war-torn countries in the course of teaching about his work, and when the things he saw threatened to overwhelm him, he would visit with a new mother and her baby. Taking time to listen to them, he would find renewed hope. Imagine whole communities of people touched, as this small group of nurses was, by the hopefulness of meaningful connection between parent and newborn. Moments of moving through mismatch to repair offered a micro-dose of hope that was meaningful not only for the babies and their parents but also for the individual nurses, the community of nurses, and the hospital as an organization. These meaningful interactions had the potential for far-reaching effects in the community. The protected time for nonjudgmental listening, for supporting movement from mismatch to repair, can serve as a kind of birthplace of hope and a seed from which to grow a healthy community.

Using Brazelton's approach with parents and newborns shouldn't be regarded as another simple solution to a complex problem. We see it as a model for embracing the uncertainty — the messiness — of all relationships. With the foundation of trust that develops as we move through mismatch to repair, we can find our way into others' experiences.

REDISCOVERING CONNECTION WITH THE STILL-FACE PARADIGM

In our society today, we see people tenaciously holding rigid positions with fear dominating their social interactions. Empathy dissipates. Forfeiting opportunities to work through difficult moments and experience repair together, they lose the source of energy that moves them forward.

A 2020 presidential candidate became embroiled in a controversy over a local food preference for combining salsa and ranch. An article on the subject revealed that "a whopping 43 percent of respondents said they had never tried the combination and never would." That's close to half of them clinging to certainty. The humor of the story may engage the smart vagus and help people connect. But the message is serious and sobering. A dangerous fear of difference pervades our world today. Yet the very messiness of a diverse society made up of varied races, ethnicities, genders, and sexual orientations lies at the core of our nation's strength. When we reach one another by listening, moving through the inevitable mismatch that such differences engender, the power of the repair gives us potential for greatness.

In his op-ed "How to Repair the National Marriage," *New York Times* columnist David Brooks sees the polarizing views gripping our society as analogous to a troubled marriage. He looks to a number of recent books about marriage in search of solutions to our current situation. His conclusion will by now ring familiar to readers of this book: "And as the saying goes, the only way to get out of this mess is to get into it."

Many of the almost seven hundred online comments on Brooks's article exemplify the trouble people are having listening to one another, which suggests that none of them are ready to apply his metaphor to the political situation. The divide between adults has become too vast. As an exercise, perhaps we need to picture one another as babies, some of whom were listened to and some of whom were not. The still-face video takes us inside the experience of parent and infant in a way that words cannot. Over and over, we hear people from many walks of life and from around the world describe how the still-face experiment changed their understanding of the nature of connection and disconnection. We get requests to use the video both for parents and for professionals in a wide variety of settings, including mental health clinics, childcare centers, and even law enforcement organizations.

At a time when people are increasingly disconnected, the still-face paradigm can help us rediscover connection. The mother and baby, each with her own set of meanings, intentions, and motivations, make the effort to move from mismatch to repair and discover new meanings together. In the process, their connection strengthens and deepens. We need to learn from them and do the same. When you do not share the same intentions, motivations, and meanings as the people you encounter in your life, then, rather than run the other way, you need to engage and find a way to repair, as the infant and mother do. Only then will we as a society grow.

The more widely the implications of the still-face paradigm are understood, the more they can enlighten the way we raise our children, navigate as a part of a couple, and relate to others in our personal, work, and civic lives. They transform our understanding of the nature of trauma and resilience and the process of healing in psychotherapy. The still-face paradigm informs social policy by highlighting the critical role of investing in infants and parents.

In an episode of the podcast *On Being*, host Krista Tippett spoke with historian Lyndsey Stonebridge about a "culture of forgiveness." Stonebridge explained, "A mature political community needs the capacity for forgiveness to accept that things go wrong. People make mistakes." Tippett expanded on that notion, saying, "It is allowing the complexity of reality in. And it's always messy."

Our sense of belonging grows not from holding on to an inflexible position but in engaging in the messiness of human interaction. When we listen to one another's stories with curiosity, not always having the right answer to a problem, we create communities of connection. As unique individuals, we will always have different motivations and intentions. When we engage in the messy process of figuring things out together, we grow and change together. We become better prepared for the inevitable next moment of disconnection and repair. For all relationships, parents with children, adult children with parents, spouses, siblings, friends, and colleagues, the message is this: Don't be afraid to disagree. Make mistakes. Stomp around. Allow the turbulence to happen. But figure out a way to repair and reconnect, to find your way through.

Making meaning anew requires patience, time, and fumbling around. We need to let ourselves be in the difficult moments when we don't quite know what's going on. That state can be unpleasant and sometimes even painful. The dynamic wonder of the human condition is that when we find release from anxious clinging to certainty, we can learn to trust one another and trust that when things go wrong, we will be able to repair the problem. Only then will we be able to move beyond polarizing conflict, become flexible in our thinking, and develop the ability to engage together in creatively building a healthier world.

ACKNOWLEDGMENTS

WRITING A BOOK TOGETHER is in and of itself an exercise in the messiness of relationships. Our smart, kind, and endlessly patient agent, Lisa Adams, held us both through the disorganizing process of transforming our separate bodies of work into a coherent whole. Shepherding the proposal through countless revisions, she led us to Little, Brown Spark, where our wonderful and ceaselessly supportive editor, Marisa Vigilante, provided an invaluable perspective in her reading of our work. Our freelance editor, Joan Benham, always understood exactly what we were trying to say and with her magnificent editing helped us translate our language into a clear and accessible form.

We are indebted to leaders in the field who have influenced us over the years. Bob Pyles and Jerry Fromm listened to us through countless moments of mismatch and repair. T. Berry Brazelton taught us to value disorganization, and Jerome Bruner taught us how to make meaning. Both still whisper in our ears. Our many colleagues, including Beatrice Beebe, Marjorie Beeghly,

ACKNOWLEDGMENTS

Jeff Cohn, Peter Fonagy, Andy Gianino, Bruce Perry, Stephen Porges, Lou Sander, Arietta Slade, Nancy Snidman, and Katherine Weinberg, each made significant contributions to our thinking.

Faculty of the University of Massachusetts Boston Infant-Parent Mental Health Certificate Program Dorothy Richardson, Marilyn Davillier, Alex Harrison, Silvia Juarez-Marazzo, and Kristie Brandt and all the Boston and Napa fellows over the past sixteen years inspire and support us with their fortitude, creativity, and friendship. Spending time in their presence never fails to energize us.

We are grateful to the many families we have encountered in our clinical work and research who generously welcomed us into their lives and became our greatest teachers.

And last but not least, we would like to thank our respective life partners, Marilyn and Joe, who offered wisdom, guidance, and endless good humor through all of our messiness. Both are masters of repair.

NOTES

INTRODUCTION: ORIGINS

4 **standardized diagnostic assessments for attention deficit hyperactivity disorder:** The practice used the Vanderbilt ADHD diagnostic ratings scales; see *Caring for Children with ADHD: A Resource Toolkit for Clinicians* (Itasca, IL: American Academy of Pediatrics, 2011).

5 **what Winnicott termed the *true self*:** D. W. Winnicott, *The Maturational Processes and the Facilitating Environment: Studies in the Theory of Emotional Development* (New York: International Universities Press, 1965), 140–52.

10 **my first book, *Keeping Your Child in Mind*:** Claudia M. Gold, *Keeping Your Child in Mind: Overcoming Defiance, Tantrums, and Other Everyday Behavior Problems by Seeing the World Through Your Child's Eyes* (Boston: Da Capo, 2011).

14 **When I looked at the program website:** See https://www.umb.edu/academics/cla/psychology/professional_development/infant-parent-mental-health.

16 **This scene comes from a videotape of a psychological experiment:** See https://www.youtube.com/watch?v=apzXGEbZht0.

17 **But all the emphasis was on the mother's behavior:** The majority of the research has been done with mothers, so while the work has implications

for all types of relationships, when describing the experiments, we generally use the word *mother.*

18 **I set up the first still-face experiment:** E. Tronick et al., "The Infant's Response to Entrapment Between Contradictory Messages in Face-to-Face Interaction," *Journal of the American Academy of Child Psychiatry* 17, no. 1 (1978).

19 **we asked pairs of adults:** E. Z. Tronick, "Why Is Connection with Others So Critical?," in *Emotional Development,* ed. J. Nadel and D. Muir (Oxford: Oxford University Press, 2005), 293–315.

20 **proclaimed that he planned to study love:** Harry Harlow, "The Nature of Love," *American Psychologist* 13 (1958): 673–85.

21 **He found that babies with fake mothers:** G. C. Ruppenthal et al., "A Ten-Year Perspective of Motherless Mother Monkey Behavior," *Journal of Abnormal Psychology* 85 (1976): 341–49.

22 **I designed a low-tech experiment:** W. Ball and E. Tronick, "Infant Responses to Impending Collision: Optical and Real," *Science* 171 (February 1971): 818–20.

22 **the process by which babies make sense of the world:** Jerome Bruner, *Acts of Meaning* (Cambridge, MA: Harvard University Press, 1990).

CHAPTER 1: REPAIR AS FOOD FOR THE SOUL

37 **Previous infant research had reflected the assumption:** J. Cohn and E. Tronick, "Mother-Infant Face-to-Face Interaction: The Sequence of Dyadic States at Three, Six, and Nine Months," *Developmental Psychology* 23 (1987): 68–77.

37 **In subsequent frame-by-frame analysis:** E. Tronick and A. Gianino, "Interactive Mismatch and Repair: Challenges to the Coping Infant," *Zero to Three* 6, no 3. (February 1986): 1–6.

38 **We drew on observations from typical interactions to get a clear picture:** F. E. Banella and E. Tronick, "Mutual Regulation and Unique Forms of Implicit Relational Knowing," in *Early Interaction and Developmental Psychopathology,* ed. G. Apter and E. Devouche (Cham, Switzerland: Springer, 2017).

40 **the term we borrowed from Jerome Bruner:** Jerome Bruner, *Acts of Meaning* (Cambridge, MA: Harvard University Press, 1990).

40 **When we performed the experiment with parent-infant dyads:** E. Tronick, *The Neurobehavioral and Social-Emotional Development*

of Infants and Children (New York: W. W. Norton, 2007), 274–92, 322–38.

42 **Louis Sander, psychoanalyst and pioneer of infant research:** Louis Sander, "Regulation of Exchange in the Infant Caretaker System: A Viewpoint on the Ontogeny of 'Structures,'" in *Communicative Structures and Psychic Structures*, ed. N. Freedman and S. Grand (Boston: Springer, 1977), 1–34; Louis Sander, "Thinking Differently: Principles of Process in Living Systems and the Specificity of Being Known," *Psychoanalytic Dialogues* 12 (2002): 11–42; https://doi.org/10.1080/10481881209348652.

42 **described what he called an *open space*:** Sander, "Thinking Differently," 38.

44 **the still-face experiment with fifty-two infants and their mothers:** A. Gianino and E. Tronick, "The Mutual Regulation Model: The Infant's Self and Interactive Regulation and Coping and Defensive Capacities," in *Stress and Coping*, ed. T. Field, P. McCabe, and N. Schneiderman (Hillsdale, NJ: Lawrence Erlbaum Associates, 1988), 47–68.

44 **We gained a new level of insight into the significance of our original findings:** C. Reck et al., "The Interactive Coordination of Currently Depressed Inpatient Mothers and Their Infants During the Postpartum Period," *Infant Mental Health Journal* 32, no. 5 (2011): 542–62; E. Tronick and M. Beeghly, "Infants' Meaning-Making and the Development of Mental Health Problems," *American Psychologist* 66, no. 2 (2011): 114–15.

47 **This shared experience is well captured by the phrase *moment of meeting*:** Sander, "Regulation of Exchange," 15.

47 **Open dynamic systems theory describes how all biological systems:** Tronick and Beeghly, "Infants' Meaning-Making," 107–19.

48 **In his book *A Brief History of Time*:** Stephen Hawking, *A Brief History of Time* (New York: Bantam, 1988), 124–25.

51 **a particular gene may lead to depression:** M. Potiriadis et al., "Serotonin Transporter Polymorphism (*5HTTLPR*), Severe Childhood Abuse, and Depressive Symptom Trajectories in Adulthood," *British Journal of Psychiatry Open* 1, no. 1 (September 2015): 104–9.

51 **Dutch Hunger Winter of 1944:** T. Roseboom et al., "Hungry in the Womb: What Are the Consequences? Lessons from the Dutch Famine," *Maturitas* 70, no. 2 (2011): 141–45; https://linkinghub.elsevier.com/retrieve/pii/S0378512211002337.

51 **One long-term follow-up study of men:** P. Ekamper et al., "Independent and Additive Association of Prenatal Famine Exposure and Intermediary

Life Conditions with Adult Mortality Between Age 18–63 Years," *Social Science and Medicine* 119 (2014): 232–39.

53 **Rachel Yehuda of the Icahn School of Medicine at Mount Sinai:** R. Yehuda et al., "Vulnerability to Posttraumatic Stress Disorder in Adult Offspring of Holocaust Survivors," *American Journal of Psychiatry* 155, no. 9 (September 1998): 1163–72.

56 **what Winnicott termed a *position of dependency*:** D. W. Winnicott, *The Maturational Processes and the Facilitating Environment: Studies in the Theory of Emotional Development* (New York: International Universities Press, 1965), 141.

57 **Eric's story of healing is confirmed by psychotherapy research:** J. D. Safran, J. C. Muran, and C. Eubanks-Carter, "Repairing Alliance Ruptures," *Psychotherapy* 48, no. 1 (2011): 80–87; http://dx.doi.org/10.1037/a0022140.

58 **Psychoanalyst Leston Havens:** Leston Havens, "The Best Kept Secret: How to Form an Effective Alliance," *Harvard Review of Psychiatry* 12, no. 1 (2004): 56–62.

59 **Meaning-making occurs across a continuum:** E. Tronick and B. D. Perry, "The Multiple Levels of Meaning Making: The First Principles of Changing Meanings in Development and Therapy," in *Handbook of Body Therapy and Somatic Psychology*, ed. G. Marlock et al. (Berkeley, CA: North Atlantic Books, 2015), 345–55.

61 **"Love and work are the cornerstones of our humanness":** Letter to Marie Bonaparte, quoted in Ernest Jones, *The Life and Work of Sigmund Freud*, vol. 2 (New York: Basic Books, 1955).

CHAPTER 2: AIMING FOR GOOD ENOUGH

63 **video from an experiment using the still-face paradigm:** M. Weinberg et al., "A Still-Face Paradigm for Young Children: 2½-Year-Olds' Reactions to Maternal Unavailability During the Still-Face," *Journal of Developmental Processes* 3, no. 1 (2008): 4–20.

66 **"What is the normal child like?":** D. W. Winnicott, *The Collected Works of D. W. Winnicott*, vol. 3, ed. L. Caldwell and H. Taylor Robinson (Oxford: Oxford University Press, 2017), 45.

68 **psychoanalyst Steven Cooper:** Steven H. Cooper, "An Elegant Mess: Reflections on the Research of Edward Z. Tronick," *Psychoanalytic Inquiry* 35, no. 4 (2015): 337–54; https://doi.org/10.1080/07351690.2015.1022477.

69 **"one of the basic rules of the universe"**: *Into the Universe with Stephen Hawking*, documentary, Discovery Channel, released April 25, 2010.

69 **This behavior is the result of an immature brain:** Kate Wong, "Why Humans Give Birth to Helpless Babies," *Observations* (blog), *Scientific American*, August 28, 2012; http://blogs.scientificamerican.com /observations/why-humans-give-birth-to-helpless-babies/.

70 **"ordinary devoted mother":** D. W. Winnicott, *Winnicott on the Child* (Cambridge, MA: Perseus, 2002), 12–18.

70 **the *good-enough mother*:** D. W. Winnicott, *Playing and Reality* (New York: Routledge Classics, 2005), 14.

71 **"Taken for granted here":** Ibid., 187.

71 **"I would rather be the child of a mother":** Winnicott, *Winnicott on the Child*, 102.

78 **his book *Touchpoints*:** T. B. Brazelton and J. Sparrow, *Touchpoints: Birth to Three*, 2nd ed. (Cambridge, MA: Da Capo, 2006), xx.

80 **Google search for the term *perfectionism*:** S. Sherry and M. Smith, "Young People Drowning in a Rising Tide of Perfectionism," Medical Xpress.com, February 6, 2019; https://medicalxpress.com/news/2019-02 -young-people-tide-perfectionism.html.

80 **Multidimensional Perfectionism Scale:** P. L. Hewitt et al., "The Multidimensional Perfectionism Scale: Reliability, Validity, and Psychometric Properties in Psychiatric Samples," *Psychological Assessment* 3, no. 3 (1991): 464–68; http://doi.org/10.1037/1040-3590.3.3.464.

80 **One study demonstrated a 33 percent increase:** T. Curran and P. Andrew, "Perfectionism Is Increasing over Time: A Meta-Analysis of Birth Cohort Differences from 1989 to 2016," *Psychological Bulletin*, December 28, 2017.

80 **The study's lead author told the *New York Times*:** Jane Adams, "More College Students Seem to Be Majoring in Perfection," *New York Times*, January 18, 2018; https://www.nytimes.com/2018/01/18/well/family /more-college-students-seem-to-be-majoring-in-perfectionism.html.

80 **Parenting expert Katie Hurley:** Katie Hurley, *No More Mean Girls: The Secret to Raising Strong, Confident, and Compassionate Girls* (New York: Penguin, 2018), 97.

80 **Developers of the perfectionism scale:** P. L. Hewitt and G. L. Flett, "Perfectionism in the Self and Social Contexts: Conceptualization, Assessment, and Association with Psychopathology," *Journal of Personality and Social Psychology* 60 (1991): 456–70; doi: 10.1037/0022-3514.60.3.45.

82 *holding environment*: D. W. Winnicott, *The Maturational Processes and the Facilitating Environment: Studies in the Theory of Emotional Development* (New York: International Universities Press, 1965), 49.

CHAPTER 3: FEELING SAFE TO MAKE A MESS

85 video of a six-month-old: E. Tronick and M. Beeghly, "Infants' Meaning-Making and the Development of Mental Health Problems," *American Psychologist* 66, no. 2 (2011): 109–10.

87 Stephen Porges, a neuroscientist: Stephen Porges, *The Polyvagal Theory: Neurophysiologic Foundations of Emotions, Attachment, Communication, and Self-Regulation* (New York: W. W. Norton, 2011).

89 "social engagement system emerges from a heart-face connection": Stephen Porges, *The Pocket Guide to the Polyvagal Theory* (New York: W. W. Norton, 2017), 147.

90 Research demonstrates that loneliness increases: J. House, K. Landis, and D. Umberson, "Social Relationships and Health," *Science* 241, no. 4865 (1988): 540–45.

93 article in the *Daily Telegraph*: Hannah Furness, "Prince Harry: I Sought Counselling After 20 Years of Not Thinking About the Death of My Mother, Diana, and Two Years of Total Chaos in My Life," *Daily Telegraph*, April 19, 2017; https://www.telegraph.co.uk/news/2017/04/16/prince-harry-sought-counselling-death-mother-led-two-years-total/.

94 "Heads Together": See https://www.headstogether.org.uk/.

95 Nancy Snidman and Jerome Kagan: J. Kagan et al., "The Preservation of Two Infant Temperaments into Adolescence," *Monographs for the Society for Research in Child Development* 72, no. 2 (2007): 1–75.

97 singing and playing a wind instrument: Porges, *The Polyvagal Theory*, 253.

99 Circle of Security: See https://www.circleofsecurityinternational.com/.

100 children's song "Baby Shark": A. J. Willingham, "Baby Shark Has Taken over the World. Here's Who's Responsible," CNN.com, January 15, 2019; https://www.cnn.com/2019/01/15/entertainment/baby-shark-pinkfong-song-trnd/index.html.

105 "Singing requires slow exhalation": Porges, *Pocket Guide to the Polyvagal Theory*, 25.

CHAPTER 4: STOPPING THE BLAME GAME

111 **Winnicott's writing on the capacity to be alone:** D. W. Winnicott, *The Maturational Processes and the Facilitating Environment: Studies in the Theory of Emotional Development* (New York: International Universities Press, 1965), 30–33.

112 **We observed variation when we analyzed videotapes:** M. K. Weinberg et al., "Gender Differences in Emotional Expressivity and Self-Regulation During Early Infancy," *Developmental Psychology* 35 (1999): 175–88.

113 **an adult still-face demonstration:** Sue Johnson and E. Tronick, "Love Sense: From Infant to Adult," DrSueJohnson.com, February 5, 2016; http://drsuejohnson.com/uncategorized/love-sense-from-infant-to-adult/.

118 **J. Ronald Lally:** J. Ronald Lally, "The Human Brain's Need for a 'Social Womb' During Infancy," For Our Babies Campaign, April 2014; https://forourbabies.org/wp-content/uploads/2014/04/The-Human-Brains-Need-for-a-Social-WombFINALApril2014.pdf.

119 **scene by a lake on a hot and sunny afternoon:** Claudia M. Gold, *Keeping Your Child in Mind: Overcoming Defiance, Tantrums, and Other Everyday Behavior Problems by Seeing the World Through Your Child's Eyes* (Boston: Da Capo, 2011), 58.

120 **co-creation of meaning:** E. Tronick, "Emotions and Emotional Communication in Infants," *American Psychologist* 44, no. 2 (1989): 113.

122 **divide mothers and babies into two groups:** E. Tronick, "An Acute Maternal Stress Paradigm" (manuscript in preparation).

124 **genes associated with behaviors of impulsivity:** M. Nikolas et al., "Gene × Environment Interactions for ADHD: Synergistic Effect of 5HTTLPR Genotype and Youth Appraisals of Inter-Parental Conflict," *Behavioral and Brain Functions* 6 (2010): 23; https://behavioraland brainfunctions.biomedcentral.com/articles/10.1186/1744-9081-6-23.

126 **Lynne Murray and Peter Cooper:** E. Netsi et al., "Association of Persistent and Severe Postnatal Depression with Child Outcomes," *JAMA Psychiatry* 75, no. 3 (2018): 247–53; doi: 10.1001/jamapsychiatry .2017.4363; L. Murray and P. Cooper, "The Role of Infant and Maternal Factors in Postpartum Depression, Mother-Infant Interactions, and Infant Outcome," in *Postpartum Depression and Child Development*, ed. Lynne Murray and Peter Cooper (New York: Guilford, 1997), 129–30.

128 **Pulitzer Prize–winning novel:** Richard Powers, *The Overstory* (New York: W. W. Norton, 2018).

128 **"How to Become a Plant Parent":** Daniela Cabrera, "How to Become a Plant Parent," *New York Times,* May 14, 2018; https://www.nytimes .com/2018/05/14/smarter-living/indoor-plant-garden.html.

CHAPTER 5: RESILIENCE RECONSIDERED

132 **We use the word *quotidian* or *everyday* resilience:** J. DiCorcia and E. Tronick, "Quotidian Resilience: Exploring Mechanisms That Drive Resilience from a Perspective of Everyday Stress and Coping," *Neuroscience and Biobehavioral Reviews* 35 (2011): 1593–1602.

133 **Psychoanalyst Erik Erikson:** E. Erikson, *Childhood and Society* (New York: W. W. Norton, 1993), 268–69.

134 **Researchers at the Center on the Developing Child:** J. Shonkoff and A. Garner, "The Lifelong Effects of Early Childhood Adversity and Toxic Stress," *Pediatrics* 129, no. 1 (2012): 232–46.

135 **Adverse Childhood Experiences (ACE) study:** Centers for Disease Control and Prevention, "Adverse Childhood Experiences (ACEs)," May 13, 2014; http://www.cdc.gov/violenceprevention/acestudy/.

139 **an episode of *60 Minutes*:** Oprah Winfrey, "Treating Childhood Trauma," *60 Minutes,* CBS, aired March 11, 2018; https://www.cbsnews .com/news/oprah-winfrey-treating-childhood-trauma/.

139 **Perry's model fits with the model we have developed:** B. Perry, "Applying Principles of Neurodevelopment to Clinical Work with Maltreated and Traumatized Children," in *Working with Traumatized Youth in Child Welfare,* ed. N. B. Webb (New York: Guilford, 2006), 46; B. Perry, "Examining Child Maltreatment Through a Neurodevelopmental Lens: Clinical Applications of the Neurosequential Model of Therapeutics," *Journal of Trauma and Loss* 14 (2009): 240–55.

141 **the lovely phrase *going on being*:** F. R. Rodman, ed., *The Spontaneous Gesture: Selected Letters of D. W. Winnicott* (Cambridge, MA: Harvard University Press, 1987), 17–19.

141 **Winnicott formulated the idea in terms of actual minutes:** D. W. Winnicott, *Playing and Reality* (New York: Routledge Classics, 2005), 131.

142 **We have observed in our lab that the longer the interval:** M. Muller et al., "What Dyadic Reparation Is Meant to Do: An Association with Infant Cortisol Reactivity," *Psychopathology* 48 (2015): 386–99.

142 Briefly elevated cortisol levels may help a person: B. S. McEwen, "Central Effects of Stress Hormones in Health and Disease: Understanding the Protective and Damaging Effects of Stress and Stress Mediators," *European Journal of Pharmacology* 583 (2008): 174–85; doi: 10.1016/j.ejphar.2007.11.071.

CHAPTER 6: GAMES WE PLAY: LEARNING TO BELONG

155 "It is in playing and only in playing": D. W. Winnicott, *Playing and Reality* (New York: Routledge Classics, 2005), 73.

157 we explored the role of games: F. E. Banella and E. Tronick, "Mutual Regulation and Unique Forms of Implicit Relational Knowing," in *Early Interaction and Developmental Psychopathology*, ed. G. Apter and E. Devouche (Cham, Switzerland: Springer, 2017).

159 southwestern Kenya: E. Tronick, *The Neurobehavioral and Social-Emotional Development of Infants and Children* (New York: W. W. Norton, 2007), 134–52; E. Tronick and M. Beeghly, "Infants' Meaning-Making and the Development of Mental Health Problems," *American Psychologist* 66, no. 2 (2011): 112–13.

161 conference on the science of representation: Duality's End: Computational Psychiatry and the Cognitive Science of Representation (Stockbridge, MA, September 2018); https://kripalu.org/presenters -programs/duality-s-end-computational-psychiatry-and-cognitive -science-representation.

163 Jerome Bruner used to tell a fable: Jerome Bruner, personal communication, 1971.

167 shortly before his death at the age of ninety-nine: T. Berry Brazelton, interview with Ellen Galinsky, 2010 Families and Work Institute's Work Life Legacy Award, Mind in the Making, https://www.facebook .com/Mindinthemaking/videos/fwi-2010-legacy-award-berry-brazelton /10156310019352958/.

167 Neonatal Behavioral Assessment Scale (NBAS): T. B. Brazelton and J. K. Nugent, *Neonatal Behavioral Assessment Scale*, 4th ed. (London: Mac Keith, 2011).

167 J. Kevin Nugent and colleagues: J. K. Nugent et al., *Understanding Newborn Behavior and Early Relationships: The Newborn Behavioral Observations (NBO) System Handbook* (Baltimore: Paul H. Brookes, 2007).

CHAPTER 7: TECHNOLOGY AND THE STILL-FACE PARADIGM

171 **the addictive nature of social media:** T. Haynes, "Dopamine, Smartphones, and You: A Battle for Your Time," *Science in the News* (blog), Harvard University Graduate School of Arts and Sciences, May 1, 2018; http://sitn.hms.harvard.edu/flash/2018/dopamine-smartphones-battle-time/.

171 *Reclaiming Conversation*: Sherry Turkle, *Reclaiming Conversation: The Power of Talk in a Digital Age* (New York: Penguin, 2015), 107–8.

174 *Le Monde* **published an article:** Hervé Morin, "L'exposition des jeunes enfants aux écrans est devenue un enjeu de santé publique majeur," *Le Monde*, May 31, 2017.

175 **cell phone use and Asperger's syndrome:** Turkle, *Reclaiming Conversation*, 108–9.

177 **cell phone use and stress, depression, and anxiety:** J. Elhai et al., "Problematic Smartphone Use: A Conceptual Overview and Systematic Review of Relations with Anxiety and Depression Psychopathology," *Journal of Affective Disorders* 207 (2017): 251–59.

177 **"When we're anxious":** Tracy Dennis-Tiwary, "Taking Away the Phones Won't Solve Our Teenagers' Problems," *New York Times*, July 14, 2018; https://www.nytimes.com/2018/07/14/opinion/sunday/smartphone-addiction-teenagers-stress.html.

178 **Vogel aims to untangle this question:** Erin Vogel et al., "Social Comparison, Social Media, and Self-Esteem," *Psychology of Popular Media Culture* 3, no. 4 (October 2014): 206–22.

179 **Psychoanalyst Danielle Knafo offers a case study:** Danielle Knafo and Rocco Lo Bosco, *The Age of Perversion: Desire and Technology in Psychoanalysis and Culture* (New York: Routledge), 62–80.

181 **high-end "fake babies":** Ibid., 121.

CHAPTER 8: WHEN MEANING GOES AWRY

185 **a post from a parenting blog:** R. Norman, "Avoiding the Trap of the Present but Absent Parent"; https://amotherfarfromhome.com/present-but-absent-parent/.

187 **"Madness here simply means a *break-up*":** D. W. Winnicott, *Playing and Reality* (New York: Routledge Classics, 2005), 131.

188 **Richard Friedman wondered**: Richard Friedman, "Suicide Rates Are Rising: What Should We Do About It?," *New York Times*, June 11, 2018; https://www.nytimes.com/2018/06/11/opinion/suicide-rates-increase-anthony-bourdain-kate-spade.html.

188 **"Suicide in the Age of Prozac"**: Robert Whitaker, "Suicide in the Age of Prozac," *Mad in America* (blog), August 6, 2018; https://www.madinamerica.com/2018/08/suicide-in-the-age-of-prozac/.

195 **"This process of *discovering the infant*"**: A. F. Lieberman, M. A. Diaz, and P. Van Horn, "Perinatal Child-Parent Psychotherapy: Adaptation of an Evidence-Based Treatment for Pregnant Women and Babies Exposed to Intimate Partner Violence," in *How Intimate Partner Violence Affects Children*, ed. S. A. Graham-Bermann and A. A. Levendosky (Washington, DC: American Psychological Association, 2011), 47–68.

195 **The negative impact on children's development**: E. Netsi et al., "Association of Persistent and Severe Postnatal Depression with Child Outcomes," *JAMA Psychiatry* 75, no. 3 (2018): 247–53; doi: 10.1001/jamapsychiatry.2017.4363.

196 **depressed mothers look away more**: M. K. Weinberg and E. Z. Tronick, "Emotional Characteristics of Infants Associated with Maternal Depression and Anxiety," *Pediatrics* 102 (1998): 1298–304.

197 **One classic study offers dramatic evidence**: René Spitz, "The Role of Ecological Factors in Emotional Development of Infancy," *Child Development* 20, no. 3 (1949): 149.

197 **when orphanages for young children**: Group homes and residential treatment centers for older children and adolescents still exist today.

198 **child psychiatrist Charles Zeanah**: C. Zeanah et al., "Institutional Rearing and Psychiatric Disorders in Romanian Preschool Children," *American Journal of Psychiatry* 166, no. 7 (2009): 777–85.

199 *Forbes* **tellingly titled "It's the Orphanages, Stupid!"**: Maia Szalavitz, "It's the Orphanages, Stupid!," *Forbes*, April 20, 2010, https://www.forbes.com/2010/04/20/russia-orphanage-adopt-children-opinions-columnists-medialand.html#71ef91fd21e6.

201 **Tiffany Field, a researcher at the University of Miami**: E. Tronick and M. Beeghly, "Infants' Meaning-Making and the Development of Mental Health Problems," *American Psychologist* 66, no. 2 (2011): 114.

201 **When research assistants in our lab played with the babies**: E. Tronick and T. Field, eds., *Maternal Depression and Infant Disturbance* (San Francisco: Jossey-Bass, 1987).

202 **In one particularly striking set of still-face experiments:** I. Mueller et al., "In a Heartbeat: Physiological and Behavioral Correlates of Event Memory at 4 Months," *Frontiers in Psychology* (under review).

204 **psychoanalyst Robert Furman:** Robert Furman, "Attention Deficit Hyperactivity Disorder: An Alternative Viewpoint," *Journal of Infant, Child, and Adolescent Psychotherapy* 2, no. 1 (2002).

207 **the 5-HTT gene:** A. Caspi et al., "Genetic Sensitivity to the Environment: The Case of the Serotonin Transporter Gene and Its Implications for Studying Complex Diseases and Traits," *American Journal of Psychiatry* 167, no. 5 (2010): 509–27.

207 **infants with the S-allele:** R. Montirosso et al., "Social Stress Regulation in 4-Month-Old Infants: Contribution of Maternal Social Engagement and Infants' 5-HTTLPR Genotype," *Early Human Development* 91, no. 3 (2015): 173–79.

208 **daily mindfulness practice:** R. Davidson and B. S. McEwen, "Social Influences on Neuroplasticity: Stress and Interventions to Promote Well-Being," *Nature Neuroscience* 15 (2012): 689–95.

208 **S version of the 5-HTT gene:** M. Nikolas et al., "Gene × Environment Interactions for ADHD: Synergistic Effect of 5HTTLPR Genotype and Youth Appraisals of Inter-Parental Conflict," *Behavioral and Brain Functions* 6 (2010): 23; https://behavioralandbrainfunctions .biomedcentral.com/articles/10.1186/1744-9081-6-23.

209 **evidence of brain changes with a variety of different types:** D. Linden, "How Psychotherapy Changes the Brain — the Contribution of Functional Neuroimaging," *Molecular Psychiatry* 11 (2006): 528–38.

CHAPTER 9: HEALING IN A MOSAIC OF MOMENTS OVER TIME

214 *The Body Keeps Score*: Bessel van der Kolk, *The Body Keeps Score: Brain, Mind, and Body in the Healing of Trauma* (New York: Viking, 2014).

214 **Shakespeare in the Courts:** Ibid., 342–44.

216 **Actor Stephan Wolfert:** See https://www.decruit.org/cry-havoc/.

219 **"These forgotten great beams of light":** Charles Siebert, "What Does a Parrot Know About PTSD?," *New York Times*, January 28, 2016; https://www.nytimes.com/2016/01/31/magazine/what-does-a-parrot -know-about-ptsd.html.

219 **A recent study showed that female war veterans:** Boston University School of Medicine, "Screening Women Veterans with Fibromyalgia for Childhood Abuse May Improve Treatment," *ScienceDaily*, August 8, 2018; www.sciencedaily.com/releases/2018/08/180808134211.htm.

220 **the value in a multitude of different forms:** A. Horvath, "The Therapeutic Relationship: From Transference to Alliance," *Journal of Clinical Psychology* 56, no. 2 (2000).

222 **"We all hope that our patients will finish with us":** D. W. Winnicott, *Playing and Reality* (New York: Routledge Classics, 2005).

CHAPTER 10: FINDING HOPE IN UNCERTAINTY

225 **In a brilliant essay entitled "The Dangers of Certainty":** Simon Critchley, "The Dangers of Certainty: A Lesson from Auschwitz," *New York Times*, February 12, 2014; https://opinionator.blogs.nytimes.com /2014/02/02/the-dangers-of-certainty/.

226 **Tara Westover in *Educated*:** Tara Westover, *Educated* (New York: Penguin, 2018).

231 ***The Empathy Exams*:** Leslie Jamison, *The Empathy Exams* (Minneapolis: Graywolf, 2014), 5.

233 ***When Breath Becomes Air*:** Paul Kalanithi, *When Breath Becomes Air* (New York: Random House, 2016), 133.

CHAPTER 11: THROUGH DISCORD TO CONNECTION AND BELONGING

242 **Hello It's Me Project:** See https://www.helloitsmeproject.org/.

245 **presentation to their nursing colleagues:** D. Lyle and J. Dallmeyer, "Using the Newborn Behavioral Observations (NBO) System to Promote Healthy Relationships Between Parents and Infants" (presentation, Association of Women's Health, Obstetric and Neonatal Nurses Conference, Atlanta, GA, 2019).

246 **"a whopping 43 percent of respondents":** T. Carman, "We Hear You, Pete Buttigieg. Salsa and Ranch Really Do Taste Great Together," *Washington Post*, August 2, 2019; https://www.washingtonpost.com /news/voraciously/wp/2019/08/02/we-hear-you-pete-buttigieg-salsa -and-ranch-really-do-taste-great-together/.

247 **"How to Repair the National Marriage"**: David Brooks, "How to Repair the National Marriage," *New York Times*, June 4, 2018; https://www.nytimes.com/2018/06/04/opinion/partisanship-tribalism-marriage-bipartisan-debate.html.

248 **podcast *On Being***: K. Tippett, "The Moral World in Dark Times: Hannah Arendt for Now," *On Being*, May 18, 2017; https://onbeing.org/programs/lyndsey-stonebridge-the-moral-world-in-dark-times-hannah-arendt-for-now-jun2018/.

INDEX

ADHD (attention deficit hyperactivity
    disorder)
  as adaptive behaviors, 204–6
  diagnostic assessments for, 4, 10,
    124, 206
  and 5-HTT gene, 208
Adverse Childhood Experiences
    (ACE) study, 135–36,
    185, 187
adversity, 130, 135–40, 143, 144, 182,
    191, 234
advice, culture of, 81, 82
agency
  development of, 65
  and games, 158–59
  and mismatch-repair process, 43, 45,
    65, 120
  and play, 155
  as power to act effectively in world,
    43, 65
  and sense of self, 66
Alive and Kicking (film), 108
anger
  acknowledgment of, 64, 72
  and disconnection, 4, 10
  fixed meanings of, 234
  and listening with curiosity, 9

  and parents' view of child's
    true self, 6
  and sense of self, 108
  and unrepaired mismatch, 109, 117
Anna Freud Centre, London, 9
annihilation, 196–97
anxiety
  and disconnection, 173–74
  and experience of mismatch, 40
  and gene expression, 51, 54–55
  and meaning, 45, 224
  perfectionism correlating with,
    80, 81
  and repair, 190
  and sense of self, 200–201
  and social media, 177–78
  and stress-related problems, 142
  and too-good mother, 73, 74
Asperger's syndrome, 175
Astaire, Fred, 36
attachments, 3, 9
attachment theory, 20–21
attention, 126–27, 155
authoritarian parenting, 229
authoritative parenting, 229
autism spectrum disorder, 95, 97, 104,
    105, 174–77

autonomic nervous system (ANS)
  and meaning-making, 42, 59, 86, 100
  and sense of safety, 86, 87, 89, 90, 92,
    98, 99, 100, 103, 105
  and stress response, 142

"Baby Shark" (song), 100
bad stress, 134–35, 143
behavior problems
  blaming parents for, 13–14
  finding meaning in, 7, 9,
    100–103, 109
  listening as technique for
    understanding, 6, 8, 10, 12–13
  management techniques for, 4
  and occupational therapists,
    124, 125
  role of relationships in, 13
  and trauma-informed care, 139, 140
belonging, sense of
  and games, 152, 154–59
  and messiness of interaction, 248
  and mismatch-repair process, 150
  and mistakes, 165
  and repeated patterns of
    interaction, 32
  and sense of self, 3
Berkshire Psychoanalytic Institute, 4–5,
    9, 14
"Bike Song, The" (song), 193
blame, 14, 124–25, 127, 129
Boston Change Process Study
    Group, 163
Boston Children's Hospital, 23, 167
boundaries, formation of, 68, 71
Bourdain, Anthony, 187–88
Bowlby, John, 21
brain
  development of, 69, 70, 139,
    208–9, 239
  effect of rapid alternating movements
    on, 67
  and games, 158, 161–64
  and interaction, 30
Brandt, Kristie, 14
Brazelton, T. Berry
  and Jerome Bruner, 22–23
  empathy of, 231–32

hopefulness of, 245
  on imperfection, 78–79
  on social competence of newborn
    babies, 17, 23–26, 167–68, 240,
    242, 246
  study of psychoanalysis, 23
  Touchpoints model of, 78–79
  on uncertainty, 228, 238
Brazelton Institute, Boston Children's
    Hospital, 167
breastfeeding, 45–47
breathing, 98, 125, 217, 227, 233
Brooks, David, 247
Bruner, Jerome, 22–23, 40, 42, 163

Catherine, Duchess of Cambridge, 94
Ceaușescu, Nicolae, 198–99
cell phone use, 171–72, 173, 175
Center on the Developing Child,
    Harvard University, 134
Centers for Disease Control, 135
certainty
  danger of, 32
  holding on to, 235–36, 246, 249
  in interactions, 238–39
  tyranny of, 226–28
Charles, Prince of Wales, 92
childhood sexual abuse, 135
ChildTrauma Academy, Houston,
    Texas, 139
Circle of Security, 99
Coleman, Kevin, 214–15
colic, management of, 10–12
Company (musical), 107
compliance, and false self, 72–73
connection. See also disconnection;
    reconnection
  fundamental importance of social
    connection, 19
  hopefulness of, 245
  infants wired to demand
    back-and-forth connection, 18
  and parasympathetic nervous system,
    87, 88–89
  range of social connections, 3
  and self-comforting behaviors, 129
  and self-regulation, 113
  and still-face paradigm, 246–49

contingency, and play, 155
Cooper, Peter, 126–27
Cooper, Steven, 68
cortisol, 51, 53–54, 116, 142–43
Critchley, Simon, 225
Cry Havoc! (one-man show), 216–17
culture
  of advice, 81, 82
  defining of, 152
  of families, 152–54
  of perfectionism, 32, 61, 80–83
  of workplace, 164–66
curiosity, listening with, 6, 8, 9, 231,
  237–38, 240–41

dancing, 108, 144, 155–56, 163
Darwin, Charles, 50, 89
Dennis-Tiwary, Tracy, 177–78
depression
  and adverse childhood experiences,
   136, 137
  and grief, 131
  and interaction, 126–27, 201–2, 204
  perfectionism correlating with, 80
  postpartum depression, 11, 12,
   126–27, 193, 195–96
  and repair, 190
  and still-face paradigm, 44
  and unrealistic expectations, 235
Diana, Princess of Wales, 92–93
disconnection
  and cell phone use, 173–74
  changing pattern of, 147–50
  messiness of, 8
  moving to reconnection, 10, 30, 144,
   248–49
  psychotherapy as controlled
   disconnection, 220–22
  and range of connection, 3, 37
  repairing of, 9, 10
  and still-face experiment, 16–17, 37,
   247–48
discord
  and culture of families, 154
  differing experiences with, 34, 35
  fear of, 33–35, 56
  and holding environment, 82
  resistance of, 58

role in growth and change, 31, 50,
  68, 83, 231
  withdrawal in moments of,
   57, 232
  and workplace culture, 166
disorder
  fear of, 32
  and imperfection, 75–76, 79
  and sense of self, 65–66
disruption in relationships
  and holding environment, 82
  moving to repair, 235
  and resilience, 132, 133, 139, 141
  and sense of safety, 84–85
  and sense of self, 65–66
  survival of, 58
distracted behavior, 41
DNA, 50–51, 208
Duality's End, 161
Dutch Hunger Winter of 1944,
  51–52, 59

Eight Ages of Man, 133
emotional state
  achieving calm through physical
   activity, 117–18
  changing, 38
  communication of, 64
  effect of rapid alternating movements
   on, 67, 77
  and messiness of relationships,
   56–57, 66
  and open state systems theory, 50
  and play, 155
  and pre-language emotional
   experience, 60
  and resilience, 133, 143
  and self-regulation, 107–8, 118,
   120–21, 127, 135
empathy, 125, 231–34, 243
endocrine system, 59
epidemiologic studies, 136
epigenetics, 50–52, 52–53, 152, 206–9
epigenome, 207–8
Erikson, Erik, 133
errors. *See also* mistakes
  in evolutionary change, 50
  and good-enough mother, 70–71

errors *(cont.)*
  in interactions, 61–62
  and open dynamics systems theory,
      47–49
  and self-regulation, 71
evolution, 50
executive function, 122
experiences
  of discord, 34, 35
  of mismatch, 6, 29, 37–38, 47, 49, 62,
      107, 116, 132
  mistakes in relational experiences, 69
  of repair, 40–41
  and sense of self, 30

false self, 72–73
feelings
  of hopelessness, 79, 133, 187, 201,
      233, 236
  multilayered levels of, 42
  negative feeling arising from
      mismatch, 38, 40, 109, 116
  positive feeling from mismatch-
      repair process, 38
Field, Tiffany, 201–2
fight-or-flight response, 87–88, 100
5-HTT gene, 207–8
Flett, Gordon, 80
Fonagy, Peter, 9
forgiveness, 248
Fox, Nathan, 198
Freud, Sigmund, 20, 61, 72
Friedman, Richard, 188–89
Furman, Robert, 204

games
  aberrant games, 162
  and brain organization, 158, 161–64
  greeting game of Gusii tribe, 159–61
  messiness of, 156
  and movement, 158–59, 162,
      163–64
  peekaboo, 156–57
  and play, 154–59
  and repetitive activities, 151–52,
      156–57, 161, 203, 228
  and sense of belonging, 152, 154–59
  and still-face paradigm, 157–58

understanding ourselves with, 150
  in workplace, 164–66
gaze, in interpersonal relationships, 159
genes
  culture embedded in, 152
  and Dutch Hunger Winter of 1944,
      51–52
  expression of, 30, 50–51, 52, 53,
      206–8
  intergenerational transmission of
      environmental influence on, 53–55
  and meaning-making, 42, 50–52, 59
Gibson, James, 22
going on being concept, 141–42, 143,
      157, 187–88, 197
Gold, Claudia, 28, 31, 61, 81–82
good stress, 134–35, 143
Gordon, Bryony, 93
Grey, Jennifer, 36
grief
  and miscarriages, 181–82, 192–93, 194
  for parent's death, 93–94
  and parents' view of child's true
      self, 6
  and resilience, 130–31, 133, 143
  and self-regulation, 108
Gusii tribe, 159–61

Harlow, Harry, 20–21, 26, 190
Harrison, Alexandra, 163
Harry, Duke of Sussex, 92–94
Harvard Center for Cognitive
      Studies, 22
Harvard Center on the Developing
      Child, 209
Harvard Medical School, 17, 19
Havens, Leston, 58
Hawking, Stephen, 48–50, 58, 69, 70, 225
Heads Together, 94
healing relationships
  learning from war trauma, 215–20
  and new interactions, 32, 45,
      213–15, 220
  and new relationships, 222–24,
      234, 235
  and path of development, 13
  and psychotherapy as controlled
      disconnection, 220–22

and repair of alliance ruptures, 58
and resilience, 144
heart-face connection, 89
Heisenberg, Werner, 225
Hello It's Me Project, 242–43
helplessness, 43, 44
Hewitt, Paul, 80
holding environment, 82–83, 112, 119–20
Holocaust survivors, and intergenerational transmission of environmental influence on genes, 53–55
hopefulness
  of connection, 245
  and meaning-making, 40, 243, 244, 245–46
  and mismatch-repair process, 45, 62, 190, 233–34
  and resilience, 131, 133
  and still-face paradigm, 32
  and uncertainty, 231–34
hopelessness
  feelings of, 79, 133, 187, 201, 233, 236
  and meaning, 45, 224
  and meaning-making, 190, 191, 209
  and repair, 62
  and resilience, 144
hormonal system, 152
HPA (hypothalamic-pituitary-adrenal) axis, 87, 142
human development
  imperfection in, 69–73
  role of mismatch and repair in, 31, 36, 39, 49
  role of play in, 155
  role of relationships in, 5, 13
  and sense of belonging, 152
human research subjects, 29
Hurley, Katie, 80

immune system, 59, 60, 90, 142
imperfection. See also perfection
  T. Berry Brazelton on, 78–79
  in human development, 69–73
  importance of, 32, 66–69, 70
  in problem solving, 75–76
  of relationships, 63, 76–77

implicit relational knowing, 163
infants
  accommodation of mothers' failures, 70–71, 73, 229
  brain organization in, 69, 70, 239
  communication style of, 25
  development of, 15–16, 17, 18–19, 29
  meaning-making process of, 43, 59, 217
  mental health of, 14, 28
  as participant in parent-child relationship, 17, 21, 25, 26
  perception of, 22
  premature infants, 12
  self-comfort ability of, 24, 25, 44, 113, 121
  and sense of belonging, 155
  six distinct states of consciousness, 24
  skills to interact with environment, 42–43, 44
  social competence of newborns, 17, 23–26
  strategies for stress management, 43, 44, 113, 132–33
Institutional Review Board (IRB), 29
intentions
  attribution of, 86
  and games, 156
  recognition of, 9, 239, 240
  and uncertainty, 238
interactions
  and aberrant games, 162–63
  blame in, 124–25, 127
  certainty in, 238–39
  and development of attention, 126–27
  errors in, 61–62
  and games, 159, 162
  intimacy of moment-to-moment interactions, 32, 37
  messiness of, 30, 36, 37, 39, 41, 45, 49, 50, 57, 59, 66, 81, 84–85, 103–4, 164, 177, 192, 218–22, 238–39, 248

interactions *(cont.)*
  moment-to-moment mismatch-repair
    process, 45, 60, 65, 106, 107, 108,
    116, 126, 129, 134–35, 145, 173,
    174, 189, 212–13
  new interactions, 32, 45, 91–94, 108,
    213–15, 220
  opportunities for repair in, 39,
    218, 219
  patterns of, 162, 163, 168–69
  patterns of interactive coping, 44
  play in, 239
  problematic meanings associated
    with, 91
  repair as crux of, 38
  and self-regulation, 106, 107, 122,
    125, 126, 129, 200
  and sense of self, 30, 72, 108
  and serve and return, 110–11
  still-face experiment on, 15–16, 17,
    18–19, 29
  uncertainty in, 72, 239
intimacy
  capacity for, 32, 57, 107, 108, 207, 231
  and capacity to be alone, 110
  and mismatch-repair process, 36, 58,
    59, 62, 233
  and self-reliance, 112

Jamison, Leslie, 231
Jaws (film), 99–100
Johnson, Sue, 113–15
judgment, 9, 14

Kagan, Jerome, 95–96
Kaiser Permanente, 135
Kalanithi, Paul, 233
Keeping Your Child in Mind (Gold),
    10, 119
Klein, Melanie, 196–97
Knafo, Danielle, 179–82

Lally, J. Ronald, 118
Leave No Trace (film), 218–19
Leonardo da Vinci, *Madonna and
    Child*, 36
LeVine, Robert, 159
Lieberman, Alicia, 195

listening
  with curiosity, 6, 8, 9, 231, 237–38,
    240–41
  open-endedness of, 230
  open-ended questions for, 6–7
  to others' perspectives, 75, 76, 77,
    246–47
  and reconnection, 7–8
  and uncertainty, 231
  understanding behavior problems
    with, 6, 8, 10, 12–13
loneliness, 3, 90–91
Love, Lilly, 219

McGarrigle, Anna, 193
McGarrigle, Kate, 193
meaning
  and anxiety, 45, 224
  in behavior problems, 7, 9,
    100–103, 109
  distorted meanings, 219–20
  fixed meaning, 149–50, 209, 234–35
  mother-child co-creation of, 120–21
  negative meanings, 43, 45
  shared meanings, 106
  words conveying, 42, 43, 59, 85, 86,
    94, 158
meaning-making
  and autonomic nervous system, 42,
    59, 86, 100
  and breastfeeding, 45–46
  Jerome Bruner on, 22, 42
  and cell phone use, 173
  co-creation of, 120
  and epigenetics, 206–9
  and games, 155, 157
  and genes, 42, 50–52, 59
  and hopefulness, 40, 243, 244,
    245–46
  and hopelessness, 190, 191, 209
  of infants, 43, 59, 217
  and lack of love, 197–200
  messiness of, 149–50, 249
  in mismatch-repair process, 41, 60,
    62, 116, 187, 213, 240, 245, 247–48
  and movement and sensation, 78
  of newborns, 24
  and not feeling known, 193–97

as ongoing process, 189
paradigm of, 59
and patterns of interactive coping, 44
and relational experiences, 68
and sense of safety, 85–86, 89, 90, 121
and sense of self, 120, 191–97, 204
and sensory system, 42, 59, 217
and still-face experiment, 42, 43, 59
and suicide, 187–88
and symptoms as coping, 203–6
symptoms reflecting emotional
    distress, 200–203
Meghan, Duchess of Sussex, 92, 94
memory
    of interactions, 202–3
    relational memory, 157
mentalization, 9
messiness
    and culture of families, 153, 154
    and culture of perfectionism,
        80, 83
    of discord, 166
    of diverse society, 246
    of games, 156
    of interactions, 30, 36, 37, 39, 41, 45,
        49, 50, 57, 59, 66, 81, 84–85,
        103–4, 164, 177, 192, 218–22,
        238–39, 248
    of play, 168
    of relationships, 56–57, 66, 83, 107,
        149, 223–24
    and sense of safety, 32, 50, 59, 66, 83,
        84–85
    and sense of self, 229
    and uncertainty, 228–29
methylation, 51
microbiome, 59
Mills Brothers, 180
miscommunications, 8
mismatch
    experiences of, 6, 29, 37–38, 47, 49,
        62, 107, 116, 132
    negative feeling arising from, 38, 40,
        109, 116
    percentage of time spent in, 37–38,
        39, 47
    unrepaired mismatch, 91, 109, 116,
        117, 124, 129, 134, 145, 146, 173,
    174, 186, 187, 189, 212, 213,
        234, 235
mismatch-repair process
    and agency, 43, 45, 65, 120
    and breastfeeding, 45–47
    as central to human development,
        31, 36, 39, 49
    in evolutionary change, 50
    and games, 157
    and gene expression, 54
    and growth in relationships, 35, 36,
        39, 49, 57, 77–78, 82, 128, 177,
        184, 234
    and healing relationships, 224
    and infant's strategies for stress
        management, 43, 44, 64–65
    in infants with depressed mothers,
        44–45, 121, 184
    insufficient experience with, 64, 91,
        135, 189–90, 212, 224
    and intimacy, 36, 58, 59, 62, 233
    length of interval in, 142–43, 189
    meaning-making in, 41, 60, 62, 116,
        187, 213, 240, 245, 247–48
    and mistakes, 61–62
    and moment-to-moment
        interactions, 45, 60, 65, 106, 107,
        116, 126, 129, 134–35, 145, 173,
        174, 189, 212–13
    ongoing context of, 40
    and parent-child martial arts
        classes, 103–4
    and perfectionism, 74–75
    and play, 169
    and positive feeling, 38
    power of, 246–47
    resilience developed through, 32,
        132, 134–35, 138, 140, 143, 144,
        145, 182, 187
    and sense of belonging, 150
    and sense of safety, 86, 106, 157
    and sense of self, 113, 116, 117, 211
    and sensory processing variations,
        96–97, 104
    strategies learned in, 38–39, 40, 43,
        44, 211
    and uncertainty, 232–33, 236
    in workplace, 165

missed cues, 8
mistakes. *See also* errors
  and games of workplace, 164–65
  leading to growth and change, 82
  as opportunities to heal and grow,
    61–62
  in relational experiences, 69
  and sense of belonging, 165
moment of meeting, 47, 244
mother-child relationship
  John Bowlby on, 21
  and co-creation of meaning, 120–21
  and good-enough mother, 70, 71–72,
    111–12, 229
  and greeting game of Gusii tribe,
    159–61
  Harry Harlow's study of, 20–21
  intergenerational effect of mother's
    love, 21, 74
  mother's responses to child, 17, 21
  and sense of safety, 85–86
  and still-face experiment, 15–16, 17,
    18–19, 29, 37, 40, 44, 63–64, 134
  and stress, 122–23
  too-good mother, 73–75
  value of, 5
motherese, 196
motivations, 9
motor system, 42, 59
Mount Auburn Hospital, Cambridge,
  Massachusetts, 23
movement
  culture embedded in, 152
  and games, 158–59, 162, 163–64
  and play, 155
  rapid alternating movements, 67, 77
  repetitive activities, 144
Mulcahey, Kaitlin, 230
Multidimensional Perfectionism
  Scale, 80
Murray, Lynne, 126–27
mutual dysregulation, 121, 123–24, 179
mutual regulation model, 120–21, 123,
  137–38, 175, 183

National Science Foundation, 159
nature versus nurture
  and epigenetics, 50–52

false dichotomies of, 30, 104,
  206, 213
and sense of safety, 104–5
Nelson, Chuck, 198
Neonatal Behavioral Assessment Scale
  (NBAS), 24–25, 167–68
neural exercise, 98
neuroarchitects, 30, 209
neuroception, 87–88, 90, 91, 97
neuroplasticity, 30
neuroscience, 14
Newborn Behavioral Observations
  (NBO) system, 25, 167–68,
  195, 240
NICU Network Neurobehavioral Scale
  (NNNS), 25, 240
Nugent, J. Kevin, 167

obesity, causes of, 135
occupational therapists, 124
open dynamics systems theory, 47–50,
  58, 79
open space, 42
optimistic expectation, 43
orphanages, 197–200

"Paper Doll" (song), 180
parasympathetic nervous system, 87,
  88, 95
parent-child relationship
  and capacity to be alone, 111–12
  coping strategies developed in, 144
  disruption in, 17
  infant as participant in, 17, 21, 25, 26
  and intrusive parent, 40, 91,
    113, 190
  and mutual regulation, 137–38
  and parental authority, 229–30
  and parent's withdrawal, 191–93, 196
  and sense of safety, 98–104
  and still-face experiment, 38–39,
    102
  and stress, 137, 169, 174
  and tantrums, 53, 74, 100–104,
    209, 231
parents
  with depressive symptoms, 44–45,
    121, 184

spending time alone together, 108–9
  view of child's true self, 6
pediatric bipolar disorder, 10
perfect girl syndrome, 80
perfection. *See also* imperfection
  cultural expectation of, 32, 61, 80–83
  and parent-child relationships, 169
  and too-good mother, 73–75
Perry, Bruce, 67, 139–40, 200
PIM3 gene, 52
play
  and games, 154–59
  in interactions, 239
  and observation of newborns, 167–69
  open play, 245
pleasure, 38, 108
polyvagal theory, 88, 102, 192, 221
Porges, Stephen, 87–89, 95, 97–98, 105
position of dependency, 56, 72
positive stress, 134
postpartum depression, 11, 12, 126–27,
  193, 195–96
poverty, 137
premature infants, 12
primitive vagus (unmyelinated vagus),
  88–91, 93, 100, 102, 103,
  192, 221
psychoanalysis, 9, 23, 163, 181, 202, 221
psychotherapy, 220–22, 224
PTSD (post-traumatic stress disorder),
  216, 219

Raphael, 36
rapid alternating movements, 67, 77
RealDoll, 181–82
Reborn, 181–82
reconnection
  and listening, 7–8
  moving from disconnection to, 10,
  30, 144, 248–49
  pleasure of, 63
  and self-regulation, 113
regulatory scaffolding, 133, 135, 139–40
relational memory, and still-face
  paradigm, 157
relationships. *See also* disruption in
  relationships; healing
  relationships; mother-child

relationship; parent-child
  relationship
  blame for struggles in, 14
  as buffers against adversity, 135–40,
  143, 191, 234
  as building blocks, 28–30
  and capacity to be alone, 110
  effect of technology on, 170
  emotional suffering in context of
  derailed relationships, 32
  and games, 161–64
  holding environment in, 82–83, 112
  imperfection of, 63, 76–77
  impermanence of early relationship
  patterns, 45
  messiness of, 56–57, 66, 83, 107, 149,
  223–24
  and mismatch-repair process, 35, 36,
  39, 49, 57, 77–78, 82, 128, 177,
  184, 234
  new relationships, 222–24, 234
  problematic relationships, 45
  role in human development, 5, 13
  and still-face experiment, 16
  survival of disruption in, 58
  technology as replacement for,
  179–83
repair. *See also* mismatch-repair
  process
  of alliance ruptures, 58
  as crux of human interactions, 38
  and culture of advice, 81
  lack of opportunity for, 40–41, 98,
  136, 190, 221
  opportunities in moments of
  interaction, 39, 218, 219
  and still-face experiment, 29
  and trust, 38, 39, 58, 62, 82, 117, 135,
  157, 189, 233, 246, 249
repetitive activities
  and games, 151–52, 156–57, 161,
  203, 228
  and self-regulation, 144, 200
resilience
  and adversity, 130, 135–38, 144, 182
  development through mismatch-
  repair process, 32, 132, 134–35,
  138, 140, 143, 144, 145, 182, 187

resilience *(cont.)*
and mutual regulation, 137
and optimistic expectation, 43
as overcoming odds, 130
and regulatory scaffolding, 133, 135, 139–40
and relationships as buffers, 135–40, 143, 191, 234
and still-face paradigm, 32
and stress, 132–33, 141, 144
and time, 141–45
responsibility and empowerment, 127
rhesus macaques, 21, 26
risk factors, in environment, 137
Rogers, Ginger, 36
Romania, 198–99

safety, sense of
and disruption in relationships, 84–85
and gene expression, 54, 55
and meaning-making, 85–86, 89, 90, 121
and messiness of interaction, 32, 50, 59, 66, 83, 84–85
and neuroception, 87–88, 90, 91, 97
and new interactions, 91–94
and parent-child relationship, 98–104
sensory perceptions of, 94–98
and social engagement, 90–91
and still-face paradigm, 85–86, 97, 102
and uncertainty, 83
and vagus nerve, 87, 88–90, 91, 92, 93, 98
Sander, Louis, 42, 47, 163, 244
scaffolding
and games, 155, 156
and meaning-making, 120, 200
regulatory scaffolding, 133, 135, 139–40
and self-regulation, 121
and still-face paradigm, 112–13, 186–87
screen time, 169–70
security, role of repair in, 38
self. *See* sense of self

self-comfort behaviors, 24, 25, 44, 113, 121, 129
self-esteem, 3, 178
self-regulation
and capacity to be alone, 110–12
co-regulation process, 122, 123, 127, 136, 139
effect of stress on, 137
and emotional state, 107–8, 118, 120–21, 127, 135
and errors, 71
and executive function, 122
and holding environment, 112, 119–20
importance of, 121–25
and interactions, 106, 107, 122, 125, 126, 129, 200
and mutual dysregulation, 121, 123–24, 179
and mutual regulation model, 120–21, 123, 137–38, 175, 183
and repetitive activities, 144, 200
and still-face paradigm, 112–15
and technology, 175
self-reliance, 108–9, 112
sense of self
and capacity for intimacy, 207, 231
and capacity to be alone, 110–12, 113
development of, 3, 30, 31, 65–66, 68, 72, 108, 211, 213
and going on being, 141–42, 143, 187
and meaning-making, 120, 191–97, 204
from multilayered levels of feeling, 42
and play, 155
and social media, 178
and stress, 141–42
and uncertainty, 72, 229
sensory system
culture embedded in, 152
and meaning-making, 42, 59, 217
sensitivity of, 12, 94–98, 104, 105, 123–25, 137, 175
Serenity Park, Los Angeles, 219
serve and return, 110–11
Shakespeare, William, 216–17
Shakespeare in the Courts, Lenox, Massachusetts, 214–15

shame, 6
Shonkoff, Jack, 134
sibling rivalry, 5–6
singing, 68–69, 97, 105
smart vagus (myelinated vagus), 88–90,
    92, 93, 98, 102, 105, 246
smiling eyes, 89
Snidman, Nancy, 95–96
social engagement
    need for, 90–91, 92
    and parent-child relationship, 100
    and sensitivity to sensory input, 97,
        98, 104
    and vagus nerve, 88–90, 98
social isolation, 90–91
social media, 80, 171, 177–78, 182
social womb, 118
Society for Research in Child
    Development, 20, 27
Sondheim, Stephen, 107
Spade, Kate, 187–88
Spitz, René, 197–98, 199
Stern, Dan, 163
still-face experiment
    development of, 26–28
    and disconnection, 16–17, 37, 247–48
    duration of still-face segment, 15–16,
        43, 64
    and infants' skills to interact with
        environment, 42–43, 44
    insights of, 28–29, 30, 36–37, 39, 61,
        184, 185–86
    and meaning-making at multiple
        levels of experience, 42, 43, 59
    and mother-child relationship,
        15–16, 17, 18–19, 29, 37, 40, 44,
        63–64, 134
    and parent-child relationships,
        38–39, 102
still-face paradigm
    concept of, 14, 28
    and connection, 246–49
    and depression, 44
    and games, 157–58
    and hope and resilience, 32
    and meaning-making, 209
    and memory of interactions, 202–3
    and psychotherapy, 221

and role-play of adult couple,
    113–15, 190
and self-regulation, 112–15
and sense of safety, 85–86, 97, 102
significance of, 29, 31, 245
and technology, 32, 170, 171–73
and trauma-informed care
    model, 139
Stonebridge, Lyndsey, 248
stress
    and behaviors of impulsivity and
        inattention, 124
    and capacity for self-regulation,
        137
    and 5-HTT gene, 207
    and gene expression, 51, 53–54
    infants' strategies for management
        of, 43, 44, 113, 132–33
    and mother-child relationship,
        122–23
    and parental authority, 229–30
    and parent-child relationship, 137,
        169, 174
    range of, 134–35, 143
    and resilience, 132–33, 141, 144
    and sense of self, 141–42
    stress-response system, 54, 87–88,
        116, 134, 142–43, 200, 217
    and unrepaired mismatch, 116
stress hormones, 87, 116, 134, 142–43
substance abuse, 135, 138–40, 185–86,
    187, 189, 243
success, definition of, 62
suicide, 187–89
Swayze, Patrick, 36
sympathetic nervous system, 87–88,
    90, 100
Szalavitz, Maia, 199–200

tantrums
    and parent-child relationship, 53, 74,
        100–104, 209, 231
    and resilience, 133
    and self-regulation, 109, 174
    and sense of identity, 146
    and technology use, 176
    and trauma-informed care, 139,
        140

technology
  adaptive function of, 179
  and autism, 174–77
  relationships affected by, 170
  as replacement for relationships,
    179–83
  and self-regulation, 175
  and still-face paradigm, 32, 170,
    171–73
temperament, 96, 104–5
time, sense of, 141–45, 155
Tippett, Krista, 248
tolerable stress, 134
toxic stress, 134
transference, 72, 202, 221, 226
transformative moments, 6
trauma
  everyday trauma across generations,
    145–46
  learning from war trauma, 215–20
  and pattern of disconnection, 147
  trauma-informed care, 139, 140
  D. W. Winnicott on, 141
Trauma Research Foundation, 214
Tronick, Ed, 6, 9, 14, 31, 68, 163
true self
  parents' view of child's true self, 6
  D. W. Winnicott on, 5, 7, 72, 93
trust
  and capacity to be alone, 113
  development of, 9, 81–82
  role of repair in, 38, 39, 58, 62, 82,
    117, 135, 157, 189, 233, 246, 249
Turkle, Sherry, 171–72, 174, 175

ugly stress, 134, 143
uncertainty
  acceptance of, 82
  and empathy, 231–34
  Heisenberg's uncertainty
    principle, 225
  in interactions, 72, 239
  and new relationships, 223–24
  opening space for, 228–31, 242, 243,
    245, 246
  and sense of safety, 83

and sense of self, 72, 229
  tolerating of, 225–26, 235
  and tyranny of certainty, 226–28
  value of, 32, 67
University of Massachusetts Boston
    Infant-Parent Mental Health
    Program, 217

vagus nerve, 87, 88–93, 98, 100, 102–3,
    105, 192, 221
van der Kolk, Bessel, 214–15
Vogel, Erin, 178
voice, prosody of, 89

Westover, Tara, 226–27
Whitaker, Robert, 188–89
William, Duke of Cambridge, 92, 94
Williams, John, 99
wind instruments, 97
Winfrey, Oprah, 139
Winnicott, D. W.
  on capacity to be alone, 111, 112
  clinical theory of, 78
  on going on being, 141–42, 157,
    187, 197
  on good-enough mother, 70,
    71–72, 111
  on holding environment, 82, 119
  on imperfection, 69
  on madness, 187
  on position of dependency, 56, 72
  on primary maternal preoccupation,
    229, 232
  on psychotherapy, 222
  on role of play in development, 155
  on sense of self, 65–66
  study of psychoanalysis, 23
  on trauma, 141
  on true self, 5, 7, 72, 93
  truths distilled from clinical work, 9
Wolfert, Stephan, 216–17

Yehuda, Rachel, 53
yoga, 144

Zeanah, Charles, 198

ABOUT THE AUTHORS

Ed Tronick, PhD, a developmental neuroscientist and clinical psychologist, is a University Distinguished Professor of Developmental and Brain Sciences at the University of Massachusetts Boston and a Research Associate in the Division of Newborn Medicine at Harvard Medical School. He is internationally recognized for his research on infant neurobehavior and infant social-emotional development. He formulated the still-face paradigm, and the mutual-regulation model and its repair-mismatch theory of interactions and therapeutic interactions. He has done research on child development and parenting in Kenya, Zambia, Peru, Grenada, and diverse communities in the United States. His current research focuses on infant memory for stress and epigenetic processes affecting infants' and parents' behavior. He has published more than four hundred scientific articles, five books, and several hundred photographs and has appeared on national radio and television programs. His research is funded by the National Institutes of Health and the National

Science Foundation. He has lectured internationally, including in London, Rome, Bangkok, Melbourne, Lisbon, Pretoria, and multiple cities in the United States.

Claudia M. Gold, MD, is a pediatrician and writer who practiced general and behavioral pediatrics for more than twenty years and now specializes in early childhood mental health. She is on the faculty of the University of Massachusetts Boston Infant-Parent Mental Health Program, the Brazelton Institute at Boston Children's Hospital, and the Berkshire Psychoanalytic Institute. She is a clinician with FIRST Steps Together, a program for pregnant and parenting women recovering from opioid dependence, and director of the Hello It's Me Project, a community-based program supporting parent-infant relationships in rural western Massachusetts. Dr. Gold speaks frequently to a variety of audiences, including parents and professionals. She is the author of *The Developmental Science of Early Childhood*, *The Silenced Child*, and *Keeping Your Child in Mind*, and writes regularly for her blog, *Child in Mind*.